The Ageless
Agatha Christie

The Ageless Agatha Christie

Essays on the Mysteries and the Legacy

Edited by J.C. BERNTHAL

McFarland & Company, Inc., Publishers
Jefferson, North Carolina

LIBRARY OF CONGRESS CATALOGUING-IN-PUBLICATION DATA

Names: Bernthal, J. C., 1989– editor.
Title: The ageless Agatha Christie : essays on the mysteries and the legacy / edited by J.C. Bernthal.
Description: Jefferson, N.C. : McFarland & Company, Inc., Publishers, 2016. | Includes bibliographical references and index.
Identifiers: LCCN 2016002459 | ISBN 9781476663135 (softcover : acid free paper) ∞
Subjects: LCSH: Christie, Agatha, 1890–1976—Criticism and interpretation. | Christie, Agatha, 1890–1976—Appreciation. | Christie, Agatha, 1890–1976. | Authors, English—20th century—Biography.
Classification: LCC PR6005.H66 Z554716 2016 | DDC 823/.912—dc23
LC record available at http://lccn.loc.gov/2016002459

British Library cataloguing data are available

**ISBN (print) 978-1-4766-6313-5
ISBN (ebook) 978-1-4766-2397-9**

© 2016 J.C. Bernthal. All rights reserved

No part of this book may be reproduced or transmitted in any form or by any means, electronic or mechanical, including photocopying or recording, or by any information storage and retrieval system, without permission in writing from the publisher.

Front cover image © 2016 iStock/Plastock

Printed in the United States of America

*McFarland & Company, Inc., Publishers
Box 611, Jefferson, North Carolina 28640
www.mcfarlandpub.com*

Table of Contents

Preface	1
Introduction: Mystery and Legacy	3
Agatha Christie in Dialogue with *To the Lighthouse*: The Modernist Artist 　Merja Makinen	11
England's Pockets: Objects of Anxiety in Christie's Post-War Novels 　Rebecca Mills	29
Queer Girls, Bad Girls, Dead Girls: Post-War Culture and the Modern Girl 　Sarah Bernstein	45
"With practised eyes": Feminine Identity in *The Mysterious Mr. Quin* 　Charlotte Beyer	61
"The sumptuous and the alluring": Poirot's Women, Dragged Up and Dressed Down 　J. C. Bernthal	81
"The Encyclopedic Palace of the World": Miss Lemon's Filing System as Cabinet of Curiosities and the Repository of Human Knowledge in *Agatha Christie's Poirot* 　Meg Boulton	98
"One must actually take facts as they are": Information Value and Information Behavior in the Miss Marple Novels 　Michelle M. Kazmer	114

And Then There Were Many: Agatha Christie in Hungarian
  Translation
    BRIGITTA HUDÁCSKÓ   130

Mother of Invention: Agatha Christie, the Middlebrow
  Detective Novel and Kerry Greenwood's Postcolonial
  Tribute Series
    JILLY LIPPMANN   145

Autobiography in *Agatha* (1979): "An imaginary solution to
  an authentic mystery"
    SARAH STREET   161

Editorial: Fans Have the Final Word
    J. C. BERNTHAL   176

About the Contributors   181
Index   183

Preface

This edited collection considers the crime writer Agatha Christie (1890–1976) in an international, interdisciplinary context. It is the first major scholarly collection of essays on Christie in English. The ten contributors consider Christie as a writer and a media figure, each from a distinct perspective. One essay unpacks Christie's relationship with modernism; another approaches her later texts from a queer theorized perspective. An essay considers the organization of knowledge in television adaptations; two others look at Christie in translation and explore her celebrity status in heritage cinema. Additional essays consider objects in the post-war novels, information behavior theory, feminism, gender studies and postcolonial tribute novels. The final word is given to fans, in an editorial that collates testimonies from readers, collectors and enthusiasts the world over, providing a valuable source for those wishing to study Christie's popularity and fan communities. This ground-breaking volume provides a wide-ranging handbook for students and scholars in many disciplines who are interested in Agatha Christie's texts or her legacy. By focusing on lesser-discussed Christie titles, it introduces new discussions, broadening horizons for study and scholarship.

Introduction: Mystery and Legacy

The detective fiction writer Agatha Christie (1890–1976) is hardly obscure. She remains the best-selling author in history, the unchallenged Queen of Crime. She created the enduring detectives Hercule Poirot and Miss Marple, and authored the longest-running West End play in history ("The Mousetrap," which opened in 1952). Back in 1980, the novelist and scholar Robert Barnard noted that no one was more widely-read, not only in geographical terms—Christie's books had already been translated into every known language—but also by people from all social backgrounds "and intelligence brackets."[1]

Despite these unique credentials, Christie has received only limited critical attention. Nearly a century has passed since her debut novel, *The Mysterious Affair at Styles* (1920) was published. In that time, neither Christie nor her legacy has been the subject of an edited collection of essays attached to an academic publisher. Why is it that Christie, a writer more widely read—including, surely, by academics and theorists—than James Joyce, Virginia Woolf or any canonical name, has not yet been afforded this dignity?

There is a history of academic study related to Christie's work, of course, but the overall mood of this scholarship, for a long time, was somewhat self-deprecating. Barnard's own book typified the tone of the time with its careful preface insisting that "this appreciation … does not pretend to be literary criticism."[2] A year previously, H. R. F. Keating had edited a collection of reflections from Christie's rivals, called *Agatha Christie: First Lady of Crime*. They discussed her plotting, and analyzed her popularity.[3] It was not, however, until the 1990s that Christie scholarship became truly and transatlantically academic.

When Alison Light considered Christie as a "conservative modernist" in 1990, she opened up a range of possibilities for studying her work, which had previously been dismissed as "part of 'popular' culture, nothing more than lighthearted, entertaining fiction, the genteel creation of a carefully brought up, modest Victorian lady."[4] Throughout the 1990s the criticism flowed, Britain following at the heels of the United States, where Christie had long interested students of popular culture. However, few critical approaches to Christie—or, indeed, to female-authored detective fiction—were serious. Marty S. Knepper observed a tendency towards "inaccurate ... truisms" and "dubious assertions" in Christie criticism, and her own work in the 1990s did much to raise the author's profile.[5] However, it was not until the rise of middlebrow studies that a great many women writers from the early and mid-twentieth centuries, including Christie, were judged worthy of thorough consideration.

Since Nicola Humble's *The Feminine Middlebrow Novel, 1920s to 1950s* (2001), a wealth of criticism and discussion has surrounded previously neglected texts, and the derogatory word "middlebrow" has been somewhat reclaimed. Whereas previous criticism of popular-but-intelligent writers had either explained away or simply denied their "middlebrow" status, a number of studies, including ones in the present volume, do not apologize for their interest in the genre. Woolf despised the middlebrow writer, whom she considered

> neither one thing nor the other[; an individual] of middlebred intelligence who ambles and saunters now on this side of the hedge, now on that, in pursuit of no single object, neither art nor life itself, but both mixed indistinguishably, and rather nastily, with money, fame, power, or prestige.[6]

However, since Humble's ambitious challenge to Woolf's elitism, we have been able to see both merit and critical potential in the unique "betwixt and between" status of the accessible yet ambitious work that so alarmed Woolf and her peers.

Now Christie is taught in university courses, iconic essays have been published and monographs are not uncommon. Pioneering projects have indicated that Christie is crucial to heritage film studies, post-structural theory, rhetoric and linguistics, feminist literary analysis, the social sciences, translation history and development, queer theory and more.[7] Christie has been investigated within a tradition of feminine self-expression, as a commentator on the insincerity and performances of modernity and as a staple of Britain's film and television culture.[8] Some of the people behind these pioneering publications have contributed to this volume, and others are engaged with here.

A new "Agatha Christie" is emerging. Christie's own description of herself as a "lucky woman who had established a happy knack of writing what quite a lot of people wanted to read" is only the beginning.[9] This fresh Christie we have to contend with is many things. She is a significant historical figure and a genre innovator. She is a cultural commentator and a shrewd businessperson who dominated a literary marketplace hostile to her sex. She developed into an expert stylist whose prose carries so much more than one meaning.

This volume offers the first wide-ranging and international collection of scholarly investigations into the functions, influences and subtexts of Christie's work and its multi-media legacy. Before discussing the contributions, I wish to draw attention toward one thing they share, which is evidence of the authors' desire to take Christie seriously: each contributor has carefully historicized his or her findings. For too long, Agatha Christie has been spoken of and written about as a vaguely interwar novelist, belonging to some airily-defined olden days that exists chiefly in the mind of the reader. In fact, her first publication, a poem about trams, appeared within months of Queen Victoria's death in 1901, and she went on to write about space travel, electric dishwashers, teddy boys and computers. She wrote through two world wars, two waves of feminism and the dissolution of the British Empire. When she died in 1976, she was still writing.

But can we read this crowd-pleaser, this unblushing Queen of the Marketplace, on a par with her elite forebears and contemporaries? Our first contributor, Merja Makinen, points out that "Virginia Woolf and Agatha Christie are two names not usually placed alongside each other," but argues that they should be: Christie is clearly and inevitably influenced by the modernist stylings of Woolf and others. Placing Christie's *The Hollow* (1946) in dialogue with Woolf's *To the Lighthouse* (1927), Makinen makes the case for a "direct and contemporary" influence, while also drawing much-needed attention to the literary fiction Christie published under the pseudonym Mary Westmacott. It is, however, only in "the slimmed-down popular genre format" that Christie was able to deal, uniquely and significantly, with literary themes. While Woolf posed open questions for women struggling to choose between marriage and a career, Christie's "workaday middlebrow" ethic enabled the "comfort" of solutions "within and alongside marriage."

Looking at objects in Christie's post–World War II novels, Rebecca Mills sets out to "take seriously Christie's literary and imaginative response to the war and the following era of technological advances, international tension and change." There is a lot to be found in small everyday objects, Mills claims. Starting with a war novel, *The Moving Finger* (1943), and progressing through analyses of *After the Funeral* (1953) and *The Pale Horse* (1961), Mills explores the deadly sentimentality attached to relics of the past and the faceless anonymity of mass-produced post-war objects: "the real evil is capitalism … it is a dangerous world."

The years following World War II have traditionally been neglected in Christie scholarship and, like Mills, Sarah Bernstein considers Christie as an alert social commentator who adapted her work to reflect the changing concerns of post-war Britain. Bernstein explores the theme of children—specifically delinquent girls—in some of the most individual but critically underappreciated novels from the latter half of Christie's career. Bernstein ties up the presentation of childhood in literature with dominant post-war rhetoric surrounding children as the innocent inheritors of the new world. An adolescent girl is "suspended in a state of non-adulthood ... a form of legal strangeness." What happens when she refuses her social duties to "reproductive futurism" (as a woman) and to family (as a child)? She causes disorder; she threatens, she kills, she dies.

As we progress through the volume, it becomes noticeable that Christie is getting more quotes—more direct analysis. Charlotte Beyer's essay is strongly influenced by Makinen's work here and elsewhere—but this time Christie's texts alone and in their own right are under the microscope. Given the reputation for social conservatism that Christie has yet to shake off, some of Beyer's revelations may be surprising. Beyer reveals that femininity can be an important quality in the male lead, by considering the gossipy, ladylike protagonist Mr. Satterthwaite. Such a "fluid position" regarding male heroism allows the author to "exceed genre boundaries and ... experiment." Beyer goes on to interrogate "femininity [and] agency" in the Quin short stories. Women in these stories are faced with an unsatisfactory choice between unhappy marriage and dishonorable excess. Finally, and ultimately, they are misunderstood.

In my own essay, I make the case for reassessing Christie as a gendered parodist. Not only is Poirot a mockery of Sherlock Holmes, his sidekick Captain Hastings can be read as both a send-up of the inevitable Dr. Watson and an unsubtle satire on heterosexuality itself. But what of Poirot's women? His flamboyant equivalent to Holmes's Irene Adler is read as a drag artist, while his machine-like secretary Miss Lemon is digested with a pinch of salt: "the books adopt a conservative, even misogynistic, worldview—but perhaps the 'c' is back-to-front." To emphasize the queer playfulness of Christie's prose, I contrast these women to versions of them that have appeared on-screen, in the long-running television series *Agatha Christie's Poirot* (1989–2013). Perhaps nostalgia prohibits irony; perhaps identity in the books is not clear-cut like it is on the screen.

Nonetheless, for many people in the twenty-first century, Agatha Christie *is* those immersive period whodunits on the television. Meg Boulton uncovers geographies and psycho-geographies in "the (tele)visual versions of Christie's books," considering Miss Lemon and her ubiquitous filing system as loci for endless, categorized and taxonomized knowledge. This "cabinet of curiosities" "contain[s] all the Poirot-verse within its cataloged confines." It imposes order and generates new knowledge. The cabinet, in short, is an active part of and a monument to "the deductive process," and Boulton proposes that the viewer is ultimately a part of the filing system itself—as we build up a dynamic and multifocal significance for "Agatha Christie."

Knowledge and information is at the heart of Michelle M. Kazmer's essay, too. Kazmer brings a completely different, and an essential, perspective to Christie, from her background in information science and communication. Kazmer considers how knowledge is evaluated and disseminated within the ever-popular Miss Marple books. "This approach," Kazmer points out, "can also increase our understanding of how information value is co-constructed in real-life contexts" because all the time, the information in a detective story is being tailored to real-world readers. Kazmer's investigation draws attention to the tactics Marple employs to uncover and manipulate information, by presenting herself as irresponsible or harmless and by knowing how to extract information in each specific context. As Marple herself points out in *A Murder Is Announced* (1950), "we old women always do snoop. It would be very off and much more noticeable if I didn't."[10]

For a quintessentially British writer, Christie has enjoyed remarkable popularity all over the world. As a translator, Brigitta Hudácskó provides another perspective on the Christie phenomenon, detailing (an aspect of) this author's complicated translation history into Hungarian. Hudácskó's keyword is "foreignness." How does a country so politically removed from that in which Christie wrote confront its own position as "other" in the texts, and how does it deal with "the foreignness of crime fiction" itself for native readers? How are foreign accents and idiolects conveyed in translation, and to what effect? As Hudácskó shows, some translators have taken quite drastic liberties with the source texts to bring them into line with contemporary political climates. The three translations Hudácskó considers, invested in Christie's "non-threatening foreignness," reflect changing politics and public appetites; they also reflect Christie's shifting status as an author-in-translation, from "lowbrow" to "highbrow" to canonical.

Christie took pride in calling herself a lowbrow, by which she probably meant "not highbrow." The tricky terrain of the "middlebrow" is mentioned by Makinen and Hudácskó, but Jilly Lippmann runs with it by considering Christie's middlebrow legacy. Lippmann takes seriously Christie's role as a figurehead for a school of fiction that is both middlebrow—substantial yet accessible—and tied to its imperial context. Considering Kerry Greenwood's Australian mysteries, Lippmann reads the flapper detective Phryne Fisher in the tradition of Christie's protagonists Tuppence Beresford, Miss Marple and even Poirot, uncovering a subtle but unapologetic intertextual tribute in the broader context of "settler postcolonial ambivalence." Lippmann understands Christie as an authority figure, who warrants more critical attention in the field of postcolonial studies.

8   Introduction

Finally, reading Agatha Christie as "an author whose celebrity exceeded her writing," Sarah Street reminds us of the mysteries of Christie's own life and the complicated ways in which her image has been constructed by others. Street details the troubled production of *Agatha* (1979), a film based on Kathleen Tynan's speculative novel, which concerned Christie's infamous disappearance, the media event of 1926. Street does not attempt to reconstruct Christie's "lost" eleven days, rather considering issues relating to celebrity, authenticity, memory and fiction. Perhaps all solutions to the Agatha Christie mystery fall short, because, as an artist, a celebrity and a woman, Agatha Christie is more than one mystery. As Street concludes, Christie's story is "an enigma, continuing to fascinate with … apparently endless possibilities for re-writing."

The contributors, by and large, do not focus on Christie's best-known publications. *The Murder of Roger Ackroyd* (1926), *Murder on the Orient Express* (1933), *Death on the Nile* (1937), and *And Then There Were None* (1939) are mentioned, of course, and a lot of good work continues to be done on them. But for this landmark volume, the point is to discover new angles on an iconic writer of the twentieth century, who is also an influential presence in the twenty-first. In a similar vein, I have encouraged all contributors to preserve their own distinctive voices in their essays; ultimately, granting Christie long-overdue academic attention is about more than absorbing her work into a colorless canon to be studied by rote with received formulae and uninspired if technically correct vocabulary. In this spirit, I have given the final word to what Agatha Christie Limited calls "superfans"—those enthusiasts and collectors who have kept the Christie brand afloat. The closing editorial collates testimonies and reflections from a cross-section of fans, and provides a useful resource for anyone wishing to study fan communities. It is also a tribute to the unusual affection that readers—academic or otherwise—have for Christie.

This volume started life as a conference at the University of Exeter. Then as now, two things struck me: the huge scope of interest and the genuine enthusiasm of participants. Something about that sheer joy in study and in writing has produced a set of essays that is diverse but also quite definitely distinctive. When Charlotte Beyer calls her primary texts "complicated and fascinating," and when Meg Boulton inserts "a confessional moment" about growing up watching *Agatha Christie's Poirot* on the television, each is strengthening their unique analysis of the Agatha Christie phenomenon. It is an international, multimedia phenomenon, made up of many voices.

This volume does not answer the question that most vexes Christie scholars: why is she still so successful? Nor does it simply raise further questions about Christie's popular status, and the value of genre texts in academic discourse. Instead, it indicates the richness and diversity of discussion surrounding her remarkable body of work. The contributions to this volume serve as an introduction to an emerging plethora of scholarship and discourse. This volume is, then, a celebration of that writer Light called "the Queen of the 'middlebrows'"[11]: a phenomenally successful novelist whose work and legacy warrant an almost boundless range of interdisciplinary scrutiny. This volume offers some solutions but encourages further investigations into the mysteries and legacies of Agatha Christie.

Perhaps Christie deserves the final word. In her autobiography, she responded to various questions about the long run of "The Mousetrap." In an international, interdisciplinary academic context, we may apply her words to her entire oeuvre: "I suppose ... that there is a bit of something in it for almost everybody."[12]

NOTES

1. Robert Barnard, *A Talent to Deceive: An Appreciation of Agatha Christie* (London: Collins, 1980), p. 11.
2. *Ibid.*, p. 7.
3. H. R. F. Keating (ed.), *Agatha Christie: First Lady of Crime* (London: Weidenfeld and Nicholson, 1979).
4. Odette l'henry Evans, "Croquet and Serial Killers: Feminism and Agatha Christie" in Gina Whisker (ed.), *It's My Party: Reading Twentieth Century Women's Writing* (London: Pluto Press, 1994), pp. 174–180 (p. 175). See Alison Light, *Forever England: Femininity, Literature and Conservatism Between the Wars* (London: Routledge, 1991).
5. Marty S. Knepper, "Reading Agatha Christie's Miss Marple Series: The Thirteen Problems" in Mary Jean DeMarr (ed.), *In the Beginning: First Novels in Mystery Series* (Bowling Green: Bowling Green State University Popular Press, 1995), pp. 33–58 (p. 34).
6. Virginia Woolf, "Middlebrow" in *Collected Essays,* vol. 2 (London: Hogarth Press, 1966), pp. 196–202 (p. 198).
7. Sarah Street, "Heritage Crime: The Case of Agatha Christie" in Robert Shail (ed.), *Seventies British Cinema* (Basingstoke: Palgrave Macmillan, 2008), pp. 105–116; Pierre Bayard, *Who Killed Roger Ackroyd? The Murderer Who Eluded Hercule Poirot and Deceived Agatha Christie* (London: Fourth Estate, 1999); Marc Alexander, "Rhetorical Structure and Reader Manipulation in Agatha Christie's Murder on the Orient Express," *Miscelánea: A Journal of English and American Studies* (2009), pp. 13–27; Merja Makinen, *Agatha Christie: Investigating Femininity* (Basingstoke: Palgrave Macmillan, 2006); Linden Peach, *Masquerade, Crime, and Fiction* (Basingstoke: Palgrave Macmillan, 2006); Marjolijn Storm, "A Corpus-Driven Analysis of Translations of Agatha Christie's Detective Novels into Dutch and into German" (Unpublished PhD thesis, University of Birmingham, 2012); J. C. Bernthal, "'Every Healthy Englishman Longed to Kick Him': Masculinity and Nationalism in Agatha Christie's Cards on the Table," *Clues: A Journal of Detection* 32.2 (2014), pp. 103–114.
8. Susan Rowland, *From Agatha Christie to Ruth Rendell: British Women Writers in Detective and Crime Fiction* (Basingstoke: Palgrave Macmillan, 2001); R. A. York, *Agatha Christie: Power and Illusion* (Basingstoke: Palgrave Macmillan, 2007); Mark Aldridge, "Love, Crime and Agatha Christie" in Karen A. Ritzenhoff and Karen Ran-

dell (eds.), *Screening the Dark Side of Love: From Euro-Horror to American Cinema* (Basingstoke: Palgrave Macmillan, 2012), pp. 83–94.
    9. Agatha Christie, *Elephants Can Remember* (London: HarperCollins, 2002), p. 18. The words refer to Christie's fictional alter-ego, the crime writer Ariadne Oliver.
    10. Agatha Christie, *A Murder Is Announced* (New York: Black Dog & Leventhal, 2007), p. 127.
    11. Light, *Forever England*, p. 75.
    12. Agatha Christie, *An Autobiography* (London: Harper, 2010), p. 510.

Bibliography

Aldridge, Mark. "Love, Crime and Agatha Christie" in Karen A. Ritzenhoff and Karen Randell (eds.), *Screening the Dark Side of Love: From Euro-Horror to American Cinema*. Basingstoke: Palgrave Macmillan, 2012, pp. 83–94.

Alexander, Marc. "Rhetorical Structure and Reader Manipulation in Agatha Christie's *Murder on the Orient Express*." *Miscelánea: A Journal of English and American Studies* (2009), pp. 13–27.

Barnard, Robert. *A Talent to Deceive: An Appreciation of Agatha Christie*. London: Collins, 1980.

Bayard, Pierre. *Who Killed Roger Ackroyd? The Murderer Who Eluded Hercule Poirot and Deceived Agatha Christie*. London: Fourth Estate, 1999.

Bernthal, J. C. "'Every Healthy Englishman Longed to Kick Him': Masculinity and Nationalism in Agatha Christie's Cards on the Table." *Clues: A Journal of Detection* 32.2 (2014), pp. 103–14.

Christie, Agatha. *An Autobiography* (1977). London: Harper, 2011.

_____. *Elephants Can Remember* (1971). London: HarperCollins, 2002.

_____. *A Murder Is Announced* (1950). New York: Black Dog & Leventhal, 2007.

Evans, Odette l'henry. "Croquet and Serial Killers: Feminism and Agatha Christie" in Gina Whisker (ed.), *It's My Party: Reading Twentieth Century Women's Writing*. London: Pluto Press, 1994, pp. 174–180.

Light, Alison. *Forever England: Femininity, Literature and Conservatism Between the Wars*. Abingdon: Routledge, 1991.

Rowland, Susan. *From Agatha Christie to Ruth Rendell: British Women Writers in Detective and Crime Fiction*. Basingstoke: Palgrave Macmillan, 2001.

Storm, Marjolijn. "A Corpus-Driven Analysis of Translations of Agatha Christie's Detective Novels into Dutch and into German." Unpublished PhD thesis, University of Birmingham, 2012.

Street, Sarah. "Heritage Crime: The Case of Agatha Christie" in Robert Shail (ed.), *Seventies British Cinema*. Basingstoke: Palgrave Macmillan, 2008, pp. 105–116.

Woolf, Virginia. "Middlebrow" in *Collected Essays*, vol. 2. London: Hogarth Press, 1966, pp. 196–202.

York, R. A. *Agatha Christie: Power and Illusion*. Basingstoke: Palgrave Macmillan, 2007.

Agatha Christie in Dialogue with *To the Lighthouse*
The Modernist Artist

Merja Makinen

In his *Anxiety of Influence*, Harold Bloom argues that "criticism teaches ... a language in which poetry is already written, the language of influence, of the dialectic that governs the relations of poets *as poets*,"[1] that later poets are always writing in a complex and denied hidden dialogue with the writers that they position as their great precursors. Although this theory was devised in the 1970s, Terry Eagleton has recently argued that it is still the most insightful of Bloom's work.[2] Bloom's "antithetical criticism" enables us not only to read a poet through their repressed influences but also to re-read the precursor through the later poet. If we shift the analysis from poetry to the novel, then this is the examination in process here, since the echoes of Virginia Woolf's *To the Lighthouse* (1927) reverberate through Christie's *The Hollow* (1946), as both explore the role of the modernist female artist—Lily Briscoe on holiday with the Ramsays, and Henrietta Savernake on holiday with the Angkatells. A re-reading of the Woolf text through the lens of Christie's work allows a different perspective on both authors, but also raises questions about literary influence and the implicit rivalry between what has been termed "highbrow" and "middlebrow" writing.

Critics have consistently discussed the modernist focus of Christie's popular writing since Alison Light's chapter in *Forever England* and Gillian Gill has noted frequent references to T. S. Eliot in her work.[3] Although Virginia Woolf and Agatha Christie are two names not usually placed alongside each other, given Christie's interest in modernism, it should not seem surprising that Woolf's major semi-autobiographical novel, published one year after Christie embraced the role of a professional writer as a divorced single mother needing to provide an upkeep for her household, should have proved of interest. Woolf is surprisingly absent in the discussions about Christie, a woman writer known to be influenced by modernism, evoking Bloom's thesis that the influenced writer disavows their anxieties through denial and elision of the influencer. Christie was happy to speak of other modernist novelists who influenced her writing, such as D.H. Lawrence and May Sinclair, in the *Autobiography*,[4] but Woolf is markedly absent except, perhaps, by contradiction. Why, for example, was Christie so often keen to stress that she could write anywhere, in any corner of a room, that all she needed was a table for her typewriter, if she was not implicitly rebuffing Woolf's 1929 *A Room of One's Own* which argued a woman needed her own room to be able to write? Christie's *Autobiography*, which describes the distractions created by her daughter's nurse, who was instructed not to disturb her when working— "maddened I would rise from my chair ... and jerk open the door"—implicitly confirms Woolf's need for seclusion.[5] But the later Christie insisted she did not need a room, just a table, and was photographed working alongside her second husband, each at their own desk, in their Devon home Greenway.

Bloom argues that the influenced writer creates their work in a dialectic, "a wrestling with the precursor" that involves "misreading" the original text in order to create the space they need for their own composition, and (ignoring his arcane terminology),[6] that British writers tend to "swerve" from the original in a "creative revisionism" of misinterpretation,[7] while the American writers try to "complete" the precursor, since they "deceive themselves into believing they are more tough-minded than their predecessors."[8] While I would challenge the male-focus of Bloom's discussion and the Freudian family romance invoked in this oedipal son/father dialectic of influence, his theorization of a necessary misreading, of swerving and of a willfully distorted completing of the original prove fruitful in the comparison of my two texts. But rather than the model of an oedipal father/son or even mother/daughter struggle of composition, I want to evoke a different familial battle—that of sibling rivalry. The influence of *To the Lighthouse* is more direct and contemporary than at first appears, because there is an interim text that needs to enter the equation: the literary novel *Giant's Bread*, published under the pseudonym Mary Westmacott, follows a similar trajectory to *The Hollow*, and was published in 1930, just three years after Woolf's novel first appeared. So the hypothesis of an anxiety of influence becomes an immediate and direct response to the precursor, later rethought and refined after another sixteen years. (Woolf died in 1941, five years before *The Hollow* was published.) It is well known that Agatha started writing stories because her elder sister had successfully published one and challenged her to do the same, so the trajectory of sibling rivalry in relation to composition has some purchase.

The precursor, Woolf, viewed through the lens of the later two Christie novels in the spirit of Bloom's antithetical criticism, re-creates a dialectic and literary dialogue that both copies and swerves from and, more importantly for the central Christie theme of the balancing of love, desire and marriage with the artist's need to create, attempts to re-write the Woolf in order to "complete" it, by correcting its resolution. Christie's direct revision in a similarly literary novel proved ineffective; it takes the slimmed-down popular genre format to clarify the "completion." In tackling the thematic referencing, however, *The Hollow* is a more literary text than usual. Poirot only arrives halfway through and Christie is on record as saying she felt his entrance spoilt the novel (indeed, his character was removed from the later transition into a successful play in 1951). But it could be argued that the rivalries between the literary and the popular, the "highbrow" modernism and the "lowbrow" crime, prove to be fruitful tensions for the composition of *The Hollow*, which is often cited as a favorite among twenty-first century feminist readers.

Reading *To the Lighthouse* (1927) through the lens of Christie's two texts delivers a thinned-down version of the themes in Woolf's novel, but also an interestingly differing one. Indeed, it is only through re-reading the Woolf for this project that I noticed that the holiday home is described as "in a hollow, on an island."[9] The novel is set on a Scottish island, where the affluent Ramsay family and invited guests holiday. Critics note that Woolf draws on childhood memories of her parents and family holidays in Cornwall. The text is set across two days, one before the war, when the family contemplates a boat trip to the lighthouse in the bay and Lily starts a painting, and one after the war, when they finally take the boat trip and Lily completes her painting. The two days become two parts, separated by a further short middle part, "Time Passes," in which seemingly off-hand parentheses frame the deaths of a number of characters as well as World War I. Separated by the war, the first part, "The Window," encapsulates the Edwardian era and Mrs. Ramsay's desire to arrange all women into wives. The third part, "The Lighthouse," negotiates a more modern era and alternative, less self-denying roles for women, as Lily embraces spinsterhood and completes her painting. Christie's first riposte to Woolf, *Giant's Bread* (1930), has the modernist composer, Vernon Deyre, rejecting the wife and hereditary house to live with his mistress and create the modernist masterwork in a place of license, Russia. This novel's structure is also divided by World War I, in a plot similar to Rebecca West's *Return of the Soldier* (1918). Vernon is reported killed in action, but returns—the shock of discovering his wife's remarriage makes Vernon lose his memory in a psychic "fugue."

The title of *Giant's Bread* refers to the lovers sacrificed to create Vernon's music (the great modernist atonal opera is called "The Giant") and the novel raises the question of whether the driven artist can have the conventional marriage. Christie's initial artistic endeavor was to be a professional concert pianist, but her shyness prevented the requisite public performative persona. Whole sections of *Giant's Bread*, such as Vernon's lonely childhood invention of friends, his lifelong nightmare of "the Beast," the fugue and its psychiatric treatment, draw on Christie's childhood and early adult memories, informing Christie's figuring of the role of the modern artist. Christie's later return to this idea in *The Hollow* shifts the debate again, coiling back on the various themes in the Woolf's work even more directly. Poirot is invited to lunch at a country house of the Angkatells where family and guests are spending a long weekend holiday in the country. Dr. Christow appears to be shot by his wife Gerda, as revenge for a fling with an old flame; Gerda is protected by the doctor's newer mistress, the modernist sculptor Henrietta. The opening chapters shift between the main protagonists in long, semi-stream-of-consciousness developments of the characters' present and their pasts (two are located round the minutes it takes for a mutton lunch to slowly congeal). These shifts evoke the more experimental style of the later Westmacott novels. The first half of *The Hollow* dwells on the characters' relationships in depth, until the tighter generic format develops with Poirot's arrival at the murder scene. In *The Hollow*, the artist is restored to being a woman, giving it a stronger analogy than *Giant's Bread* to Woolf's writing, despite being further away from *To the Lighthouse* chronologically.

An antithetical critical analysis of the two Christie novels in relation to the Woolf text reveals six major tropes at play in each of the three works (and indeed in the case of the final one, has no intrinsic structural function apart from its reference to the precursor):

1. A setting that is an escape from the every-day demands; a place of license and holiday.
2. The obsession of the (woman) artist with creating new and modernist art.
3. Familial/generational expectations of normative gender roles and conventional marriage.
4. The balancing of love, desire and marriage with the artist's drive to create.
5. Grief for those who die enabling artistic creation.
6. Middle class complacency with regard to money and leisure.

These six themes reappear in different combinations across each of the three texts, like a re-shaken kaleidoscope where the same pieces of colored glass create different patterns and shapes.

A Setting as a Place of License

As the earlier description of each novel indicates, each has a setting that is an escape from the everyday demands, a place of license and holiday. In

To the Lighthouse, this is a holiday home on a Scottish island, where all the furniture is cast-off and the children's cricket ball can smash the greenhouse without complaint. The sense of space, ease and informality on holiday beside the sea allows characters to wander off and arrive late for meals, focused on their own interests away from the demands of mundane work and social expectation. *Giant's Bread* has no such holiday setting, but instead, Vernon and his mistress Jane are forced to leave the cultural demands and expectations of England (to prevent his wife's bigamy being made public) and flee to Moscow where the revolutionary license allows them to live together unmarried without opprobrium and allows him to write his different music. The bohemian setting of the Russian capital, their place of permissiveness and escape, is so distanced from the English setting that it is never represented directly, but only shown via letters and reminiscences. But it is the setting that nurtures Vernon's creation of his opera. The Hollow, Lucy and Henry Angkatell's home, is the site for the other characters' weekends away and the early pages describe each character's delighted anticipation of the relaxation and escape afforded by the expansiveness of the countryside in fall. While this setting is not the site for Henrietta's artistic creation, since she has a studio in London, it is the scene for what Poirot calls her artistic obfuscation of the evidence.

The Obsession of the (Woman) Artist to Create New and Modernist Art

In the first part of *To the Lighthouse* Lily has to contend with Charles Tansley's sexist denigration, "women can't paint, women can't write,"[10] through which Woolf evokes the Edwardian "Angel in the House," a heteronormative ideal that positioned women in subordinate and supportive roles to men. In the final, modern part, Lily gains more perspective on this denigration and creates her painting. Across both parts Lily explores the compulsion of being an artist:

> Drawn ... out of community with people into the presence of the formidable ancient enemy of hers—this other thing, this truth, this reality, which suddenly laid hands on her, emerged stark at the back of appearances and commanded her attention.[11]

Lily needs to lose her consciousness, yielding the self to the rhythms of the brush across the canvas. Determinedly non-representational—Mrs. Ramsay becomes a purple triangle—she explains her method to the botanist, William Bankes, and his "scientific mind" comprehends her composition; "the question being one of the relation of masses, of lights and shadows"[12] and the balancing of shadow and light, mass and space into a unified composition. The representation of the finished vision links to the post-impressionist exhibitions organized in London by Woolf's friend Roger Fry:

> Beautiful and bright it should be on the surface, feathery and evanescent, one colour melting into another like the colours on a butterfly's wing; but beneath the fabric must be clamped together with bolts of iron.[13]

The novel ends with Lily completing the painting and hence confirming the importance of this theme of the woman artist. "Yes, she thought, laying down her brush in extreme fatigue, I have had my vision."[14] *Giant's Bread* is as strongly semi-autobiographical and literary as *To the Lighthouse*. In both novels, the art is transferred to a different medium; *Giant's Bread* also makes the artist male in a further distancing technique. The novel opens with Vernon's opera's success, staged for the opening night of London's new National Opera House, attended by royalty, the press, the fashionable and the musical experts. It is an opera consisting of the music and spectacle with weird lighting effects representing Man's move through the stone age to machinery/skyscrapers and finally glass, a new glacial age. The elderly distinguished critic gives it the accolade of a work of genius as the music of the future, and links it to British composers such as Holst, Vaughan Williams, Arnold Bax, but modulated through the "Russian Revolutionary School."[15] Twice the text insists on the highbrow status of the music, which will not be commercial. Once it moves from the prologue, the novel's focus is on the modernism of Vernon's creation—connecting it to Vladimir Tatlin and Vsevolod Meyerhold's work in Moscow, Sergei Prokofiev, Igor Stravinsky and the unappreciated Arnold Schoenberg. Linking to Albert Einstein's theory of relativity, Vernon argues that music needs to move away from the representational to something more scientific and "absolute," arguing with a "white-hot conviction" that "there are notes they don't use—notes they ought to use."[16] Needing new instruments to get the sound he requires, he turns to glass goblets despite the ridicule of his friends. Modernist music has to have "the courage to disregard tradition,"[17] and is obsessive: "You couldn't write music unless you gave your whole time, your whole thoughts, your whole soul to it."[18] *The Hollow* opens with Henrietta's sculpting of a "Nausicca," with obsessive weeks of agony, "driving her, harrying her … that urgent incessant longing,"[19] ruined by the spitefulness of the model being translated into the clay and tarnishing her vision for the piece. Henrietta's perfectionism causes her to sacrifice the piece, despite the experience of destroying her own flesh and blood. Here too the model is disappointed that it is not a likeness, but an abstract, where planes and shapes suggested by individual bodies are developed into a more stylized form. The pear-wood "The Worshipper" is destined for the International Group's exhibition, signifying both Henrietta's modernism and her success. She is described as a genius and Lucy Angkatell insists that she does not keep to feminine subjects such as animals and children (as D. H. Lawrence has his female artist, Gudrun, do in *Women in Love*), but she also "does" big constructions alongside the abstract figures, "advanced things, like that curious affair in metal and plaster that she exhibited at the New Artists last year. It looked like a Heath Robinson step-ladder. It was called Ascending Thought."[20]

The scientific endorsement and understanding of her work, where modernist techniques are linked to a more objective, rationalist approach, as with Lily and her botanist and Vernon and the mathematician, comes from the medical doctor Christow, who recognizes his wife's essence in the powerful abstract form. He denounces Henrietta as "unscrupulous" in using the resemblance, but she is not unscrupulous; she supports Gerda through the social gathering at the Hollow and then through the murder investigation. John's adjective is biased, and the epithet consistently assigned to Henrietta is "detached"; the quality of detachment is portrayed as allowing her an unconventional clarity of view. Tied to her artist's eye, this characteristic gives her an attractive unsentimental rigor, in contrast to Vernon's blind self-absorption. The female artist in *The Hollow* is allowed the most direct and accurate viewpoint, on a par with Poirot's own. All three novels have artists wrestling with the modernist difficulties of being new and comment on the driven, obsessive nature of their calling.

Familial/Generational Expectations of Normative Gender Roles and Conventional Marriage

In the Edwardian part of *To the Lighthouse*, Mr. and Mrs. Ramsay encapsulate the Edwardian binary gendered division of roles. Men have arduous public roles and deal in facts and reality, while women are unable to read a compass and, like Mrs. Ramsay, concentrate more on people's feelings and support their men's emotional inarticulacy. At the opening of the novel, this is conveyed through the parents' comments to the young son regarding his desired trip to the lighthouse. His father speaks to the facts of the weather making it impossible, and is angered by his wife's rejection of what he sees as the truth. She is upset at his insistence on dashing the loved son's wish, and prefers an irrational hope that it might be possible. To her, women's only purpose is to marry and support their men, and she is forever working to bring this about, matchmaking Paul and Minta, Lily and William Banks (both of whom are equally content with their work). Those who are not married are to be pitied, particularly "poor Lily," whose lack as a sexual object leaves her valueless under Mrs. Ramsay's terms, and Lily's painting is viewed as a compensatory hobby to help fill her empty life. The moment when "arriving late at night, with a light tap on one's bedroom door, wrapped in an old fur coat (for the setting of her beauty was always that—hasty but apt),"[21] she comes to discuss the evening and to urge Lily to marry, chimes with a significant characterization of Lucy Angkatell, in *The Hollow*, who disturbs her guests' sleep for similar reasons. Mrs. Ramsay's beauty, her eight children, her constant emotional self-sacrifice to her husband's needs and the successful dinner party stand testimony to an Edwardian concept of the successful wife. Lily is represented as constantly having to battle this evaluation and desire, and its undermining of her confidence is represented by her inability to complete her painting until Mrs. Ramsay has died. After her death, however, Lily, Mr. Ramsay, Cam and James renegotiate the gender roles in less patriarchal, authoritative and less femininely self-sacrificial ways, which are shown to be viable.

Giant's Bread has a similar generational division between Vernon's mother and father as the binaries of the past; he is reticent but honest and factual, while she is emotionally dishonest and histrionic, rejecting truth to live false normative roles of domesticity. Christie's earlier novel takes a more phallocentric view of woman's emotionality, in contrast to Woolf's feminist twist. Here, as elsewhere, Christie ties this to heredity, giving the Deyres an artistic bohemian side; following desire is designated as "weak-willed, self-indulgent and attractive,"[22] a trajectory shared by his father, aunt and cousin Joe, as well as Vernon himself, in choosing the honesty of desire despite conventionality, and the consequent social disaster for the women. The father insists on giving this the accolade of "courage." On the maternal Bent side, Vernon inherits the bourgeois "drive," whether for music or business, though it is notable that this skips the selfish, damaging mother for the male side through the uncle. Both mother and uncle strive to marry off Vernon to his cousin, in a subplot that Vernon avoids, making his own choice, although his own wife, Nell, embraces similar marital stereotypes. The main issue of the past that Vernon has to battle is his ability to make enough money as a traditional husband to be able to afford the upkeep and restoration of his beloved family home, Abbots Puissant. This family house stands as the tradition at odds with his need to write music.

In *The Hollow*, Lucy and Henry Angkatell serve as the Edwardian generation; he is the professional, ordered, matter-of-fact male with a public, imperial past as a governor of a British colony,[23] she occupies the Mrs. Ramsay role as irrational, beautiful and charming, and determined to marry Edward off as a way to save the ancient family home. Here the Edwardian woman recovers the charm and attractiveness of an irrational emotionality, which aligns her more closely to Mrs. Ramsay. Lucy differs, though, in her ignoring of conventionalities, as she contemplates shooting people if they prove inconvenient to her matchmaking. *To the Lighthouse* has Mrs. Ramsay sacrificing herself to support her husband—*The Hollow* reverses the gendered nurturing and has Henry constantly worrying what his wife might do next. Her extraordinary appeal prevents her from being unattractive, although she borders on a sexist construction of irrational, in need of male protection, from her husband's attitude to the butler who conceals the gun beneath the eggs. What is interesting is that all three texts create past heteronormative roles, where the men are rational and the women irrational, but give differing textual valuations to this phallocentric depiction, set in the Edwardian near past. The focus around traditional values includes an expectation of traditional marriage, which the artist has to contend with and in both Christie novels the marriage is given further traditional urgency by the need to protect an ancient family home.

The Balancing of Love, Desire and Marriage with the Artist's Obsession to Create

This theme is the major focus of Christie's Bloomian "swerve from" and serve "to correct and complete" what is misread as Woolf's theme, allowing the space for Christie's own meditation on the needs and demands of the driven woman modernist. It allows, coincidentally, the most insightful re-reading of *To the Lighthouse.*

To the Lighthouse uses Paul and Minta's relationship to explore Lily's distance from sexual desire. This is constructed, as is so much in this complex text, as having two perspectives, one of love and romance, which Lily gets caught up in, wishing to help Paul's chivalric hunt for Minta's lost brooch, "so beautiful and exciting, … odes have been sung to love; wreaths heaped and roses."[24] But the other side is of male lust, "the heat of love, its horror, its cruelty, its unscrupulosity" which has "fangs" that women are victims "exposed" to.[25]

> It is the stupidest, the most barbaric of human passions and turns a nice young man with a profile like a gem (Paul's was exquisite) into a bully with a crowbar (he was swaggering, he was insolent) in the Mile End Road.[26]

Lust is so appalling that it transforms nice middle class gentility into working class East End aggression. Lily authoritatively states that women are dissatisfied with this sexual aspect of love, feeling, "This is not what we want; there is nothing more tedious, puerile, and inhumane."[27] And she grasps her role as artist as one that saves her from such horrors:

> For at any rate, she said to herself, catching sight of the salt cellar on the pattern, she need not marry, thank heaven: she need not undergo that degradation. She

was saved from that dilution. She would move the tree rather more to the middle.[28]

Lily believes that time shows that Mrs. Ramsay's Edwardian obsession was wrong because, by this time, "the marriage had not been a success,"[29] Minta has taken lovers, insolently coming home at all times of night, while Paul, lonely and miserable, frequents coffee shops to play chess. However, the final image of this failed marriage in the modern era is a fascinating one given Christie's later texts.

> They were "in love" no longer; no, he had taken up with another woman, a serious woman with her hair in a plait and a case in her hand (Minta had compared her gratefully, almost admiringly), who went to meetings and shared Paul's views … far from breaking up the marriage, that alliance had righted it. They were excellent friends.[30]

Lily triumphs over Mrs. Ramsay's spirit, arguing that friendship is more valid between the sexes in the modern world than an outmoded view of love. "It has all gone against your wishes. They're happy like that. I'm happy like this. Life has changed completely."[31]

This same theme is the main focus of *Giant's Bread*—Vernon's desire for love, romance and sex is encapsulated by the two women in his life. Nell, the conventional and pretty wife, fulfilling all the normative roles of domesticity and sympathy but unable to understand an artist's needs and afraid of his creativity, has his love, represented very similarly to Woolf's romance as unreal and intensely emotional. The mistress, successful classical singer Jane Harding, has his desire, linked to her understanding of his obsession, and her emotional honesty challenges him to face the truths of a situation and ignore the conventions. Where Nell tricks him into marriage, fearing Jane and his genius, Jane sacrifices her own voice to build his career, indicating the novel's positive evaluation of sexual desire stripped from false and self-seeking conventional trappings. In case the reader misses the structuring, when Vernon returns after the war to find Nell married to a rich American, she refuses to forgo her luxurious comfort in his family home, and he moves to Russia with Jane to allow Nell to remain married, and to concentrate on his music, thus living out the argument the experienced Jane made much earlier in the text that music demands everything of its creator. The youthful Vernon had aimed to rescue his family house and marry his love while becoming both financially successful and a great composer but Jane argues that devoting his whole focus may allow him to achieve just one of these four goals, since "Life isn't like a penny novelette."[32] When Vernon challenges her experienced view, she responds that "to get what you want, you must usually pay a price or take a risk" and that if he chooses music "it will swallow up all the rest."[33] Vernon ignores her advice, trying to achieve all four goals and his friend Sebastian opines, "I don't think a genius wants to be married to a real person. He wants to be married to someone quite negligible—someone whose personality won't interfere."[34] His concern at this point is that Jane is too strong a personality—but Jane will take her own advice and sacrifice her voice and career to love one person fully.

In this novel, focused on the clashing demands of tradition and the need to be new, the demands of overwhelming love and the obsession with creation, the artist's genius comes from a dramatic rejection of marriage and family, enabling him to live in an honest relationship of sexual desire that enables him to focus on artistic creation. One of the problematic figures here, as in the Westmacott novel *The Rose and the Yew Tree* (1947) is that the man's success comes at the expense of the mistress's self-sacrifice, and this is considered acceptable because it is the woman's freely given choice.[35] The gendered stereotype of the woman devoting herself to her man's success, while perhaps more accommodated in the 1940s, raises real problems to twenty-first century audiences. The idea that so much has to be sacrificed to create great art links to the giant in the title of both the novel and its opera; when the critic questions who and what was sacrificed to go into the making of this Giant's bread, intertextually citing the nursery rhyme, "fee, fi, fo, fumb," leading to our final realization at the close that Vernon has sacrificed everything to it. Placing the success of his genius at the opening structures our evaluation of marriage and desire in relation to the artist's need to create. Nell's unattractive and selfish character juxtaposed with Jane's selfless honesty ensures we favor the choice of the supportive mistress. In many ways, this text, by shifting the main creator to a male character, seems to reinforce Lily's view that women cannot have an encompassing sexual relationship and be a painter or singer. Women get sacrificed as bones to make the artistic bread, while men can find a viable compromise between creation and desire outside of marriage.

In *The Hollow*, Christie splits the dialogue on professional obsession at odds with overpowering love and desire between the male doctor's scientific research and the woman artist's sculpting. John Christow's research, the focus of his professional life, was threatened by his youthful romantic obsession with the actress Veronica Cray, who egotistically expected him to sacrifice his work to devote himself to her. This is depicted as selfish and egotistical. Instead, the woman artist's need for both sex and companionship, kept at a distance from her artistic obsession, is solved with Henrietta's adulterous relationship with Christow. This relationship is allowed a much more positive frame than Jane Harding's, since Henrietta is strong enough to refuse to sacrifice her art to love. Henrietta achieves the necessary balance of love and sexual pleasure alongside devotion to her art precisely because she does not live with John and is not engrossed by domesticities, which allows her to compartmentalize her competing desires. This Gerda-John-Henrietta love triangle, it should be noted, exactly mirrors the final view we are given of Minta and Paul's system in the modern section of *To the Lighthouse*, with Paul married to Minta but finding sex and a meeting of minds with his mistress. Lily's thesis that "far from breaking up the marriage, that alliance had righted it" is borne out in detail. John is able to have a conventional family with two children and a wife who sentimentalizes her subservience, and a satisfying sexual relationship with Henrietta, whose "unswerving rectitude" and genuine interest supports his research into Ridgeway's disease.[36] When he is stuck, he flees to Henrietta, seeking escape through sex, but she gently steers him towards uncovering the clinical solution. His loss of self, pacing, as his mind races, and then the exhaustion of peace when he solves the problem, directly echoes Henrietta's experiences as she wrestled with sculpting Nausicca, two chapters previously. Both characters share this obsession with bringing something new to the world. The only thing that John sacrifices is an overpowering, all-consuming love of a sort he finds unattractive in his maturity, when he refuses to "risk" (that Christie word) either his family or his relationship with Henrietta.

Henrietta too has love and sexual desire and her need for equal intellectual companionship satisfied through her love for John, while the unconventional role of mistress allows her the space to focus on her sculpture. What she "sacrifices," as a woman artist, is marriage and family, but it is clear she is not interested in these (as she refuses Edward's third proposal), and since she does not want to break up the marriage, she also proves no threat to Gerda's lifestyle. In supplying John with the intelligent conversation Gerda's character cannot (she is fashioned as Sebastian's "someone quite negligible—someone whose personality won't interfere"), Henrietta does "right" the marriage for John and serves as Gerda's protector after his murder. *The Hollow* therefore takes up the ending of *To the Lighthouse*'s 1920s meditation on sexual desire and artistic obsession, "swerves" to make it the focus of the precursor novel and proceeds to complete it with a claim for clear-sighted "tough-mindedness" that is open about female sexual desire, "misreading" the original text in order to create the space needed for Christie's own composition that argues the co-existence of healthy sexuality alongside the driven need to create, in the very different context of the mid-1940s.

In this novel Christie explores, through John and Henrietta's relationship, John's entrenched conventional view alongside his appreciation of the independent equality he shares with her, and here retracts the further gendered expectations the woman artist faces. Henrietta is aware that "after a while—I got between John and what he was thinking of. I affected him as a woman. He couldn't concentrate as he wanted to concentrate—because of me."[37] Poirot thinks that Henrietta prioritizes her love for John in refusing to claim a status for their relationship beyond their extramarital affair, but in fact she is content with the status quo while it is John who wants more. Still, John's jealousy of her sculpture is always punctuated with textual signals ("he knew he was unfair") as he acknowledges that "it was only on very rare occasions that her absorption with some inner vision spoiled the completeness of her interest in him. But it always roused his furious anger."[38] The word Christie uses to signify Henrietta's distance from obsessive love is "detachment" and Henrietta acknowledges that part of her will always belong to her art. The text allows her to voice her sense of the artist's burden: "'But I,' she thought, 'am not a whole person. I belong not to myself, but to something outside of me.'"[39] Henrietta does not subordinate her work to loving him, just as Christie has John refuse to subsume his work in loving Veronica Cray. With John's unreasonable demands of Henrietta, the text quietly notes the unequal expectation men level against women in the same situation, and hence the strength that professional women artists need to resist social convention.

Christie seems to have directly lifted Woolf's triangle and developed it to allow emotional and sexual satisfaction for the female artist, rejecting Lily's fear of sex as victimizing the woman and damaging her profession, while appearing to agree the impossibility of the conventional Edwardian marriage. Hence the focus on female self-sacrifice and subservience and the necessary resistances to it. Both Jane Harding and Henrietta Savernake are constructed, in their vitality, irony and clear-eyed honesty in making choices, to refute victimhood to male sexual appetite as they fulfill their own desires. Jane does sacrifice her voice to the better (male) artist but Henrietta, just after World War II, can inhabit a bohemian lifestyle that requires much less sacrifice of the self, as she continues to sculpt her modernist pieces. And, Christie's text argues, her support for both the husband and the wife situates her as the most attractive of the characters, allowing the adulterous mistress the moral high-ground, a view Poirot endorses at the close: "I have admired you, always, very much."[40]

Grief for Those Who Die Enabling Artistic Creation

Fascinatingly, each text closes with artistic accomplishment linked to a sense of loss and grief. In the first section of *To the Lighthouse*, Lily questions whether her modernist representation of Mrs. Ramsay with James, the mother and child composition, is indeed "a tribute," since she is solely concerned with shape and color.[41] Its completion in the final section is accompanied by her memories; her grief: "'Mrs. Ramsay! Mrs. Ramsay!' she cried, feeling the old horror come back—to want and want and not to have. Could she inflict that still?"⁴² But Mrs. Ramsay's spirit takes up the necessary position in her chair, to allow a shadow to fall across the step that enables Lily to complete the painting: "with a sudden intensity, as if she saw it clear for a second, she drew a line there, in the centre. It was done; it was finished."⁴³

The improbable conclusion of *Giant's Bread* finds all corners of Vernon's love triangle aboard the sinking *Titanic*, and Vernon, having a split second to save only one of the two women as they slide past him into the waves, chooses the wrong woman, Nell. This gives him the final grief-stricken focus to compose the "Giant." Finally realizing, now that he has lost her, his true love for Jane, he pours his grief into the music and in creating becomes happy: torn between "agony and wild exultation," the closing lines echo the ruthless cruelty of art, using peoples as victims to its inception.⁴⁴ Where Lily's art allows for a resolution to her grief, and an acknowledgement of Mrs. Ramsay's kindness in her complex memory of her, Vernon's art is both a more simplistic and a more divisively bitter and guilt-stricken rendition. Grief is not resolved but overwhelmed in the artistic endeavor. Despite the determined modernism of his music, it is a very romantic construction of the artist.

The Hollow also ends with the artist's grief for a dead person inspiring a composition. Where Lily's grief allows her to complete a painting, Christie's artists' grief proves the inspiration for new work in both novels. Henrietta, finally able to give in to her grief for John, is horrified as in her paroxysm she begins to envisage a cowled, elongated figure epitomizing her sorrow; "She thought.... I cannot love—I cannot mourn—not with the whole of me."⁴⁵ Henrietta differs from Vernon in that she is guiltless of John's death. This is reinforced by her encouragement to John's patient to get well for his sake, as a testament to his scientific cure for Ridgeway's Disease, his vision. Directly after, she is inspired by her a new vision which becomes "exhibit no. 58. 'Grief.' Alabaster. Miss Henrietta Savernake."⁴⁶ In *The Hollow*, however, there are no human victims sacrificed for the art work. It is a purely internalized conflict and pain, and the art no longer demands the whole person but just a part of them, allowing a more attractive, less selfish characterization. All three novels end with grief enabling artistic creation, but only Christie explores how this links to the love of a sexual partner, and the artist riven between their devotion to their art and to their lover, since Lily has eschewed any sexual complications.

Middle-Class Complacency in Relation to Money and Leisure

There is little structural reason for this theme in *The Hollow*, but some in *Giant's Bread*, apart from each text being complexly in dialogue with *To the Lighthouse*. Charles Tansley in the Woolf novel, the impoverished doctoral student supporting his sister's education while denigrating Lily's painting, is allowed to comment on the Ramsay's complacent affluence and class solipsism. However, this is portrayed negatively as the chip on the shoulder of a disagreeable guest. He is portrayed as harping on about smoking cheap tobacco, has an unattractive lack of social ease and rejects polite conversation as "talking nonsense." These, alongside his cruel sexist comments on Lily's painting, leave him little space to mount a serious critique of the very present leisured affluent solipsism. But he needs to be registered since his function is echoed in *The Hollow*. *Giant's Bread* has a number of characters who challenge English middle-class solipsism, none more so than Sebastian Levine, a Jewish millionaire (this character allows Christie to examine British anti-Semitism). In relation to poverty, there is also Nell's annoyance at Vernon's sentimental view that poverty is unimportant if they have love, and her resentment of his total ignorance. However, in *Giant's Bread* poverty is really a decline from affluence to lower-middle-class drudgery, this time from the woman's viewpoint—the drudgery of trying to keep up appearances without the income for pretty new clothes. Nell, like Charles Tansley, is an unsympathetic character and so the critique again lacks power. While the issue of poverty, and the ignorance exhibited by the affluent over what it means, are present, there is not enough focus to consider poverty a theme. There is also an absence of awareness concerning the actual nature of poverty.

In *The Hollow*, the young David Angkatell effectively takes the Tansley role of disdaining the socialite frivolity of the party. However, since he will inherit Ainswick if Edward does not breed a legitimate heir, he clearly cannot speak for the poor. Midge, the impoverished cousin who has to make her living as an assistant in an up-market fashion shop is a positive, central character who serves this function, irritated into speech at Edward Angkatell's comfortable incomprehension of the ugliness of life. "She thought with rancor: 'they don't know *anything!*'"[47] Once again the conception of poverty is a middle-class rendition of the hardship of being bullied and patronized as a shop-assistant (and includes a highly problematic representation of the Jewish owner). The text does refer to the working class hardship of Mrs. Crabtree and Mrs. Pearstock (as *To the Lighthouse* has its Mrs. McNab), but insists with a complaisant solipsism all of its own that the "Poor with a capital P" are all the same, "under the skin."[48] In both Christie novels, this representation of a resentment of upper-middle class ignorance around the hardship of poverty has only minimum correspondence to the main themes of the artist's need to create the new, in conflict with the desire for companionship and sex. The real explanation for their presence comes in the fact that it is also a vestigial non sequitur in the precursor text.

Harold Bloom's theorization of the anxiety of influence allows a reading of Christie's dialogue with *To the Lighthouse* that has her "swerving" to explore the driven compulsion to create something new and modernist and the effect this has on the artist's personal and emotional needs. Both Christie texts examined challenge Woolf's thesis of virginal dedication but acknowledge that conventional marriage may be incompatible, particularly for the woman artist. However, Christie always assumes that men and women have equally healthy sexual appetites and the solution seems to be long-term commitment outside of and alongside of marriage. In *The Hollow*, Christie takes Woolf's representation of the modern flawed marriage and crafts it into a workable *ménage à trois*, as a direct resolution to Lily's abstemiousness. While Bloom's theory reveals a tension between the Mary Westmacott persona, experimenting with form in ambitious "middlebrow" literary novels and the popular Christie detective fiction, it also demonstrates that both genres are deemed viable to contradict the modernist vision of Virginia Woolf. Both formats engage in a creative contextual struggle of denial and restitution with the contemporary writer, revealed by their secret intertextuality of theme and sub-theme. However, the reasons for why these two Christie novels create dialogues with the Woolf must necessarily remain a hypothesis for the reader's fictional creation of Christie (as Foucault illustrates all biographical creations of the author are), whether Christie imagined herself as the conflicted artist, in relation to emotional commitments; justified her choice of the "workaday middlebrow" crime fiction in contrast to the tortured status of the modernist, in order to live a more comfortable emotional life with commercial success; or simply saw the dislocation and tensions as interesting fictional puzzles, is open to an array of interpretations. What can be argued with more certainty is that Harold Bloom's antithetical criticism is one way of allowing a serious engagement with "middlebrow" novels, granting them equal status in literary terms with modernist dialogues on artistic production, gender and desire. And while not wishing to claim that *The Hollow* is as substantial a novel as *To the Lighthouse*, it also raises questions about such implicitly discriminatory designations as "highbrow" and "middlebrow."

NOTES

1. Harold Bloom, *The Anxiety of Influence: A Theory of Poetry* (New York: Oxford University Press, 1973), p. 25.

2. Terry Eagleton, *Figures of Dissent: Critical Essays on Fish, Spivak, Zizek and Others* (London: Verso, 2005), p. 168.

3. Alison Light, *Forever England: Femininity, Literature and Conservatism Between the Wars* (London: Routledge, 1991), p. 73. Gillian Gill, *Agatha Christie: The Woman and Her Mysteries* (London: Robson, 1990), pp. 157, 158, 170.

4. Agatha Christie, *An Autobiography* (London: Fontana, 1977), pp. 198, 203-204.

5. *Ibid.*, p. 232.

6. Bloom, *The Anxiety of Influence*, p. 5.

7. *Ibid.*, p. 42.
8. *Ibid.*, p. 69.
9. Virginia Woolf, *To the Lighthouse* (London: Hogarth Press, 1960), p. 156.
10. *Ibid.*, p. 78.
11. *Ibid.*, p. 245.
12. *Ibid.*, p. 86.
13. *Ibid.*, p. 264.
14. *Ibid.*, p. 320.
15. Agatha Christie, *Giant's Bread* in *Absent in Spring and Other Novels*, written as Mary Westmacott (New York: St Martin's Minotaur, 2001), pp. 163–468 (p. 169).
16. *Ibid.*, p. 252.
17. *Ibid.*, p. 455.
18. *Ibid.*, p. 305.
19. Agatha Christie, *The Hollow* (London: HarperCollins, 2002), p. 23.
20. Christie, *The Hollow*, p. 13.
21. Woolf, *To the Lighthouse*, p. 80.
22. Christie, *Giant's Bread*, p. 149.
23. See Rowland for a useful critique of the implicit Edwardian Imperialism.
24. Woolf, *To the Lighthouse*, p. 159.
25. *Ibid.*
26. *Ibid.*
27. *Ibid.*, p. 160.
28. *Ibid.*, p. 159.
29. *Ibid.*, p. 269.
30. *Ibid.*, p. 265.
31. *Ibid.*, p. 269.
32. Christie, *Giant's Bread*, p. 306.
33. *Ibid.*, pp. 315, 316.
34. *Ibid.*, p. 317.
35. Agatha Christie, *The Rose and the Yew Tree* in *Absent in Spring and Other Novels*, written as Mary Westmacott (New York: St Martin's Minotaur, 2001) pp. 469–644.
36. Christie, *The Hollow*, p. 37.
37. *Ibid.*, p. 240.
38. *Ibid.*, pp. 69–70.
39. *Ibid.*, p. 384.
40. *Ibid.*, p. 375.
41. Woolf, *To the Lighthouse,* p. 85.
42. *Ibid.*, p. 310.
43. *Ibid.*, p. 319.
44. Christie, *Giant's Bread*, p. 466.
45. Christie, *The Hollow*, p. 383.
46. *Ibid.*
47. *Ibid.*, p. 194.
48. *Ibid.*, pp. 42–43.

Bibliography

Bloom, Harold. *The Anxiety of Influence: A Theory of Poetry*. New York: Oxford University Press, 1973.

Eagleton, Terry. *Figures of Dissent: Critical Essays on Fish, Spivak, Zizek and Others.* London: Verso, 2005.

Christie, Agatha. *An Autobiography* (1977), London: Fontana, 1978.
_____. *Giant's Bread* (1930). *Absent in Spring and Other Novels*, written as Mary Westmacott. New York: St Martin's Minotaur, 2001, pp. 163–468.
_____. *The Hollow* (1946). London: HarperCollins, 2002.
_____. *The Rose and the Yew Tree* (1948). *Absent in the Spring and Other Novels*, written as Mary Westmacott. New York: St Martin's Minotaur, 2001, pp. 469–644.
Gill, Gillian, *Agatha Christie: The Woman and Her Mysteries*. London: Robson, 1990.
Foucault, Michel. "What Is an Author?" in D. F. Bouchard (ed.), *Language, Counter-Memory, Practice: Selected Essays and Interviews*. Oxford: Basil Blackwell, 1977, pp. 113–138.
Light, Alison. *Forever England: Femininity, Literature and Conservatism Between the Wars*. London: Routledge, 1991.
Rowland, Susan. *From Agatha Christie to Ruth Rendell: British Women Writers in Detective and Other Writing*. Basingstoke: Palgrave Macmillan, 2001.
Sova, Dawn P. *Agatha Christie A to Z*. New York: Checkmark, 1996.
Woolf, Virginia. *A Room of One's Own*. London: Hogarth Press, 1929.
_____. *To the Lighthouse* (1927). London: Hogarth Press, 1960.

England's Pockets
Objects of Anxiety in Christie's Post-War Novels

Rebecca Mills

In Agatha Christie's work, objects are clues to character, motive and eventually the criminal in the accepted tradition of detective fiction, but as her oeuvre develops from the Golden Age to the post-war era, everyday objects also serve a series of increasingly complex functions. Objects are reifications of social conditions and change. They are a nexus where yearning for the past meets the dangers of nostalgia; the temporality of the plot is disrupted by the everyday items that furnish interior spaces and serve as metaphors for identities positioned between the grim post-war present and the golden past, or between theatrical artifice and the solidly real. Through their contact with the violence and trauma inherent to detective fiction, but also the legacy of World War II, the objects in *The Moving Finger* (1943), *After the Funeral* (1953) and *The Pale Horse* (1961) come to occupy multiple blurred and layered categories, as their generic function becomes saturated with symbolic and emotional affect. In this essay, by tracing the strands of material culture in Christie's less-studied post-war novels, I will not only demonstrate a tension between the presentation of objects as things to be preserved, as embodiments of ways of life, and the tendency to shatter these symbols of continuity and subvert ordinary objects into metaphors for danger and anxiety, but also take seriously Christie's literary and imaginative response to the war and the following era of technological advances, international tension and change.

This essay is informed by the cultural historian Jacques Barzun's emphasis on the significance of the physical, material elements of detective fiction that accompany cerebral deduction and psychology. As he writes in *Detection and the Literary Art*, "The raw material of detection consists of the physical objects that surround action. These become literary substance when the detective imagination has chosen and arranged them so that some are clues while others produce atmosphere, verisimilitude, suspense."[1] In Christie's post-war novels in particular, both the absence of personal items and a clutter of things can serve as indicators of both guilt and strangeness, out-of-placeness and erased or anxious individual and collective identities. Although, as Stephen Knight argues, "Christie's wartime mysteries superintend contemporary battles from a distance and with an Austenesque pattern of radical displacement, not recognizing the war as itself, but representing its effect in terms of disruptions to the normal balance of gender and social power,"[2] as in *Sad Cypress* (1940) and *The Moving Finger* (1943), the full effects of wartime and its tensions and deprivations are delayed as well as displaced. The war also leaves traces on the material culture of Christie's wartime and post-war texts; objects and the emotional and social textures of the spaces where they are positioned reveal both "disruptions" to social stability, but also to emotional mental equilibrium at collective and individual levels.

In its concern with social and cultural continuity and change after the war as well as literary style and genre, this essay also builds to some extent on Alison Light's discussion of Christie's "conservative modernism" during the interwar period. Light hints at the importance of objects in Christie's fiction; of *Peril at End House* (1933), she writes:

> *End House* is hardly a symbol of patrician bourgeois authority but of modern domestication; it offers a new image of bourgeois pleasures, one which depends upon the consumption of a commercialized culture: the gramophone, the wireless, journalism. What interests Christie is this mixing of old and new and the possibilities it creates for different kinds of desires, new species of deception.[3]

This mixing of old and new is evident throughout Christie's Golden Age work; in *The Murder of Roger Ackroyd* (1926), for instance, the crucial clues are a "Tunisian dagger" which would be at home in any Holmes story, and a Dictaphone, with its modern uncanny power of broadcasting a dead man's voice. Light seems to suggest that Christie's use of technology and items anchors her work in Christie's present, serving to locate the interwar books in their contemporary milieu. Objects in Christie's post–World War II novels, however, I would suggest, serve to dislocate the books from their period, undermining their modernity; the insistence is on legacies of the past—and the concomitant dangers of eradicating the past altogether. While objects, particularly weapons, retain what Light calls the juxtaposition of the "macabre and the familiar,"[4] the balance often tilts towards the former. But this tension between the everyday and the defamiliarized is part of the process of the detective story; as Barzun writes, "What do we gain from the details of detection? An understanding, first, of the silent life of things, and next, of the spectacle of mind at work."[5]

England Has Pockets

I begin my investigation of the "silent life of things" with the Miss Marple novel *The Moving Finger* (1943). This novel serves as an apposite starting point because it straddles the divide between Christie's explicitly wartime novels such as *N or M?* and her early 1940s novels in which the war is blanked out such as *Evil Under the Sun*. As well as offering examples of the alienating affect assigned to things, and illustrating the connection between metaphorical objects and collective or individual identity, *The Moving Finger* demonstrates the temporal dislocation revealed and concealed by objects. Set in the village of Lymstock, the narrative revolves around a series of poison-pen letters, which lead to seeming suicide, a murder and mounting paranoia among the villagers. Narrator Jerry and his sister Joanna end up in the village in search of rural peace and quiet after Jerry's accident; as the aesthete Mr. Pye, an inhabitant of the village and due to his queerness, a suspected author of the letters, comments,

> A wonderful country, England. It has pockets. Lymstock is one of them. Interesting from a collector's point of view—I always feel I have voluntarily put myself under a glass shade when I am here. The peaceful backwater where nothing happens.[6]

To belong to the village is not only to be enclosed in a pocket, but also to be an object, a static figurine isolated from the rest of England and the passage of history. Indeed, Mr. Pye refers to the elderly Miss Emily as "a charming creature…. Like a piece of Dresden," going on to emphasize her age and unsuitability for the modern world by reiterating the glass metaphor:

> Absolutely a period piece. She's not, you know, of her own generation, she's of the generation before that. The mother must have been a woman of very strong character. She kept the family time ticking at about 1870, I should say. The whole family preserved under a glass case.[7]

Glass suggests vulnerability as well as protection, however—as Gill Plain observes, "In her depiction of Lymstock under siege, Christie is more than usually explicit in her suggestion that the idyllic 'English' community is a fragile construct."[8]

Pye's seemingly casual remarks reveal the other aspect of the village; the presence of the past. The preserving glass case is not only a symbol of Miss Emily's mother's monstrous feminine power, but also enforces stagnation in the village. This is evident, again via Pye's acid commentary, through reference to objects—Miss Emily "likes to keep things as they were—but not for *le bon motif*—not because of the resultant harmony—but because it is the way her mother had them."[9] This stasis extends to the village as a whole: "And then, somewhere in seventeen hundred and something, the tide of progress swept

Lymstock into a backwater.... It turned into a little provincial market town, unimportant and forgotten."[10] Servants have a regular day out and postmen have a regular hour for deliveries; the routines are choreographed and fixed, which enables the murders and delivery of the letters. Nevertheless, the backwater has an inhabitant tormented by what Mrs. Dane Calthrop, the vicar's wife, describes as "a dark stream of poison … black inward unhappiness—like a septic arm physically, all black and swollen."[11] Poison as a motif recurs not merely through the "poison-pen" letters that allow the anxieties of the community—related to faithful partners, hidden perversions, or past sins—to rise to the surface. As Jerry remarks, "What kind of place is this for a man to come to lie in the sun and heal his wounds? It's full of festering poison, this place, and it looks as peaceful and as innocent as the Garden of Eden."[12] Eventually the poison shifts from a metaphorical and spiritual concept to materiality; it comes to light that the first fatal victim of the letters was murdered by her husband with cyanide used by the gardener to kill wasps. This is an instance of what Light describes as Christie's typical "domestication of weaponry,"[13] but there are further implications; poison is concealed, killing the body from within. The murderer and poison-pen letter-writer Mr. Symington poisons his wife because he wishes to marry his children's governess but maintain his façade of respectability as a county solicitor; he is imprisoned within the glass case of social convention, with fatal results.

Symington intended the letters as a smoke-screen. He took on the persona of a deranged woman and disseminated them in order to divert suspicion, as well as providing a motive for his wife's seeming suicide. As objects, the letters continue the theme of the intrusion of the past into the present, as the police expert describes: "The text of the letters is composed of words made up from individual letters cut out of an old printed book. It's an old book, printed, I should say, about the year 1830. This has obviously been done to avoid the risk of recognition through handwriting, which is, as most people know nowadays, a fairly easy matter."[14] The cut-out letters that make up the text mean that the police and amateur detectives are searching for a book with missing pages, an absence rather than something hidden, that echoes the absent moral code of the writer/murderer, and suggests blank spaces within the communal narrative of the village that is being re-written by the poison pen letters. It is indeed the "silent life of things" that is tracked as the police search for the hollow book and analyze the typescript. The book turns out to be a "ponderous volume of somebody's sermons,"[15] found in Miss Emily's bookshelf in the house rented by Jerry and Joanna. The book has been preserved because everything in Lymstock has been preserved. Not only does its location cast suspicion on Miss Emily, it also transforms the book of religious writing into an empty shell; the texts have been cut and rearranged for evil purpose.

It is a chance message on a piece of paper and a dream evoking the language and atmosphere of wartime that provides the final check to Symington's scheme. War has been conspicuously absent from the novel; there is no rationing, blackout, or war news, London has a plentiful supply of fashionable dress stores and restaurants and although Jerry is an injured pilot, military flying is not mentioned. As Plain comments, "Far more important [than mourning the murdered] is the novel's insistence upon communal health and gender normativity. *The Moving Finger* is firmly designed to assert stability in the face of change and to keep wartime trauma under control."[16] We see this particularly in the happy endings for Jerry and Joanna, who find true love and move to the village, rather than in any acknowledgement that Symington's two young sons will be orphaned when he is hanged. Nevertheless, there are hints of war in the escalating paranoia of the villagers and the growing sense that secrets are dangerous and the symmetry of the ending is only made possible through Miss Marple's analysis of Jerry's dreamwork: "No smoke without fire. No fire without smoke. Smoke…. Smoke? Smoke screen … no, that was the war—a war phrase. War. Scrap of paper…. Only a scrap of paper. Belgium—Germany."[17] The insistence on fire here connotes the destruction of the war, while the "scrap of paper" suggests a worthless peace treaty. From Jerry's recital of this dream, Miss Marple translates international warfare into personal conflict and deduces that Mrs. Symington's alleged suicide note was a handful appropriate words torn from a longer, innocuous message (another re-ordered text) and that the poison pen letters were a smoke screen, a diversion to conceal real intent. Jerry's dream shatters the dreamworld beneath the glass casing, the world of Dresden dolls and poisonous festering wounds; fire can be purifying as well as destructive. It is left ambiguous, however, whether Lymstock is thereby restored to modernity, or whether by moving to the village, Jerry and Joanna themselves abandon their careers as pilot and bright young thing and sink into the past.

"The tea-shop that would never be"

After the Funeral (1953) picks up on the themes of "period pieces" and change versus stasis. England's pockets are no longer backwaters forgotten by time and progress, but are emptied, sites of change and disintegration and brutal murder. Cora Lansquenet is found dead in her bed in a country cottage, hacked to death with a hatchet; the general response is that the only possible culprit capable of such senseless violence is one of the "half-witted local oafs" or "these adolescent criminals—there's a lot of them about."[18] In Christie's post-war era, the countryside no longer even has a peaceful façade; on a more imaginative level, Cora's niece Susan muses, sleepless in Cora's cottage, "How sinister the country was somehow. So different from the big noisy indifferent town."[19] There is safety in numbers in *After the Funeral*—though, of course, as is Christie's wont, the danger comes from within the closed community; as with Mr. Symington in *The Moving Finger*, the person closest to the victim here committed the crime.

Miss Gilchrist, the respectable and solidly bourgeois companion to Cora, has been playing the part of the flustered middle-aged maiden lady; in actual fact she is resentful of Cora and the restricted and subservient life of the lady-companion, and obsessed with re-establishing her tea-shop from before the war. As Nicholas Birns and Margaret Boe Birns write of Christie's interwar novels,

> Christie's use of the mask in her fiction has its roots in the nature of mystery novels, which depend on their highlighting a doubleness, a dichotomy between appearance and reality, a dichotomy which the detective in his investigations enacts rhetorically but only provisionally solves.[20]

In *After the Funeral*, this "dichotomy between appearance and reality" is negotiated through the relationships between the characters and the objects they desire and which surround them. Miss Gilchrist goes to Cora's brother's funeral dressed in Cora's clothes: "rather cushion-like in shape, and dressed in wispy artistic black with festoons of jet beads, back in the home of her girlhood, moving about and touching things and exclaiming with pleasure when she recalled some childish memory."[21] Later it becomes apparent that the alleged Cora's "cushion-like" shape was literally due to padding, and Miss Gilchrist has also appropriated Cora's "false front" of hair as well as her childhood memories and nostalgic connections to the furnishings of the house. The other implication here is that the house, or at least its above-stairs quarters, has remained unchanged for decades; this stagnation enables Miss Gilchrist to perform her role, to fake belonging to the house and the family.

After the Funeral is cluttered with things and families. While the funeral of Cora's brother Richard Abernethy and the reading of his will may seem to be the starting point of the novel, we actually start with the story of Enderby Hall, a "vast Victorian house built in the Gothic style" and furnished with "rich faded brocade and velvet" and family portraits.[22] The blinds in the windows are falling apart but have lasted a long time; the alternative, according to the butler is "Gimcrack.... The material wasn't good, or the craftsmanship either."[23] The end of an era is mourned via the kitchen of Enderby Hall: "[Cook] Marjorie turned up the gas under her large saucepan of creamy chicken soup. The large kitchen range of the days of Victorian grandeur stood cold and unused, like an altar to the past."[24] This is an altar not much respected by the younger generation of Richard's relations; the house is too old, too big and too inconvenient, and it might as well be turned into an institution.

Despite the sense of heritage and tradition, the house is gradually emptied of the family lineage; not only is "head of the family" Richard now dead, but his sons had been killed in the war and by polio. Enderby Hall and its faded drapery and period pieces are being divided and discarded. The arrangement of "a bouquet of wax flowers under a glass shade on a malachite table" is particularly important[25]; as in *The Moving Finger*, the connotations of the glass shade are artificiality, and the doubled preservation and stagnation. The glass shade here is fragile, however—even the family name is lost after Richard's death. The younger generation may have escaped stagnation but are all flawed; George is dishonest and embezzles from his business, Rosamund lacks a moral compass and is married to an egotistic, potentially murderous actor, Susan has business acumen but a blind spot for her highly neurotic, potentially murderous husband. We are meant to assume that the faded grandeur of Enderby Hall, the replacement of mansions with public institutions or cheaply built suburbs, and the shoddy craftsmanship of postwar building and factories, are metaphors for the younger generation's corruption and lack of integrity, especially since Rosamund has theatrical connections and Susan wants to repurpose "period pieces" from their place within a family's interior geography into a decorative gimmick in her commercial operation. Indeed, R. A. York comments that in *After the Funeral*,

> Christie's anxiety is obviously that the modern world is one in which morality and social stability have been undermined by egoism and hedonism. The concern with social stability is based on the assumption that an ordered society is comprehensible and therefore helps people to manage life because it defines possible types of conduct and the reactions to them that are to be expected.[26]

Nevertheless, the real danger lies in attempting to recover the social order damaged by the war. The brutal murderer Miss Gilchrist, the contemporary of Richard and Cora, is a woman from inside the glass casing, whose obsession with the past is a warning about holding onto it and its artefacts.

Miss Gilchrist and Cora live in a cottage crowded with paintings and *objets d'art*. Some paintings are by Cora's deceased husband, some are sketches by Cora herself and some are "horrible daubs" picked up by Cora at farmhouse sales.[27] Cora's furniture is "spurious cottage oak and some arty painted stuff"—the cottage is a cracked mirror of the family portraits and authentic drapes and furniture of Enderby Hall, including the "small green table painted with large purple clematis"[28] that echoes the malachite table with waxed flowers. Clues are concealed amid this insistence on clutter and inauthentic pieces of art and furniture; we are told that among Cora's messy personal possessions lie "two false fringes"[29] which Miss Gilchrist uses to impersonate her, and we later learn that the "horrible daubs" and landscapes concealed a genuine Vermeer. This Vermeer is Miss Gilchrist's motive, as she needs the money to equip her teashop. Miss Gilchrist's dreams are fueled by recollection of past glories, but rather than the comfortable Victorian days and family life of Enderby Hall at its height, she yearns for a specific place in the social order; a period and environment somewhere between the shoddy modernity of Cora's cottage and moneyed splendor—a thoroughly bourgeois interwar teashop called the Willow Tree.

Miss Gilchrist, possibly one of the "surplus women" left by World War I,[30] poured her life into the teashop, and its loss is her constant refrain. As Merja Makinen points out, Miss Gilchrist's position as a paid companion involves "poverty and paucity of experience" as well as "years of dependent drudgery."[31] Miss Gilchrist has compensated for her lack of independence and poverty not only by fixating on her pre-war life as a teashop proprietor but also by allowing the shop and its objects to replace her personality; she is as obsessed with things as Pye is in *The Moving Finger*, but with practical and pretty everyday objects rather than antique decorative pieces. Readers get several versions of the following litany:

> When my little teashop failed—such a disaster—it was the war, you know. A delightful place. I called it the Willow Tree and all the china was blue willow pattern—sweetly pretty—and the cakes really good—I've always had a hand with cakes and scones. Yes, I was doing really well and then the war came and supplies were cut down and the whole thing went bankrupt—a war casualty, that is what I always say, and I try to think of it like that.[32]

Miss Gilchrist finds comfort for her loss by subsuming its individuality into a collective national disaster. Nevertheless, the *idea* of the teashop, her specificity about its accouterments, is embedded into her character as the only authentic thing about her—the Abernethy family lawyer Mr. Entwhistle realizes that "Miss Gilchrist had a Spiritual Home—a lady-like teashop of Ye Olde Worlde variety with a suitable genteel clientele."[33] When she offers Susan tea, "the ghost of the Willow Tree hung over the party."[34] Miss Gilchrist finally cracks under Poirot's cross-examination and her motive and plans for the Palm Tree in Rye or Chichester are revealed.

> "Oak tables—and little basket chairs with striped red and white cushions..."
> For a few moments, the tea-shop that would never be seemed more real than the Victorian solidity of the drawing-room at Enderby...
> It was Inspector Morton who broke the spell.[35]

The uncanny nature of the remembered and imagined tea-shop and its objects serves as a warning about the power of the past—and the imagined—to cast a spell. Richard Abernethy's young relatives are able to move on with their lives, aided by their legacies, and the "Victorian solidity" of Enderby is broken up. However, there is also a mournful tone; England has no pockets for everyday women who want everyday things like Miss Gilchrist.

"A dangerous world"

Both *The Moving Finger* and *After the Funeral* are set primarily in the countryside; London is a site for luxury shopping and dining in the former, and comforting anonymity and bustle in the latter. In her rural novels, Christie invokes the claustrophobia of people knowing too much about each other, and the anxiety of not knowing quite enough, as well as using figurative and actual objects to explore the disturbing side of disconnection from the modern world. In her post-war urban novel *The Pale Horse* (1961), Christie navigates the uncertainties of anonymity and lack of community and connection. Objects remain crucial in supplying the material texture of the plot, however; their presence or absence shape the form of the clue-puzzle narrative, as well as the identities of the characters. If Miss Gilchrist was driven by the desire to possess material comfort and objects, in *The Pale Horse*, death itself is commodified and modern technology not only enables evil acts, it embodies evil itself. In *The Pale Horse*, the motifs of theatre and performance that recur throughout Christie's *oeuvre* become a framework and driving force for the entire plot—with appropriate props. This theatricality is central to the genre of detective fiction; as Birns and Boe Birns write, "In detective fiction, the world is to some degree a stage, and the people in it merely players, deceiving those around them and sometimes even themselves as to their true motives and actual deeds."[36] The focus of critical study so far has been on the double nature of people and characters, the hidden sides of communities. We certainly see these aspects in novels discussed here—we also see the extent to which these double lives and hidden passions are staged through objects and setting.

In *The Pale Horse*, the evil witches of pantomimes, and somewhat more seriously, the staging of *Macbeth*, form a *leitmotif*. Narrator and eventually amateur detective Mark Easterbrook, a historian of the Mogul Empire, sits in a coffee bar in Chelsea, musing "on the sinister implications of present-day noises and their atmospheric effects"[37] and reflecting that the smoke effects and trapdoors of pantomimes suggest that "it came to me suddenly that evil was, perhaps, necessarily always more impressive than good. It had to make a show! It had to startle and challenge! It was instability attacking stability."[38] This "show" of evil is repeated throughout *The Pale Horse* on two different levels, both manifested through objects, or props; ones is the evil potential of modern technology, and the other the evil of witchcraft in the traditional paranormal, supernatural, possibly Satanic sense. The first chapter opens with Mark in the Chelsea coffee bar, situated firmly within urban modernity:

> The Espresso machine behind my shoulder hissed like an angry snake. The noise it made had a sinister, not to say devilish, suggestion about it. Perhaps, I reflected, most of our contemporary noises carry that implication. The intimi-

dating angry scream of jet planes as they flash across the sky.... Even the minor domestic noises of today, beneficial in action though they may be, yet carry a kind of alert. The dish-washers, the refrigerators, the pressure cookers, the whining vacuum cleaners—"Be careful," they all seem to say. "I am a genie harnessed to your service, but if your control of me fails..."

A dangerous world—that was it, a dangerous world.[39]

York suggests that these opening paragraphs illustrate a "seriously felt tension between conservatism and the recognition that the world, like the individual, cannot go back"[40] as well as "a very strenuous effort of the part of the elderly author to grasp the changing world of the 1960s."[41] He goes on to comment that "there is already something a little absurd in this fear of the espresso machine."[42] I would suggest that there is more than a fear of progress evident here. The "silent life of things" has been transformed into noise; the "angry scream" of the airplanes, in particular, may be designed to evoke the Blitz. Even in the early 1960s, a time of relative peace and plenty, memories of the war and anxieties relating to the potential danger of machines persist. This unease about science and technology is infused with a more visceral fear—the "devilish" and hissing Espresso machine evokes Satan-as-serpent and the Garden of Eden in *Genesis*—or indeed the Apocalypse of the *Book of Revelations*. As Mrs. Dane Calthrop (presumably the same vicar's wife as in *The Moving Finger*) comments at the end of the novel, "Revelation, Chapter Six, Verse Eight. And I looked and behold a pale horse: and his name that sat on him was Death, and Hell followed with Him."[43] The fundamental fear in the novel is that technological developments validate the beliefs in the supernatural, and in the dark figures of the Bible; as Mark comments later, "The science of tomorrow is the supernatural of today."[44] The fears of the past may come true via the methods of the future. Finally, being afraid of an espresso machine *is* absurd, but Mark is not—this comment fits in with the musing on pantomimes and special effects designed to suggest evil.

The Pale Horse in the novel is a fourteenth-century inn in the village of Much Deeping that has been converted into a home for three women; the only note of its former purpose is a grimy sign of a horse and rider. Thyrza Grey, Sybil Stamfordis, and Bella are the archetypal three witches; they are known in the village to organize séances and possess second sight. On ordinary occasions, their house is furnished with "chintz and Chippendale," even if they do have the *Malleus Maleficarium* on their shelves.[45] When Mark, his fellow investigator Ginger and their allies in the police force deduce that the three women are involved with a sequence of inexplicable deaths, he consults the women in their professional capacity, pretending to accept their promise to be able to kill people far away. The pleasant everyday library has been transformed; Mark finds "purple cloth, embroidered with various cabbalistic signs," "a small brazier, and next to it a big copper basin."[46] During the proceedings an upside-down crucifix and holy water are used. Although Mark tries to tell himself that these traditional, even clichéd accessories of witchcraft are "mise-en-scene.... Meretricious trappings," he is uneasy.[47] When an "electrical contrivance of some complicated kind" is included in the ritual, and "the big box-like machine had started to emit a low hum, the bulbs in it glowed" his anxiety is compounded[48]; the sinister potential of everyday electronic objects, the dangerous world, seems too real.

The deadly ritual, which was supposed to harness both science and magic to murder, is, as Mark realizes, all play-acting. The robes and holy water, even the sacrificed cock, are all what Jerry in *The Moving Finger* would call a "smoke screen" and, indeed, Christie herself has in this novel performed something of a smoke and mirrors trick by hiding a straightforward detective story amid paranormal trappings. The solution does rely on objects, however, if not mystical ones; the real murders are committed by dangerously egotistical chemist Mr. Osborne, who substitutes the poisonous substance thallium for an everyday lotion or medicine used by the intended victim. These murders are bought by desperate or greedy customers via a middle-man; Mr. Osborne has recruited an army of "consumer researchers" to interview intended victims and find out what products they habitually use. One of these researchers is dying at the beginning of the novel, and confesses her suspicions to a priest, who is also murdered. When the police investigate the dead woman's lodgings, they find that she lived under a false name, and that "the dead woman had had curiously few personal possessions. No letters had been kept, no photographs."[49] The lack of objects here, the lack of personality, show not only the rootlessness and isolation of modern urban living, but also suggest a contrast to the women at the Pale Horse inn with their entrenched history.

The connection between consumerism, modern beauty products and medications and the practice of buying murders—euphemistically framed in terms of placing a bet—suggest that the real evil is capitalism. Death and murder are commodified, and by extension so are the victims whose deaths form part of the transactions. While the purchasers of murder have a connection to the victim—one girl is killed by her stepmother who inherits her money, for example—the visceral connection that murder ignites between killer and victim that is usually present in Christie's earlier work is outsourced to the efficient killing team of the witches, the chemist and the middle-man, and mediated and diluted via the objects used. Christie's Golden Age murderers are often despicable and sometimes sympathetic, but they are human enough to plunge the knife, pour the poison, or pull the trigger themselves. This sanitized system of murder leaves the hands of the guilty blood-free, and indeed implicates the victims themselves in their own demise, as they use the face-cream or lotion into which the thallium has been inserted.

This system works because of urban environment that Christie portrays in the novel; not only is it one of potential danger around every corner, it is one where roots and connections have been erased. The London of *The Pale Horse* shows the beginnings of the Swinging Sixties; the Chelsea coffee bar scene is full of aristocratic girls who discard their family heritage and social conventions, café owners named Luigi who speak flawless Cockney and workers without permanent jobs or homes. In a village, even in Christie's 1960s, life is regulated enough that anything, or anyone out of the ordinary, could potentially be noticed. In London, everyone is used to strangers everywhere. Evil is located in the banal, innocuous-seeming man, the shopkeeper, who wants too much power over his fellow-men and the empty people who work for him; Mr. Bradley, the middle-man who organizes the connection between the customer and the witches, sits in an anonymous office in Birmingham and wears "a dark business suit and looked the acme of respectability."[50] As a complete opposite to the antiquity, ritual and paraphernalia of The Pale Horse inn, Mr. Osborne lives in Bournemouth in a street that is "very, very new"[51]; his house is named Everest and his "small bungalow" is the "acme of neatness, though rather sparsely furnished."[52] "Everest" turns out to be a pun on "ever rest," a cheap joke worthy of a pantomime. If people in Christie's villages kill people they know, people in Christie's cities kill people they don't—and this is why it is a dangerous world.

"Somehow, that was the most frightening thing of all"

It is hard to plot a linear trajectory of development or definitive message in the use of material culture and atmospheric textures in Christie's later work, partly because of the sheer volume of her output—anxieties that can be read in Christie's post-war work range from the erasure of heritage and identity to the dangers of obsession with the past. This essay has attempted to illustrate and illuminate some of these contradictory anxieties and their implications, by moving from examining the poisonous undercurrents revealed when the metaphorical glass shade is lifted from a peaceful village, to the disintegration of tradition and the concomitant dangers of nostalgia embodied in a poor lady-companion's yearning for a place and things of her own, to the mass production of murder enabled by people's gullibility and acceptance of isolated, technologically-driven and disconnected urban existence.

Christie's use of objects to reinforce themes of stagnated communities and households and fluid or performed identities is evident throughout these novels, in the ladylike Mr. Pye and his collection of *objets d'art*, the detachable hair and padding assumed by Miss Gilchrist and the theatrical trappings of the three witches in *The Pale Horse*. Performance and props figure prominently throughout Christie's work; as York and others have observed, "theatricality is one of the basic concerns and one of the basic mechanisms of the Christie novels."[53] In these novels, the dramas become wider in scope; Mr. Symington consistently assumes the intellectual and emotional persona of a stunted, embittered middle-aged woman, Miss Gilchrist borrows Cora's mannerisms and childhood as well as her costume and false hair, and the three witches performance is a crucial link in a widespread criminal organization.

Conversely, the lack of personal objects and the resulting identity and atmosphere they lend is also a signal of danger and anxiety: an indication of a hidden and dangerous self, a negation of humanity, or an absence of a recognizable code for placing and dealing with that person. This is an aspect of Christie's work that also intensified as the century moved forwards. While detective fiction traditionally invokes atmosphere to reflect ideas of dark heritage, warped family or communal life or emotional charge—we see this in *Peril at End House, Death on the Nile* and *Nemesis*, for example—the anxieties related to a lack of atmosphere and the objects that created is a "structure of feeling" that Christie links specifically to modernity. In *And Then There Were None* (1939), a group of diverse and unrelated people are lured to an island off the coast of Devon:

> If this had been an old house, with creaking wood, and dark shadows, and heavily paneled walls, there might have been an eerie feeling. But this house was the essence of modernity. There were no dark corners—no possible sliding panels—it was flooded with electric light—everything was new and bright and shining. There was nothing hidden in this house, nothing concealed. It had no atmosphere about it.
> Somehow, that was the most frightening thing of all.[54]

It becomes apparent that these people are on the island to die in increasingly ludicrous ways in order to atone for crimes they had committed but without facing legal consequences. It is fitting that this novel that plays a complicated trick on reader expectations uses the lack of atmosphere in a generically inappropriate way; rather than an ominous setting that foreshadows, having the characters aware of the uncanny nature of a place that does not fit its feeling heightens the tension for the reader. This sinister lack of atmosphere becomes incorporated into the more conventional novels discussed here. Mr. Pye's queerness is directly linked to his home: "Mr. Pye was an extremely ladylike plump little man, devoted to his petit point chairs, his Dresden shepherdesses and his collection of bric-a-brac…. It was hardly a man's house."[55] But the danger inherent in his queerness is expressed via Jerry's observation that "it seemed to me that the curious thing was that [Pye's home] hadn't any atmosphere."[56] Mr. Pye is all poisoned tongue and Dresden china; he lacks a defined, solid identity even as he lacks a stable gender. Miss Gilchrist's own possessions are either destroyed by the war or in storage; she spends her life in someone else's house, surrounded by the artefacts of someone else's past. Forced to hide herself, she becomes driven to commit brutal murder. When Mr. Entwhistle meets her he decides that "she had one of those indeterminate faces that women of fifty so often acquire"[57]; indeed, her identity is indeterminate enough that she is able to easily slip into the identity of Cora Lansquenet. It is not until Miss Gilchrist mentions her teashop that she gains a past, although even so, Entwhistle thinks, "There must be hundreds of Miss Gilchrists all over the country [in teashops]."[58] In some ways her obsession with things makes her the converse of Mr. Pye; he has things but no identity, whereas she has nothing but carries her own atmosphere around with her. Mr. Osborne in *The Pale Horse* combines Mr. Pye's lack of atmosphere and attachment to his community with Miss Gilchrist's obsession with being recognized, attaining a suitable social position. His humanity is negated by his empty home. The "silent life of things" reinforces and affirms life in general, even if this life is bitter and murderous; without it, there is only empty, mechanical murder and an empty, mechanical society.

Notes

1. Jacques Barzun, "Detection and the Literary Art" in Robin W. Winks (ed.), *Detective Fiction: A Collection of Critical Essays* (Englewood Cliffs: Spectrum, 1980), p. 149.
2. Stephen Knight, "Murder in Wartime" in Pat Kirkham and David Thoms (eds.), *War Culture: Social Change and Changing Experience in World War Two* (London: Lawrence and Wishart, 1995), p. 163.
3. Alison Light, *Forever England: Femininity, Literature and Conservatism Between the Wars* (London: Routledge, 1991), p. 81.
4. *Ibid.*, p. 94.
5. Barzun, "Detection," p. 149–150.
6. Agatha Christie, *The Moving Finger* (London: HarperCollins, 2010), p. 32.
7. *Ibid.*, pp. 32, 152.
8. Gill Plain, "A Stiff Is Still a Stiff in This Country: The Problem of Murder in Wartime" in Petra Rau (ed.), *Conflict, Nationhood and Corporeality in Modern Literature: Bodies-at-War* (Basingstoke: Palgrave Macmillan, 2010), p. 112. Light shares this view, emphasizing the sinister underbelly of Christie's villages even in the "Golden" interwar years: "Christie's rural settings, which many have seen as hermetically sealed, provide an especially empty security, apparently representing order and harmony but quickly revealed as a 'cover' for its opposite.... The village in her novels is a community whose members ought to know each other but don't" (p. 92).
9. Christie, *The Moving Finger*, p. 31.
10. *Ibid.*, p. 8.
11. *Ibid.*, p. 97.
12. *Ibid.*, p. 93.
13. Light, *Forever England*, 94.
14. Christie, *The Moving Finger*, p. 89.

15. *Ibid.*, p. 155.
16. Plain, "The Problem of Murder," p. 113.
17. Christie, *The Moving Finger*, p. 119.
18. Agatha Christie, *After the Funeral* (London: HarperCollins, 1993), pp. 32, 36.
19. *Ibid.*, p. 117.
20. Nicholas Birns and Margaret Boe Birns, "Agatha Christie: Modern and Modernist" in Ronald G. Walker and June M. Frazer (eds.), *The Cunning Craft: Original Essays on Detective Fiction and Contemporary Literary Theory* (Macomb: Western Illinois University, 1990), p. 122.
21. Christie, *After the Funeral*, p. 15.
22. *Ibid.*, p. 7.
23. *Ibid.*, p. 8.
24. *Ibid.*, p. 11.
25. *Ibid.*, p. 153.
26. R. A. York, *Agatha Christie: Power and Illusion* (Basingstoke: Palgrave Macmillan, 2007), p. 83.
27. Christie, *After the Funeral*, p. 105.
28. *Ibid.*, pp. 35, 98.
29. *Ibid.*, p. 123.
30. A cruel term for single women who needed to work developed in public discourse around women and the workplace of the nineteenth century, and revived after the loss of a generation of men in World War I left women unmarried or widowed. See, for example, Gerry Holloway's *Women and Work in Britain Since 1840* (London: Routledge, 2005).
31. Merja Makinen, *Agatha Christie: Investigating Femininity* (Basingstoke: Palgrave Macmillan, 2006), p. 126.
32. Christie, *After the Funeral*, p. 40.
33. *Ibid.*
34. *Ibid.*, p. 107.
35. *Ibid.*, p. 247.
36. Birns and Boe Birns, "Modern and Modernist," p. 122.
37. Agatha Christie, *The Pale Horse* (London: Harper, 2002), p. 11.
38. *Ibid.*, p. 12.
39. *Ibid.*, p. 9.
40. Yorke, *Power and Illusion*, p. 83.
41. Christie, *The Pale Horse*, p. 84.
42. *Ibid.*
43. *Ibid.*, p. 331.
44. *Ibid.*, p. 208.
45. *Ibid.*, p. 96.
46. *Ibid.*, p. 231.
47. *Ibid.*, p. 234.
48. *Ibid.*, p. 238.
49. *Ibid.*, p. 43.
50. *Ibid.*, p. 165.
51. *Ibid.*, p. 141.
52. *Ibid.*, p. 142.
53. York, *Power and Illusion*, p. 41. Theatricality is the essence of *At Bertram's Hotel*, in which the hotel seems to be full of Edwardian pre-war comfort but is in fact a front for organized crime. For more discussion of the novel, see York's monograph.

54. Agatha Christie, *And Then There Were None* (London: HarperCollins, 2011), p. 79. A lack of atmosphere linked to murder also appears in *Sparkling Cyanide* (1945): "Most of that August they spent in the country at Little Priors. Horrible house! Iris shivered. A gracious well-built house, harmoniously furnished and decorated (Ruth Lessing was never at fault!). And curiously, frighteningly vacant. They didn't live there. They occupied it. As soldiers, in a war, occupied some look-out post" (London: HarperCollins, 2006), p. 370. It turns out that Ruth Lessing is a murderer, who killed both Iris's sister Rosemary and Rosemary's husband.
55. Christie, *The Moving Finger*, p. 119.
56. *Ibid.*, p. 33.
57. Christie, *After the Funeral*, p. 38.
58. *Ibid.*, p. 41.

Bibliography

Barzun, Jacques. "Detection and the Literary Art" in Robin W. Winks (ed.), *Detective Fiction: A Collection of Critical Essays.* Englewood Cliffs: Spectrum, 1980, pp. 144–153.

Birns, Nicholas, and Margaret Boe Birns. "Agatha Christie: Modern and Modernist" in Ronald G. Walker and June M. Frazer (eds.), *The Cunning Craft: Original Essays on Detective Fiction and Contemporary Literary Theory.* Macomb: Western Illinois University, 1990, pp. 120–134.

Christie, Agatha. *After the Funeral* (1956). London: HarperCollins, 1993.

_____. *The Moving Finger* (1943). London: HarperCollins, 2010. E-book.

Knight, Stephen. "Murder in Wartime" in Pat Kirkham and David Thoms (eds.), *War Culture: Social Change and Changing Experience in World War.* London: Lawrence and Wishart, 1995, pp. 161–172.

Light, Alison. *Forever England: Femininity, Literature and Conservatism Between the Wars.* London: Routledge, 1991.

Plain, Gill. "A Stiff Is Still a Stiff in This Country: The Problem of Murder in Wartime" in Petra Rau (ed.), *Conflict, Nationhood and Corporeality in Modern Literature: Bodies-at-War*, Basingstoke: Palgrave Macmillan, 2010, pp. 104–123.

York, R. A. *Agatha Christie: Power and Illusion.* Basingstoke: Palgrave Macmillan, 2007.

Queer Girls, Bad Girls, Dead Girls
Post-War Culture and the Modern Girl

Sarah Bernstein

Although a number of Agatha Christie's detective novels take their titles from children's nursery rhymes, critics of her work have tended to overlook the representation of children in her narratives. Several of Christie's post-war novels, however, feature dead or dangerous (or dangerous and so dead) children. In texts that span the post-war period, from *Crooked House* (1949) to *Nemesis* (1971), it is the figure of the girl who is the locus of particular anxiety. The problem of the "modern girl" is central to debates in the post-war era about delinquency and welfare reform, as girls' agency must be carefully managed lest they disrupt traditional gender and familial orders. Though these later texts have been much maligned by critics, Christie's enduring popularity through this period evinces her skill at filtering into her stories contemporary social changes and their attendant public anxieties.

In their representations of girlhood, Christie's post-war texts weave together motifs of crime and cultural change, suggesting the three are linked in ambivalent ways in the cultural imagination. Debates concerning the balance of care and control that emerge with the creation of the Welfare State and continue throughout the mid-century are expressed in Christie's novels as being intimately connected with the problem of the modern girl. In *No Future* (2004), the queer theorist Lee Edelman discusses the extent to which political discourse is invested in a fantasy of the future, represented by the image of the child. The figure of the child comes to represent the "telos" or culmination of the social order and, importantly, is responsible for securing and reproducing it. This conception resonates with the rhetoric of national reconstruction and modern nation building after World War II, which placed particular emphasis on the role of motherhood and domesticity as crucial to the survival of the British nation. In this context, children's behavior—particularly that of girls—must be carefully policed, so that they grow into and exercise their important reproductive capacities as mothers in order to secure the future of the nation. Edelman's conception of the child is useful in thinking about different kinds of refusals of social reproduction rendered in Christie's texts and how girls, represented in the novels as queer in various ways, are perceived as destabilizing the narrative (and social) order. Drawing, then, on Edelman's conception of the (imagined) child as a powerful image of social fulfillment and futurism, and Kathryn Bond Stockton's figurations of the queer and "dangerous" child in the twentieth century, this essay explores the ways Christie's post-war novels braid together queerness, criminality, and young femininity. I posit that, in registering changing cultural and legal mores about women, children and the mentally ill, and in eliding these categories into and under the heading of "queer," Christie's narratives reflect an anxiety surrounding certain possibilities for new womanhood that occlude or disrupt discourses of futurity. In so doing, Christie's texts highlight the fraught socio-political approach to girls at the mid-century, which held girls to be in need both of protection and of policing, of care and of control.

This essay therefore focuses on the representation of children in Christie's work in order to explore the ways in which cultural tensions circulating in the second half of the twentieth century, tensions about welfare reform, permissiveness and the family, are worked out in—and, indeed, are deeply embedded within—her narratives. In this way, the essay provides an important context for reading Christie's work, suggesting that her crime novels engage with post-war culture—and as the preceding chapters by Merja Makinen and Rebecca Mills demonstrate, culture between the wars—in ways that have not been discussed in a sustained manner. In the years following World War II, there was, as Ian Taylor writes, an "outburst of social and political anxiety over the condition of youth and its contribution to delinquency and social disorder."[1] Occasioned in part by the displacement caused by wartime evacuation of children and the separation of families, concern over dislocated and delinquent youth helped to guide public policy interventions into the family. The psychoanalyst John Bowlby's studies in the 1940s popularized the notion that problem families cause delinquency, arguing that juvenile offenders are a product of home lives in which there is a failure of attachment. Around the same time, Leslie Wilkins produced a Home Office report that claimed to prove a causal relationship between delinquency and broken families, further feeding unease over the state of the family. As Taylor explains, the linking of problem families to delinquency directly influenced juvenile justice system reforms in the 1950s and 1960s in England and Wales, particularly in the different emphasis on "care" and social rehabilitation. Thus, child welfare policy after World War II also created a new kind of child: the child *at risk*, who is in danger not only of being harmed, but of becoming delinquent. In this way, welfare reform advanced legislation that collapsed the distinction between children in need of protection and those in need of control.

Problem Children

In *The Parlour and the Suburb*, Judy Giles argues that "in Britain, in the 1950s, children (and the reproductive capacities of the mothers who bear them) became central to the programmes of successive governments for rebuilding Britain, not as it had been in the recent past, but as a 'modern' nation."[2] Giles's parenthetical statement—that women are relevant insofar as they are reproductive—takes on a particular resonance in the context of discussions about problem families. The coinciding "social" and interventionist aspects of the state created a "new politics of governmentality," which was clearly demarcated by gender.[3] As Pamela Cox writes, "one of the key ways of managing the population was to regulate those who were to literally reproduce it—to give birth to it, to mother it, to nurture it."[4] If politics, according to Lee Edelman, depends upon "reproductive futurism"—securing the future of the social order through its transmission to "the Child"—and in the post-war period, women were still largely responsible for nurturing and inculcating values to this child, then women also must be carefully handled.[5] Thus, as Cox explains, "connections between bad girls, bad mothers and bad families remained close and powerful in modern topologies of delinquency."[6]

Anxieties surrounding delinquent and vulnerable children—particularly girls—are reflected in Christie's fiction after World War II. The three novels discussed in this chapter, *Crooked House* (1949), *Dead Man's Folly* (1956) and *Hallowe'en Party* (1969), span the post-war years and feature dead girls, dangerous girls, or a combination of both. Critics Alison Light and R.A. York have already pointed up Christie's use of the nursery rhyme, with Light explaining that Christie's texts employ "the suspense that lies in the nursery rhyme ... [expressing] the child's fear of the unexpected violence which manifests itself first in the most apparently secure of places, family life."[7] The actual representation of children in Christie's novels, however, has largely been overlooked. Merja Makinen's 2006 study of Christie and femininity includes a fascinating reading of the child who kills in *Crooked House*, but her analysis assimilates the child, Josephine, into a broader discussion of femininity. In this chapter, I will read the girl-killers and girl-victims in Christie's texts in terms of their nebulous status as persons without legal personhood—as *girl* characters. The girls are not-yet-straight, not-yet-sane, and not-yet-woman, and the narratives characterize the presence of these pubescent children as ambiguous and unsettling.

Formally, the detective story is especially suited to discussions of futurity. In his 1977 work *What Will Have Happened*, Robert Champigny writes that the detective novel is a "text [that] has to be precisely oriented toward the denouement"—the revelation of the murderer's identity—but "as long as what is to be made explicit remains implicit, [the narrative] is borne by a perfect modified by a future."[8] Moving towards the future unraveling, the detective narrative is also urged along by it, the narrative's teleology amounting to the future, as Derrida writes in *Specters of Marx*, coming "back in advance."[9] The aesthetic frame that supports the detective novel is future-oriented; its telos of sequence presupposes a future reveal that will restore order to a social world disrupted by murder. And the world of the cozy mystery, especially, is domestic, middle-class, family-centered. Even after World War II, when the cozy narrative is on the decline, Christie still employs its characteristic elements, though she begins to jumble them up, anatomize and atomize them. As Alison Light writes, "The fiction may in the end work to offer 'reassurance,' but since [depicted] communities always thrive on suspicion, their insecurities can never be resolved."[10] Even familial relations become ambiguous and "thrown out of kilter."[11] In these texts, family—and by extension society—becomes estranged from itself; the resulting instability of social exchange calls into doubt any possibility of meaningful community. And futurism, according to Lee Edelman, "generates generational succession, temporality, and narrative sequence, not toward the end of enabling change, but instead, of perpetuating sameness, of turning back time to assure repetition—or to assure a logic of resemblance ... in the service of representation."[12] In retaining tropes of the conventional Golden Age detective novel (such as the country house and the extended, "respectable" family) at a time when the very basis of these institutions is being called into question, Christie's post-war texts evoke tensions about and around the role and preservation of the family.

According to Edelman, "politics remains, at its core, conservative insofar as it works to *affirm* a structure, *authenticate* social order, which it then intends to transmit to the future in the form of its inner Child."[13] Securing the future of the social order thus depends upon its transmission to "our children." This poses a problem at a time when one of the prevailing anxieties was about growing social permissiveness due to loosening familial bonds. Various strands of social scientific discourse after World War II reconstruct the modern family as a particular and peculiar case for concern. Sociologists and psychoanalysts set out to explore what they perceived as the breakdown of the traditional family, effected by social liberalization and a new culture of permissiveness. Stuart Hall et al. write that some groups felt this permissiveness would cause an erosion of moral constraints, which would, in turn, undermine the authority of the law itself. The message, then, of family-centered studies of delinquency is that "what goes wrong goes wrong early. In policy terms, this has meant early intervention and risk-focused prevention."[14] Because it requires welfare workers to identify children with the potential to become criminal, risk-focused prevention collapses the distinction between the child who needs protecting and the child who needs to be contained. In a phrase that would well fit an analysis of Christie's *Crooked House*, Paul Knepper writes that, "from this perspective, pruning young lives before they grow crooked is the most sensible means of reducing crime"; the child we fear is thus tidily telegraphed onto the image of the child we would protect.[15] Risk-focused intervention also depends upon a very specific—and ideological—model of the family, and arrangements that diverge from this paradigm are at risk of being considered a "problem" and subject to policing. In this way, governing institutions mobilize very real (and legitimate) fears about the exploitation of children in order to sharply delimit the boundaries of acceptable morality, couching it in terms of a moral renewal. For who, after all, would not claim to be on the side of those "fighting for our children"?[16]

Queer Girls, Bad Girls

Throughout the twentieth century, girls have been the special targets of discourses on moral health. As Cox has shown, while fewer girls than boys appeared before juvenile courts, girls were more often the objects of informal (and moral) reformatory projects aimed specifically at their innocence, protection and salvation. Social developments that saw more women in the workplace and more autonomy for girls were accompanied by panicked discourses of waywardness, which bespoke both criminality and imperiled moral purity. According to such discourses, the liberalizing effects of these social developments undermined parental (paternal) authority, and this, in turn, led to delinquency. This is an idea that circulates especially in Christie's texts of the late 1960s and early 1970s. In Christie's *Hallowe'en Party* (1969), which centers on the murder of thirteen-year-old Joyce, found drowned in an apple-bobbing bucket, Superintendent Spence tells Poirot, "I suspect that girls have always been partial to the bad lots, as you say, but in the past there were safeguards," and Poirot replies, "That's right. People were looking after them."[17] Rowena Drake, a not entirely disinterested character (she is the murderer), reiterates the sentiment: "I must say that mothers and families generally are not looking after their children properly as they used to," she says to Poirot.[18] It is a kind of circular reasoning in which girls are both product and propagator of generational, gender, and familial disorder.

In *Nemesis* (1971), Professor Wanstead, a criminal psychologist, is Miss Marple's ally in solving the puzzle left her by the recently deceased and wealthy financier Mr. Rafiel. He tells Miss Marple, "Girls are said to mature earlier," but at the same time, "in a deeper sense of the word, they mature late." His theory is muddled, connecting girls' wish to be "free to do what they think are grown up things" with their "wish *not* to become adult—*not* to have to accept our kind of responsibility." He relates this to girls' contemporary fashion choices—"their miniskirts … their Baby Doll nightdresses, their gymslips and shorts," which, according to Wanstead, reflects young women's "worship of childishness."[19] Tied up in Wanstead's partly censorious, partly erotic description of girls' dress is his implication of mothers in the breakdown of familial order. It is Mom "away at work," as Rafiel's solicitor and will executor Mr. Broadribb says, who trips up the correct sexual sequence, making girls at once mature too early and too late. Wanstead takes his analysis further, accusing mothers of contributing to and covering up for girls' sexual waywardness: "Girls, you must remember," he says, "are far more ready to be raped than they used to be. Their mothers insist, very often that they should call it rape."[20] Girls' delinquency, which is ostensibly caused by broken-down parental authority (specifically, owing to ineffective mothering), tends to feed back into and rupture the family unit in a perpetual and self-destructive sequence. Wanstead, as a criminal psychologist, and Broadribb, as a solicitor, are figures working in some capacity for the legislative system. That Christie's narrative singles out these two men to relate their distasteful views on delinquent girls and mothers suggests that the novel is interested, more broadly, in exploring the connections between perceived social changes as they relate to girls and systems of surveillance and legislation. The novel's correlation of changing roles and mores with the legislative system indicates, in turn, that Christie's text is engaging with the moral and actual policing of girls and women. The circular figuration of girlish delinquency conveniently stresses "the importance of managing both the natural and the social"; girls' "pubescent bodies had to be managed and their sexual energies safely channeled," while at the same time their "relationship to the wider culture … had to be carefully negotiated."[21] In Christie's narratives, it is the girls' pubescent bodies that elude narrative attempts to fix them; they are not orderly and obedient, but girls who take power where they can get it: in money, in secrets, and in bodily autonomy. Part of their agency lies in their refusal of reproductive futurism and even, in the case of *Crooked House's* Josephine, of familialism.

In her study *The Queer Child: Growing Up Sideways in the Twentieth Century*, Kathryn Bond Stockton suggests that "evidently we are scared of the child we would protect," that perhaps "we are threatened by the specter of their longings that are maddeningly, palpably opaque."[22] The child, she writes, "is the act of adults looking back ... a ghostly, unreachable fantasy."[23] As a "managed delay," and suspended in a state of futurity, the child is prevented (by adults) from growing into adulthood, and thus, having "nowhere-to-grow," queers time by growing sideways instead of up.[24] In this way, Stockton's sketches of children who are queer in various ways "horizontalize History ... making History broaden itself by growing outside and beside itself."[25] The temporal strangeness of children unsettles linear narratives of history, and also of the law. As Stockton goes on to remark, in the twentieth century, which has been termed the century of the child, laws that would protect children also produce them as a form of "legal strangeness," that is, beings more in need of protection than of freedom, who are suspended in a state of non-adulthood.[26] This very notion of children as a form of legal strangeness is a troubling motif in Christie's post-war novels.

In *Hallowe'en Party*, Poirot arrives on the scene after the body of thirteen-year-old Joyce is discovered. Ariadne Oliver tells Poirot,

> I mean, children do queer things sometimes. I mean, there are queer children about, children who—well, once I suppose they would have been in mental homes and things, but they send them home now and tell them to lead ordinary lives or something and then they do something like this.[27]

The word "queer" grows out of its original sense of "crosswise," "going wrong" and, later, "peculiar," to its more common usage, from the turn of the twentieth century, as a derogative for "gay," and Ariadne's confused use of it here seems to reflect this polyvalence. Her sentiment regarding "queer children" who might once have been institutionalized but who are now told to "lead ordinary lives" is likewise expressed by various characters. Retired Superintendent Spence tells Poirot that, in his day,

> we had our mentally disturbed, or whatever you would call them, but not so many as we have now. I expect more of them are let out of the places they ought to be kept safe in. All our mental homes are too full; over-crowded, so doctors say, "Let him or her lead a normal life. Go back with his relatives," etc. And then the nasty bit of goods, or poor afflicted fellow, whichever way you like to look at it, gets the urge again.[28]

Spence's comments evoke the seemingly irresolvable tension between care and control also at the heart of juvenile delinquency policy: like the child at risk, the released patient is a nasty bit of goods who must be contained or else he is a poor afflicted fellow in need of treatment. When a police surgeon echoes these remarks, he insists upon a historical specificity. These are social developments, he tells Poirot, of the last seven to ten years. So what happened in the late 1950s and early 1960s? After World War II, the abandoning of the Poor Law model of social welfare that had begun in earnest during the interwar period gained momentum. In general, new Welfare State policies, following more progressive interwar attitudes, turned towards a model of community care over institutional care: "regulation *within*, rather than removal *from* the community."[29] This change had particular resonances for child welfare, given that the Curtis Committee in England and Wales had "concluded in 1946 that boarding out was ... preferable to institutional care."[30] Further, the 1959 Mental Health Act sought to normalize mental illness by collapsing the distinction between psychiatric facilities and other hospitals, and by adopting an after-care policy in which local authorities would be compelled to provide "residential accommodation ... facilities for training or occupation ... [and] any ancillary or supplementary services for or for the benefit of" the mentally ill.[31] The bill, in other words, made care in the community into law. The characters in *Hallowe'en Party* reflect a broader social unease about such changes, and the manner in which they formulate this anxiety seems to have to with a fear of misrecognition. For example, of the categories of children "deprived of a normal home life" listed in the 1945–46 Report of the Care of Children Committee, those "Removed by Order of Court (delinquent or in need of care or protection)," both fell under the purview of the Home Office.[32] The feared-for child was no longer discernible from the child we feared. More generally, boarding out and care in the community helped in theory to break down markers of difference. What is frightening, for the middle-class characters in Christie, is that the people leading so-called normal lives may not be "normal" at all. It is interesting that the cast of *Hallowe'en Party* explicitly addresses these anxieties but, as Muncie points out, British social history is "replete with such 'respectable fears' in which the present is compared unfavorably with the past."[33] Christie's registering of changing cultural and legal ways is significant because of the ways in which her texts braid these together and connect the resulting changes to "queerness."

Anxiety about the "mentally disturbed" is coupled with children in two ways in Christie's fiction: first, the worry of "the things you find out in the papers," that "children don't home from school because they've accepted a lift from a stranger, although they've been warned not to."[34] And second, the fear of children's strangeness, their murderous motives. In *Hallowe'en Party*, Mrs. Goodbody tells a story of a seven-year-old girl who killed her infant brother and sister: "Beautiful little creature she was, too," she says. "You could have fastened a pair of wings on her, let her go on a platform and sing Christmas hymns, and she'd have looked right for the part. But she wasn't. She was rotten inside."[35] The solicitor Jeremy Fullerton remarks that crimes were so often associated with young people, and that it was difficult to know precisely what to *do* with such young delinquents. *Crooked House* develops this theme in more specific detail. The Assistant Commissioner tells the narrator that, for the murderers he has known, the break that operates with most of us doesn't operate for them. A child, you know, translates desire into action without compunction.... Lots of kids try to take a baby out of a pram and "drown it," because it usurps attention—or interferes with their pleasures. They get—very early—to a stage when they know that it is "wrong"—that is, that it will be punished. Later, they get to *feel* that it is wrong. But some people, I suspect, remain morally immature.[36]

If this formulation seems familiar, it is because it is, in effect, a Freudian formulation of the child, for whom the id "is the special province ... that libidinal repository of insatiable desires," the force that needs to be repressed in the interest of the social bond.[37] Freud's conception of homosexuality is also characterized by this notion of arrested development, which, as Stockton writes, is, for Freud, still a form of growth, but "growing sideways" rather than growing up.[38] In Christie's novel, it is killers who are like children, and this articulation imaginatively ties together child, killer and queer. Mental illness, delinquency and queer children thus braid together in a general fear-of-and-fear-for the child.

Makinen has argued that Christie's representation of female killers signals a certain feminist impulse in her writing. Christie, she comments, "in her villains allows women an agency, an importance and a dangerous competence to disrupt society.... Deviant women behaving badly have the potential to disrupt the textual world and the preconceptions of Christie's readership."[39] What of Christie's victims? What *Crooked House*, *Hallowe'en Party* and *Dead Man's Folly* have in common is a dead girl. Three dead girls, in fact. If we can believe Poirot's adage that one's "death [is] like so many things are in life, a result of [one's] actions," then what actions lead to the girls' deaths?[40] All three, Josephine, Joyce and Marlene, encompass the problem of fearing the child we would protect. The little power they wield lies in their unexpectedness. In *Hallowe'en Party*, Poirot says, "Children *do* see things. They are so often, you see, not expected to be where they are" (100).[41] They are killed because they know—or are thought to know—things they cannot be trusted to keep to themselves. Marlene is a blackmailer; Joyce, a boaster with a blackmailing brother; and Josephine, a girl-killer with opaque longings. They are dangerous in that they present the texts with what "for at least two centuries [has] largely been viewed as antithetical to childhood: sex, aggression, secrets, closets, or any sense of what police call 'a past.'"[42] As the texts repeatedly tell us, these are queer girls with obscure and possibly mad motives; girls who are not-yet-straight and never will be. Christie's novels conflate the thematics of mental illness, juvenile delinquency, and femininity into the notion of queerness to reflect new social unease about the logic of "reproductive futurism" that subtends, as Edelman argues, the political system in its entirety.

Within the logic of reproductive futurism, securing the future of the social order depends upon its transmission to our children. Stockton explains that "'the future' and 'our children' are always bound together in a kind of frightening (and hermetically sealed) 'reproductive futurism.'"[43] The image of the child, "not to be confused with the lived experiences of any historical children, [thus] serves to regulate political discourse."[44] Politics, according to Stockton, is now done only in the name of our children's future. The queer children of Christie's novels have no future themselves (they are dead), and while they lived, being queer and "crooked" girls, put "the goal of socially-sanctioned couplehood on perpetual delay."[45] Josephine, for example, is a queer child, ever standing on thresholds, swinging on doorways in a disused yard, emerging from the opening of the yew hedge. Her grandfather's young widow tells the narrator that Josephine "looks queer. She gives me the shivers."[46] There is something decidedly uncanny about her: she is described as "goblin"-like, "ghoulish," a "malicious gnome," her mother's "funny ugly baby ... a changeling."[47] In one sense, she is queer in that she is not-yet-straight (and never will be), yet she "is, nonetheless, a sexual child with aggressive wishes" and murderous motives.[48] Marlene and Joyce are likewise not-yet-straight (and never will be). In *Dead Man's Folly*, Inspector Bland asks whether Marlene was "fond of boys," to which Constable Hoskins responds, "I wouldn't say they'd much use for her."[49] Though Hoskins goes on to suppose that Marlene might have liked it if they had, the oblique remark seems deliberately suggestive coming from an otherwise voluble character. In the comic books found with her body, Poirot notices that Marlene has been doodling in the margins: "Jackie Blake goes with Susan Brown," "Peter pinches girls at the pictures," "Georgie Porgie kisses hikers in the words," "Biddy Fox likes boys."[50] There is a curious ambiguity in that Jackie, who goes with Susan, could be either girl or boy, and also that at fourteen, Marlene finds it suggestive that a girl her age, Biddy Fox, likes boys, and the ambivalence opens the text to a reading that considers queerness as a possibility.

Dead Girls

Unlike other girls their age, Josephine, Joyce and Marlene position themselves outside of the "going-steady" paradigm. They derive their pleasure from secrets rather than heterosexual bonding; all three girls, we are told, "get a vicarious thrill by ... spying and peering at [their] young contemporaries."[51] Instead of coupling off with boys their age or dreaming up wedding scenarios, instead of submitting to the imperative of reproductive futurism, in other words, the girls are interested in murder: the bloodier the better. And indeed all three girls divulge a predilection for gore. Josephine regretfully tells Charles that in her mother's theatrical production of *Jezebel*, "They threw her out of the window. Only no dogs came and ate her. I think that was a pity, don't you? I like the part about the dogs eating her best."[52] In *Hallowe'en Party*, Joyce says to Ariadne Oliver, "I like murders to have lots of blood," and *Dead Man's Folly*'s Marlene rues that her role as pretend corpse in the Murder Hunt calls for strangulation and not stabbing, and tells Poirot that she "like[s] sex murderers."[53] The girls' fascination with death and dismemberment brings about their own murders, as the narrative codes their enjoyment of bloody (fictional) murder as unnatural. Josephine's playing at murderer and detective is another manifestation of ego and desire running unchecked, and Marlene's interest in murder is "hungry," expressed with "avidity" and "relish."[54]

Edelman, in *No Future*, opposes "the compulsive narrative of reproductive futurism" to the death drive.[55] While the narrative of reproductive futurism underpins the Symbolic order, the death drive is what is remaindered, an "inarticulable surplus that dismantles the subject from within … the negativity opposed to every form of social viability."[56] He writes, "Queerness, therefore, is never a matter of being or becoming but, rather, of *embodying* the remainder of the Real."[57] The girls' queerness is, to be sure, also a matter of excess; they are keenly interested in blood and guts, the insides of bodies, and their own bodies seem to be everywhere all the time in the texts. Josephine's embodiedness, for instance, makes Charles uncomfortable. He remarks upon her smell, "of flowers," which is in his nose, and even on her breathing: "Josephine came nearer and breathed heavily in my face," he tells us, and she leaves the room "breathing excitedly."[58] Similarly, Joyce's murder (drowned in an apple-bobbing bucket) is recalled continually and in unnecessary detail by characters not witness to it. The texts find the girls especially troubling because, of course, they are girls, and on the cusp of fertility that they seem unlikely to put to use through proper channels. The texts code their fertility as excess, a dangerous waste. The girl corpses are evoked persistently, making them hang over the texts in an expression of claustrophobic and entropic femininity. In the case of Josephine, the narrative attempts to defuse this tension by gradually ghosting her. At first, she is "Sophia's sister, Josephine," a basically normal child with familial links: soon she becomes "a ghoulish child," "an unpleasant child," and finally, in conversation with his father and Inspector Taverner, Charles refers to her as "he, or rather she— or I'd better say *it*."[59] This is significant for two reasons. First, the narrative ghosting of Josephine speaks to the ghosting of queer children in the legal system. Stockton writes that Anglo-American "law-courts do not believe in … overtly same-sex oriented children," and that in fact "the tendency of metaphor … to reconfigure relations and time … prove[s] why fictions uniquely nurture ideas of queer children."[60] Second, Christie's narrative's ambiguous treatment of Josephine—its difficulty in naming her—is relevant in that it reflects contemporaneous tensions around and about the "modern girl." According to Cox, "successive generations of girls in England and Wales have been cast as posing an ever new threat to the social order requiring ever-new restraints."[61] The problem of the modern girl is, then, one of managing agency. If, in the newly permissive post-war world, familial roles have been unbound, girls' agency—particularly their sexual agency—needs still more to be directed into appropriate and productive channels. The girls in Christie's narratives, however, disrupt discourses of futurity that appeal to the Child by embodying the queer (girl) child who will not reproduce, and so threaten to destabilize the social order.

Crooked House, the earliest of the novels, takes up this theme most explicitly. The text's murder mystery is embedded within the story of Charles and Sophia's courtship. Sophia tells Charles at the start that she cannot marry him until her grandfather's murder is solved, and the novel ends with their engagement. The narrative of the queer child is thus subsumed into the logic and "constraining mandate of futurism."[62] This is significant, because Josephine is perceived to disrupt familial lineage. Even while Charles remarks upon her presumed resemblance to her grandfather, she is ever a changeling, nobody's child, who seems to have come from nowhere, an unexpected eruption in the family.

Charles reflects that Josephine "had been born with a kink. The crooked child of the crooked house."[63] Hers is a kind of belonging dislocated from familial bonds. She is the house's child, the child of a cottage "swollen out of all proportion," a malignant growth, a mistake.[64] When Aunt Edith drives herself and Josephine to their deaths, she claims that it is in Josephine's interest, to protect her from suffering "as I believe she would suffer if called to earthly account for what she has done."[65] But when Sophia asks Charles what would have happened to Josephine had she lived, he answers that she would likely have been sent to a reformatory for a few years before being released. As we have seen, it is likely that Josephine *would* have been released, for, as Stockton argues, a child's motive is not a publicly available concept: "children are those peculiar legal creatures … who are generally deemed by the law not to have a motive to harm, or most especially, any rational intent to kill."[66] But Edith goes further: she conceals Josephine's crime. In killing Josephine, she is protecting the extant Leonides family from the shame of association to a queer, murderous child. In killing Josephine, she is pruning, as it were, the family tree of a sick branch so that the rest of the family can grow into their futures, and the novel ends in the promise of marriage, thus reifying the logic of reproductive futurism. This speaks to the anxiety the characters in Christie's novel feel about concretizing familial roles, especially those of mothers and girls, and it is a tension that the form of the detective story ultimately cannot resolve.

The queer child is, then, a source of anxiety because she occludes discourses of futurity and because she destabilizes the very image of the child that remains, as Edelman puts it, "perpetually on the horizon of every acknowledged politics."[67] In Christie's texts, the living child whose presence threatens the social order is done away with in the interest of preserving the imagined child. Stockton writes, "In the century of the child, the child is feared to disappear."[68] This has an unexpected resonance in Christie's postwar fiction, in which the narratives kill off the child they would protect. The adult characters, over whose world hangs the specter of a dead girl, imaginatively connect this child (these children) to new welfare policies they perceive to be ineffective. Christie's texts thus reflect a more pervasive anxiety that the image of the Child, which "serves to regulate political discourse [and even] to prescribe what *will* count as political discourse" is symbolically breaking down.[69]

NOTES

1. Ian Taylor, *Crime in Context: A Critical Criminology of Market Societies* (Cambridge: Polity, 1999), p. 42.
2. Judy Giles, *The Parlour and the Suburb: Domestic Identities, Class, Femininity and Modernity* (New York: Berg, 2004), p. 162.
3. Pamela Cox, *Bad Girls in Britain: Gender, Justice and Welfare, 1900–1950* (London: Palgrave, 2013), p. 14.
4. *Ibid.*
5. Lee Edelman, *No Future: Queer Theory and the Death Drive* (Durham: Duke University Press, 2004), p. 13.
6. Cox, *Bad Girls in Britain*, p. 152.
7. Alison Light, *Forever England: Femininity, Literature, and Conservatism Between the Wars* (London: Routledge, 1991), p. 88.
8. Robert Champigny, *What Will Have Happened: A Philosophical and Technical Essay on Mystery Stories* (Bloomington: Indiana University Press, 1977), pp. 59, 21.
9. Jacques Derrida, *Specters of Marx: The State of Debt, the Work of Mourning, and the New International,* trans. Peggy Kamuf (London: Routledge, 2006), p. 10.
10. Light, *Forever England*, p. 97.
11. *Ibid.*, p. 88.
12. Edelman, *No Future*, p. 61.
13. *Ibid.*, p. 3. Emphasis original.
14. Paul Knepper, *Criminology and Social Policy* (London: Sage, 2007), p. 114.
15. *Ibid.*
16. *Ibid.*
17. Agatha Christie, *Hallowe'en Party* (Glasgow: Fontana, 1972), p. 29.
18. *Ibid.*, p. 40.
19. Agatha Christie, *Nemesis* (London: HarperCollins, 2002), p. 201. Emphasis original.
20. *Ibid.*, p. 183.
21. Cox, *Bad Girls in Britain*, p. 161.
22. Kathryn Bond Stockton, *The Queer Child, or Growing Up Sideways in the Twentieth Century* (Durham: Duke University Press, 2009), pp. 36, 126.

23. *Ibid.*, p. 5.
24. *Ibid.*, pp. 90, 124.
25. *Ibid.*, p. 36. Stockton's discussion covers the protogay child, the grown homosexual, the child queered by Freud and the normative child queered by innocence.
26. *Ibid.*, p. 64.
27. Christie, *Hallowe'en Party*, p. 23.
28. *Ibid.*, p. 32.
29. J. Clarke, quoted in John Muncie, *Youth & Crime* (London: Sage, 2004), p. 79.
30. L. Abrams, "Lost Childhoods: Recovering Children's Experiences of Welfare in Modern Scotland" in Anthony Fletcher and Stephen Hussey (eds.), *Childhood in Question: Children, Parents and the State* (Manchester: Manchester University Press, 1999), pp. 152–172 (p. 163).
31. "Bill [passed, cap. 72] to repeal the Lunacy and Mental Treatment Acts, 1890 to 1930, and the Mental deficiency Acts, 1913 to 1938, and to make fresh provision with respect to the treatment and care of mentally disordered persons and with respect to their property and affairs; and for purposes connected with the matters aforesaid [as amended by Standing Committee E]," 20th Century House of Commons Sessional Papers (*House of Commons Parliamentary Papers Online*, 1958–9). Web.
32. United Kingdom, The Home Department, the Ministry of Health, and the Ministry of Education, *Report of the Care of Children Committee 1946* (London: HMSO, 1946). Web.
33. Muncie, *Youth & Crime*, p. 51.
34. Christie, *Hallowe'en Party*, p. 32.
35. *Ibid.*, p. 131.
36. Agatha Christie, *Crooked House* (London: Penguin, 1953), p. 95. The same anecdote appears in Christie's *And Then There Were None* (1939) and *Curtain: Poirot's Last Case* (1975).
37. Chris Jenks, *Childhood* (London: Routledge, 1996), p. 72.
38. *Ibid.*, p. 24.
39. Merja Makinen, *Agatha Christie: Investigating Femininity* (Basingstoke: Palgrave, 2006), p. 134.
40. Christie, *Hallowe'en Party*, p. 166.
41. *Ibid.*, p. 100.
42. Stockton, *The Queer Child*, p. 30.
43. *Ibid.*, p. 13.
44. Edelman, *No Future*, p. 11.
45. Stockton, *The Queer Child*, p. 101.
46. Christie, *Crooked House*, p. 65.
47. *Ibid.*, pp. 71, 72, 98, 143.
48. Stockton, *The Queer Child*, p. 27.
49. Agatha Christie, *Dead Man's Folly* (London: HarperCollins, 2009), p. 97.
50. *Ibid.*, p. 190.
51. *Ibid.*
52. Christie, *Crooked House*, p. 73.
53. *Ibid.*, p. 9.
54. *Ibid.*, pp. 76–77.
55. Edelman, *No Future*, p. 23.
56. *Ibid.*, p. 9.
57. *Ibid.*, p. 25.
58. Christie, *Crooked House*, pp. 71, 74, 76.

59. *Ibid.*, pp. 71, 72, 75, 83.
60. *Ibid.*, p. 16.
61. Cox, *Bad Girls in Britain*, p. 3.
62. Edelman, *No Future*, p. 4.
63. Christie, *Crooked House*, p. 191.
64. *Ibid.*, p. 25.
65. *Ibid.*, p. 190.
66. Stockton, *The Queer Child*, p. 158.
67. Edelman, *No Future*, p. 3.
68. Stockton, *The Queer Child*, p. 37.
69. Edelman, *No Future*, p. 11.

BIBLIOGRAPHY

Abrams, L. "Lost Childhoods: Recovering Children's Experiences of Welfare in Modern Scotland" in Anthony Fletcher and Stephen Hussey (eds.), *Childhood in Question: Children, Parents and the State*. Manchester: Manchester University Press, 1999, pp. 152–172.
"Bill [passed, cap. 72] to repeal the Lunacy and Mental Treatment Acts, 1890 to 1930, and the Mental Deficiency Acts, 1913 to 1938, and to make fresh provision with respect to the treatment and care of mentally disordered persons and with respect to their property and affairs; and for purposes connected with the matters aforesaid [as amended by Standing Committee E]." 20th Century House of Commons Sessional Papers, *House of Commons Parliamentary Papers Online*, 1958–1959.
Champigny, Robert. *What Will Have Happened: A Philosophical and Technical Essay on Mystery Stories*. Bloomington: Indiana University Press, 1977.
Christie, Agatha. *Crooked House* (1949). London: Penguin, 1953.
_____. *Dead Man's Folly* (1956). London: HarperCollins, 2009.
_____. *Hallowe'en Party* (1969). Glasgow: Fontana, 1972.
_____. *Nemesis* (1971). London: HarperCollins, 2002.
Cox, Pamela. *Bad Girls in Britain: Gender, Justice and Welfare, 1900–1950* (2002). London: Palgrave, 2013.
Derrida, Jacques. *Specters of Marx: The State of Debt, the Work of Mourning, and the New International*. Trans. Peggy Kamuf. London: Routledge, 2006.
Edelman, Lee. *No Future: Queer Theory and the Death Drive*. Durham: Duke University Press, 2004.
Giles, Judy. *The Parlour and the Suburb: Domestic Identities, Class, Femininity and Modernity*. New York: Berg, 2004.
Hall, Stuart, et al. *Policing the Crisis: Mugging, the State, and Law and Order* (1977). London: Macmillan, 1978.
The Home Department, The Ministry of Health, and the Ministry of Education. *Report of the Care of Children Committee 1946*, Cmd. 6922, London: Her Majesty's Stationery Office, 1946. *House of Commons Parliamentary Papers Online*, 2015.
Jackson, Louise. *Women Police: Gender, Welfare and Surveillance in the Twentieth Century*. Manchester: Manchester University Press, 2006.
Jenks, Chris. *Childhood*. London: Routledge, 1996.
Knepper, Paul. *Criminology and Social Policy*. London: Sage, 2007.
Light, Alison. *Forever England: Femininity, Literature, and Conservatism Between the Wars*. London: Routledge, 1991.
Makinen, Merja. *Agatha Christie: Investigating Femininity*. Basingstoke: Palgrave, 2006.

Muncie, John. *Youth & Crime*. London: Sage, 2004.
Scraton, Phil. "Defining 'Power' and Challenging 'Knowledge': Critical Analysis as Resistance in the UK" in *Critical Criminology: Issues, Debates, Challenges*. London: Palgrave, 2002, pp. 15–40.
Stockton, Kathryn Bond. *The Queer Child, or Growing Up Sideways in the Twentieth Century*. Durham: Duke University Press, 2009.
Taylor, Ian. *Crime in Context: A Critical Criminology of Market Societies*. Cambridge: Polity, 1999.
York, R.A. *Agatha Christie: Power and Illusion*. Basingstoke: Palgrave, 2007.

"With practised eyes"
Feminine Identity in The Mysterious Mr. Quin

Charlotte Beyer

> "He arrived just after the curtain went down ... in time to glance round the house with practised eyes."
> —Agatha Christie, "The Face of Helen"[1]

This essay examines the representation of feminine identity in selected texts from Agatha Christie's short story collection, *The Mysterious Mr. Quin* (1930). Christie's representation of femininity has received welcome scholarly attention from Merja Makinen, among others,[2] yet the *Mr. Quin* stories are among the less examined of Christie's works. Michael Cook also comments on the lack of attention paid by critics to Christie's *Mr. Quin* short stories. He argues that this volume is among her best work, stating that "it is perhaps the least well-known of her early texts and certainly one which has received scant critical attention."[3] Cook goes on to assert that these stories constitute "some of [Christie's] finest prose and acute observation of the art of detection and its relationship with human nature."[4] This essay will explore these questions further, by focusing on the *Mr. Quin* stories and their examination of the central question of femininity in the interwar years. In terms of genre, the *Mr. Quin* tales are mystery stories and are characterized by a prominent crime dimension. The protagonist Mr. Satterthwaite functions as an amateur detective within the stories, aided by Mr. Quin, a mysterious figure who appears in the stories to alert Satterthwaite to important events, only to disappear again seemingly without trace.[5] Cook suggests that in the Mr. Quin stories, the detective function "is actually divided between the spectral Quin and the earthly Satterthwaite."[6] Satterthwaite is an elderly gentleman, who often appears marginalized in the company of the stories' younger characters.

Through his character, Christie challenges conventional cultural notions of ageing and explores alternative or ambiguous masculine roles.[7] Satterthwaite is outside the heterosexual romance plots often depicted in the Mr. Quin stories, and in terms of gender he is often shown to represent a more fluid position. As Cook suggests, although Satterthwaite solves mysteries, these stories differ from conventional crime fictions in highlighting the role and significance of intuition and emotion, through the character of Quin.[8] Through these strategies, Christie has created short stories which exceed genre boundaries and reflect a willingness to experiment.[9] As we shall see, the narratives feature a number of textual elements and ideas that suggest these short stories provide a formal and thematic bridge between genre writing and literary fiction. The way in which these stories problematize and interrogate gender and femininity in the interwar years is central to this bridging, and contributes to situating Christie's work centrally within her contemporary culture, critiquing and participating actively in that culture. As Melissa Schaub has stated, "the 1930s [were] a transitional decade, away from an older generation's vision of feminism and toward another."[10] The stories considered in my essay are crime texts which invite wider considerations of questions around women's creativity, modernism, location, and class in the interwar years.

Examining three main areas of enquiry in the *Mr. Quin* stories, I investigate Christie's use of the crime short story genre as a site for exploring strategies for the representation of femininity, agency and creativity. The *Mr. Quin* stories, "The Face of Helen," "The Bird with the Broken Wing," and "The World's End," explore differing aspects of femininity and its conflicts. In these three *Mr. Quin* stories, Christie probes with a remarkable and deceptive lightness of touch some problematic stereotypes associated with female identity and its representation in crime fiction and her contemporary culture: objectification and power, victimization and resistance and the female artist and intergenerational conflict between women. My discussion also considers the role of Mr. Satterthwaite in negotiating these gender codes. In its examination of "The Face of Helen," my chapter focuses on the depiction of female physical beauty and sexuality, and considers the role of art in contesting one-dimensional understandings of perfection and power. "The Bird with the Broken Wing" explores women's impossible choice in relation to male partners, between compatibility and safety as opposed to passion and excess.[11] Christie's examination of this topic suggests that genre writing and literary fiction both have the capacity for critical scrutiny of these social and cultural questions in relation to gender. My examination of "The World's End" centers on Christie's portrayal of a female artist figure pursuing her singular aesthetic vision regardless of the dismissive reception of her work she endures from her surroundings.[12] In all three stories, the problems experienced by female characters are foregrounded by the isolation they are experiencing. None of them are seen to enjoy close female friendships or continued closeness with their mothers or other female family members. This isolation from other women, the stories suggest, are to the detriment of these female characters, who struggle alone against an often hostile or at best indifferent patriarchal society.

Analyzing Christie's creative engagement with the short story genre in the *Mr. Quin* stories, this essay considers the specific constraints and possibilities afforded by this format.[13] I argue that the short story genre allows Christie to explore differing constructions of femininity without being tied to specific a developmental or linear progression, a dimension which potentially contributes to challenging prescribed narrative plots for women. The *Mr. Quin* stories present a special part of Christie's oeuvre, as reflected in her own assessment of these texts. Commenting that the *Mr. Quin* stories were her own personal favorites among her works,[14] these short texts appear to have within them the concentrated intensity of Christie's aesthetic vision and the questions of her contemporary time which preoccupied her. As Cook states: "The pleasure Christie gleaned from writing the Quin tales is vitally important to their appreciation.... Christie takes a step back from her conventional texts to analyse the nature of a detective."[15] These texts illustrate Christie's use of the short story genre as an experimental format through which to explore contemporary questions and ideas related to gender. In this respect, her work bears many similarities to more canonical women short story writers traditionally regarded as modernists, such as Katherine Mansfield, who enjoyed literary status generally denied to Christie. For Christie, the short story provided a fertile imaginative space for the exploration and interrogation of crime and of femininity and its construction. As we shall see, these stories expose the patriarchal domination inherent in the heterosexual marriage plot, and strive to depict female characters seeking alternatives outside the confines of this plot which allow them to articulate their creative identities free of domestic responsibilities and constraints.

Woman as Object: "The Face of Helen"

Christie's fascination with the complexities of femininity and its construction is at the heart of her *Mr. Quin* stories. In "The Face of Helen," she examines the impact of cultural mythologies of femininity and power on women's existence, problematizing cultural fear of female authority and seduction frequently associated with beauty and projected onto female characters in crime fiction and in society more generally. As Mary Evans states, commenting on the portrayal of female beauty in crime fiction: "young and attractive women ... are often the victims of murderers. In this context, crime fiction identifies one of the schisms of western culture: its veneration for female beauty but the ancient fear of its disruptive possibilities."[16] "The Face of Helen" also examines the question of female beauty and objectification in its portrayal of the vulnerable Gillian. In this story, the protagonist and amateur detective Mr. Satterthwaite becomes fascinated by a young woman called Gillian West who he notices in the audience one night while at the opera in London. We learn of Satterthwaite's admiration for Gillian's extraordinary allure, which he likens to the mythical figure of Helen of Troy.[17] Upon meeting Gillian, however, he learns that beneath her stunning looks she is an ordinary woman, troubled by two men who are competing for her affections, Philip Eastney and Charlie Burns. That same evening, after the performance has ended, their rivalry turns violent when the two suitors start brawling in the street. Satterthwaite chivalrously comes to Gillian's assistance, and breaks up the fight between Philip and Charlie. Satterthwaite's age and marginalized position sets him apart from the romance plot and enables him to gain the trust of all the characters in the story, including the would-be murderer. Furthermore, his role as confidante and companion to female friends and acquaintances, rather than a romantic lead or interest, is suggestive of his ambiguous masculine position within the texts. The role of outsider is a facet Satterthwaite shares with Christie's other eccentric male detective figure, Hercule Poirot who, according to Sarah E. H. Moore, is "the clearest example of the detective-as-outsider."[18] Towards the end of the story, Satterthwaite saves Gillian from an attempt on her life by her jilted lover Philip, a brilliant but erratic scientist who has devised an ingenious way to murder her. Failing to accomplish his murderous mission, Philip drowns himself in the Thames at the end of the story.

Gillian's beauty foregrounds the way femininity is performed and constructed within the scopic economy, and reflects the consequences of symbolic allusions to myth and powerful females. In its examination of constructions of feminine identity, power and the politics of appearance, "The Face of Helen" foregrounds the idea of performance and ritual through its use of setting. The opera represents a highly stylized and formal space centered on public spectacle. Satterthwaite's perception of performance reinforces the story's thematic focus on the dramatic, as he perceives his own role to be similar to playing a part in a theatrical performance. Self-consciously cultured in his tastes, he congratulates himself on the enjoyment he takes in mixing with great artists and the cultural elite, and is described as "an appreciator and a connoisseur of all the arts."[19] As well as being a cultural snob, Satterthwaite is a people-watcher and benign voyeur, and this activity is crucial to the story. Satterthwaite's position reflects his ambiguous role within the text as desiring participant, detective and rescuer, with Gillian as a passive object. Christie's portrayal of this process illustrates the way women are objectified, and their appearance a spectacle for male consumption. The story depicts the routine strategies Satterthwaite has devised in order to ensure maximum people-watching opportunities at the opera.[20] These observations are key to reading Satterthwaite's activity at the opera, and Gillian's role within it. Cook comments on Satterthwaite's capacity for heightened perception, stating that he "engages with that part of the psyche which is fundamental to his comprehension of events."[21] Christie describes him as "the gossip, the looker-on at life, the little man who ... recognizes drama when he sees it, and is conscious that he has a part to play."[22] Christie's reflections thus point to the highly strategic function and role for Satterthwaite within the *Mr. Quin* stories.

Christie's critique of the scopic economy is central to "The Face of Helen" and its depiction of Satterthwaite's gaze and of Gillian as a spectacle for consumption. This representation reflects John Berger's discussions of female objectification and the male gaze. Berger's ideas regarding these issues can be summarized as follows, "in the history of painting, the bodies of women are displayed for the proprietary claims of male viewers, and feminist studies of film confirm a similar representation of the female body for the male gaze."[23] In crime fiction the gaze often turns out to be dangerous or even deadly. While waiting for the performance to commence, Satterthwaite's glance falls on Gillian's head in the stalls circle, and he reflects: "There were, he knew, such faces in the world—faces that made history."[24] Helen of Troy is the mythical figure alluded to in Satterthwaite's thoughts, as he reflects: "*The face that launched a thousand ships.*"[25] These intertextual references reflect Satterthwaite's knowledge of the arts. But these mythical allusions are also used to grant Gillian's character greater symbolic power. When commended by Mr. Quin on his keen appreciation of beauty, Mr. Satterthwaite replies that he immediately recognized the exceptional charm of the young woman's head. However, Satterthwaite perceives a deeper, more profound perfection in Gillian, suggesting an abstract, non-predatory appreciation of the human form as an object of perfection, rather than a sexualized commodity for consumption. He reflects: "Beauty! ... Not charm, not attraction, nor magnetism ... just sheer beauty."[26] Satterthwaite's thoughts are a reflection of patriarchal culture and its association of charismatic and beautiful women with historic or mythical women possessing extraordinary power to command men, such as Cleopatra and Mary Stuart.[27] Linking these associations to Gillian, Christie exposes the gap between mythic constructs and reality. The story suggests that Helen of Troy and other female figures of exceptional exquisiteness have been perceived as a threat to the status quo and the patriarchal order of male dominance, and were punished as a result. In this way, Christie's story examines the parameters and definitions employed in patriarchal society to portray but most significantly diminish feminine influence.

Gillian's vulnerability as a potential victim of crime is evident from the portrayal of her relationships with males. She is pursued by two young men of contrasting dispositions and fortunes. Charlie Burns, her fiancé, is a steady and reliable shipping clerk. The other, Philip Eastney, is a handsome, brilliant but unstable scientist who tried to use his connections to help Gillian in the music world. Charlie is presented as a safe option for Gillian, unlike Philip who she cares for "like a friend" but is not in love with.[28] Philip's appearance is suggestive of his volatility and passion—a capacity for violence which Gillian herself intuits. His irregular, dynamic face furthermore presents a contrast to Gillian's classic beauty. It is the lack of regularity in Philip's facial features and the refusal of his talents to be marshaled that suggest his malevolence and obsessive nature.[29] Depicting the love triangle, Gillian and Charlie's engagement and the traumatic experiences Gillian has endured at the hands of men due to her physical allure,[30] the story incorporates features from both romance and crime fiction, highlighting how female characters are reduced to pawns in male rivalry. The threatening prospect of violent male rivalry is demonstrated in the image of Gillian's two admirers fighting over her like dogs.[31] Gillian's victimization at the hands of men due to her physical perfection reflects Cathy Cole's assertion that "beauty in crime novels is often a contributing factor to the female victim's death."[32] Charlie explains: "Gillian's had a lot of unpleasantness.… She's a good-looker, as you can see, and—well, that often leads to trouble for a girl."[33] This threat later becomes manifest when Philip, on learning of Gillian's engagement, attempts to murder her, offering her two gifts under the pretext of congratulating her on her engagement: a radio and a glass ornament. He instructs her to listen to the radio at a specific time when a famous opera singer is performing in the studio. It transpires that said opera singer is capable of hitting a unique glass-shattering note, and this will release the poison gas Philip has put into the glass ornament. The murder plot itself is constructed around the ritualistic dimension of performance. The striking appearance of the glass ornament given to Gillian by Philip echoes the story's message of the dangers for women who are objectified and exploited because of their physical appearance.

In "The Face of Helen," Christie employs the character of Gillian as a focal point for her investigation of the contradictions of femininity and power, and the challenges these pose to a conservative and male-orientated society which offers women few means for self-determination and agency. The story demonstrates that class and gender issues are both intertwined and central to the crime it portrays. "The Face of Helen" makes a number of references to social class and gender. Gillian's class status is immediately discernible to Satterthwaite, who sees her as belonging to a new "arty" class, signaled by her clothing which is bohemian but affordable.[34] Such social and artistic constructions of feminine beauty and sexuality are highlighted as contributing factors in the victimization of women. This can be seen in the story's main themes of the construction of femininity and the visual. That this is a crux question in crime fiction is emphasized in Mary Evans's assessment that

> women's beauty is written as embodying the potential for agency; a consistent theme suggesting throughout crime fiction that female beauty can both provide women with social and personal confidence and inspire men to exceptional actions.[35]

Throughout the story Gillian is subjected to the male gaze and is defined through that evaluation. These assumptions and values are shown to be enforced via enduring cultural myths and stereotypes which inform social and cultural judgment, such as the ancient Greek myth of Helen of Troy, in which a woman becomes the object of male desire and rivalry. Christie's preoccupation with these questions in "The Face of Helen" demonstrates the thematic overlap between her work and modernist literary fiction by women writers such as such as Virginia Woolf. Gillian is portrayed as a modern woman from a modest social sphere, attempting to have friendships with men, who has artistic aspirations but lacks female friendships or any meaningful female relations. Alone and symbolically motherless, wholly reliant on male acceptance and protection, Gillian is vulnerable and anxious to please her male companions in return for their protection. "The Face of Helen" portrays the precarious process young women must negotiate, of establishing social and emotional boundaries through characters' social status, modern clothing and artistic aspirations.

Female Victimhood: "The Bird with the Broken Wing"

Whereas in Christie's "The Face of Helen," the main female character escapes her murderer, though does not escape objectification, in "The Bird with the Broken Wing" female trauma and victimization are inexorable, as suggested by the story's title. My discussion here focuses on Christie's representation of femininity and trauma, the role of Satterthwaite in negotiating crime and imagery in the story. In "The Bird with the Broken Wing," Satterthwaite spends the week-end at a country house party, but finds that he is not enjoying himself and is missing his London home comforts. Sat in his armchair by the fire, he feels an outsider at the party, marginalized from the youthful company because of his age and bored by the "monotonous" séance game played by the young partygoers at the country house.[36] When he receives an invitation from his young female friend Madge Keeley to attend her party at another nearby country house, Laidell, Satterthwaite leaves to join her party. Here, he learns of Madge's engagement to Roger Graham and meets an enchanting woman called Mabelle Annesley. When Mabelle is found hanged the next morning, Satterthwaite's assistance is required to in order to reveal that her death was not suicide, and to help identify her killer. The murderer turns out to be Madge's father, an intellectually gifted man who is a bystander, overlooked in his own household.

The traditional country house setting so frequently associated with Golden Age crime fiction is employed in "The Bird with the Broken Wing" in order to focus on the positioning of female trauma inscribed within that locus. In this story, Christie imbues the country house setting with a sense of claustrophobia to illustrate young women's entrapment and relative powerlessness within the patriarchal class structures symbolized by such estates. The country house is an oft-maligned location in crime fiction. Alison Light has argued that is suggests "ancestry, settled traditions and kinship."[37] "The Bird with the Broken Wing" exploits the claustrophobic nature of the country house by foregrounding the idea of caged entrapment associated with the bird motif in the story's title. The country house location enables Christie to pose questions related to class, status, rank and authority, and to specifically foreground the position of those individuals marginalized by or rendered invisible within that setting. Reaffirming the status quo, the country house becomes a locus for compromise and unhappy marriages, isolation, abjection and rage.

This is demonstrated in the extended description of the owner of Laidell, the murderer David Keeley. Keeley is depicted as "invisible" despite his great intellect. An exceptionally gifted and intelligent mathematician, he is nevertheless perceived by his surroundings as inconsequential, unattractive and lacking in charisma.[38] Keeley is the master and owner of the stately home, yet paradoxically this status does not grant him social visibility or acknowledged authority and respect. With this character, Christie examines the figure of the invisible and marginalized male who acts out in rage. Similarly to Eastney in "The Face of Helen," Keeley in "The Bird with the Broken Wing" represents the character of the male genius who sets himself apart through his intellectual prowess, a quality which becomes excessive to the culture that surrounds him, and thereby renders him a threat to the status quo. In both stories, it is his murderous intervention which is at the center of the crime plot. Similarly, in both stories, these male figures act as alter egos to Satterthwaite, embodying the darkness and rage his benevolence negates.

"The Bird with the Broken Wing" uses dichotomous description to highlight the contradictions of femininity as a construct, and to illustrate the way in which women are pitted against one another in patriarchy, rivaling one another for male approval and attention. The female characters Madge and

Mabelle represent the emotional and sexual implications of conformity. Keeley's daughter Madge constitutes a contrast to her "invisible" father, and is described as "a fine upstanding young woman, bursting with energy and life. Thorough, healthy and normal, and extremely pretty."[39] Madge's conformity is founded on a pragmatic approach to heterosexual relations and marriage. Adhering to convention and accepting marriage as her fate, Madge's engagement to Roger Graham is an act of pragmatism based on practicality. However, it turns out that, in the longer term, Madge may risk a fate similar to that endured by Mabelle, trapped in a stale marriage and seeking passion with Roger, Madge's fiancé. Describing the two women to Satterthwaite, Roger's contrasting perceptions are evident in the clichéd language he uses to describe his feelings for them. He declares himself to be "fond" of Madge, referring to her as "a good sort," well-suited to him. In contrast, he has trouble depicting his feelings for Mabelle and finally resorts to using words such as "enchantment."[40] Madge depicts her relationship with her fiancé in unromantic terms as a "safe" choice. Their relationship is evidently based on a notion of shared interests and pursuits, rather than passionate abandon.[41] Satterthwaite's own assessment of the young couple confirms them as "good healthy sociable young folk."[42] In having opted for a relationship based on social and class compatibility, Madge and Roger reflect Makinen's point that Christie "depict[s] a whole range and diversity of femininities and masculinities that form workable relationships."[43] In "The Bird with the Broken Wing," Christie shows Madge seeking to evade dependency and victimhood, by choosing a common-sense marriage which presents a "workable" arrangement of compatibility. Like Gillian in "The Face of Helen," Madge's choice of relationship reflects her determination to remain free of all-consuming emotional and sexual involvement. Madge's rejection of a relationship of destructive passion and prioritizing a "workable" marriage, make her a survivor and enable her to retain a measure of agency and control, in a setting which would otherwise seek to diminish her influence.

In contrast, Mabelle is unable or unwilling to conform to social expectations and conventional constructions of femininity. The story illustrates this through its depiction of her peculiar allure and unhappiness. Neither vampish nor aggressively sexual, Mabelle appears vulnerable and ethereal, qualities which the story suggests are seductive and mesmerizing to men. Satterthwaite perceives that she has "something much more elusive and intangible than beauty.... She had the quality of enchantment."[44] However, Mabelle's otherworldliness and isolation also render her pitiful, as Satterthwaite recognizes.[45] This impression leads him to devise the phrase "the bird with the broken wing" for her, a term evoking traumatized femininity. There is a question over Mabelle's family background, a further reference to her traumatic past which serves to isolate her from the rest of the party. Mabelle's family has suffered a series of devastating tragedies and deaths, making them seem cursed by ill fortune.[46] Jessica Gildersleeve, in her discussion of Christie's "The Mousetrap," makes a point about female isolation and the vulnerability it engenders, which is also valid for "The Bird with the Broken Wing" and its depiction of Mabelle as "a warning about the vulnerability of the independent woman who enters a relationship without the knowledge, support, or capacity for surveillance offered by an extended familial or social network."[47]

Mabelle's music is used to illustrate the contrast between private creativity and public spectacle, and women's problematic position in relation to agency in the arts—a theme also treated in "The Face of Helen" and "The World's End." At the evening gathering at Laidell, Mabelle is asked to perform for the guests. However, when Mr. Satterthwaite passes her room upstairs, he discovers that she has not returned to the guests downstairs, but instead is sitting alone in the windowsill, playing her ukulele to herself. Mabelle's playing is regarded merely as entertainment for others, whereas for her, the music appears to signify her abjection by her family's legacy of self-destruction and death. To underline this association the musical instrument is used to murder Mabelle, as Keeley strangles her with one of its strings. It is Satterthwaite's affinity with music and artistic understanding that enables him to make this discovery, and Keeley's lack of musical understanding that leads to his undoing. Christie thus uses music and art as a strategy through which to foreground the contrasting masculine positions presented by the cultured Satterthwaite and the scientific Keeley. "The Bird with the Broken Wing" offers a poignant image of the ethereal Mabelle hypnotically playing her ukulele alone in a room upstairs, evoking a dream-like sense of unreality. The music she is playing is defiantly traditional and quaint, eschewing more fashionable music forms such as jazz.[48] The tension within Mabelle's character is evident: as a married woman having an affair she could be seen as a seductress; yet, she is not described in overtly sexualized terms. Rather, Mabelle's ethereal sexuality and solitary nature render her vulnerable and, ultimately, a victim.

"The Bird with the Broken Wing" suggests that excessive passion in women is dangerous and leads to emotional damage and erasure of self. As in "The Face of Helen," Mabelle is without female companionship and wholly dependent on her relationships with males. This male dependency and lack of female bonds, the story suggests, places women in a position of vulnerability, an aspect which signals danger in a crime narrative. Makinen argues that Christie's young modern women seek new ways of redefining marriage for themselves that will empower them and allow them to retain agency.[49] To some extent, Madge's character is an embodiment of this agency, whereas Mabelle continues to rely on male control and ultimately succumbs to it. The fragments of text remaining from Mabelle's burnt letters to Roger Graham suggest her emotional dependency on him. Satterthwaite's role is to provide the symbolic link between these two female characters. He is sympathetic to both women and communicates an understanding of their predicaments and their choices. With his "practised eyes," Satterthwaite is positioned on the edge of conversations and the social sphere in both country houses. He remains a marginalized figure, until he steps in able to solve the mystery, but it is his outsider position that enables him to see and understand.

Conventionally, detective fiction has tended to portray female characters in victim roles as a means of interrogating the gender coding of crime. In "The Bird with the Broken Wing" the motif of the bird foregrounds the association of female with victimhood in crime fiction, but also specifically echoes the ways in which this motif has been used by women writers in literary fiction. As Ellen Moers shows, nineteenth- and twentieth-century women writers often employ the bird as a complex metaphor for female entrapment and resistance within patriarchy.[50] Mabelle's appearance and her musicality both underline her association with birds. The motif of the bird is central both to the story's crime plot and to its investigation of femininity. A bird with the broken wing is trapped and defenseless, an easy prey for an opportunistic killer. Christie's story shows how the motif of the bird serves to bridge the genres of crime writing and literary fiction, and to reflect critically on contemporary social and cultural change. Both Madge and Mabelle represent female acquiescence to the marriage plot; however, they occupy contrasting positions in the romance narrative. Both positions illustrate the compromises and pressures women face in having to make choices that limit them, between accepting a marriage of class compatibility and social convenience or, as in Mabelle's case, the pain of emotional dependency and victimhood.

The Woman Artist: "The World's End"

The story "The World's End" further interrogates the objectification and victimization of women. This is achieved by countering these compromised female characters with alternative depictions of femininity which also reflect a renewed preoccupation in Christie's contemporary society with the woman artist. Contrary to "The Face of Helen," "The World's End" does not present the female artist figure as the passive object of the male gaze or a victim of crime. Exploring the gender-political implications of these representations and their linguistic and contextual significance, my analysis of this story foregrounds Christie's complicated engagement with the woman artist and her contemporary society. My discussion of "The World's End" focuses on Christie's treatment of the themes of female artistry and the gender politics of creativity explored in the story.

"The World's End" depicts Mr. Satterthwaite on holiday in Corsica with his friend, the Duchess of Leith. In Corsica, he meets a young female artist called Naomi Carlton-Smith, a relation of the Duchess who is also staying at their hotel. The Duchess asks Naomi to show them her paintings, which are experimental in style to the Duchess' great dismay. Ignoring the Duchess' criticisms of the work, Satterthwaite is impressed by Naomi's paintings and purchases one of them. The next day, they go for drive in the mountains and reach a remote village, referred to by Naomi as "The World's End." Here, they meet the well-known popular actress Rosina Nunn and her travelling party eating lunch while sheltering from bad weather.[51] The rather unfocused Rosina Nunn regales her companions with the story of the theft of her precious gemstone. It transpires that the thief accused of stealing the gem is Naomi's fiancé, who is a playwright and now in prison. However, it is revealed that Rosina mislaid the gemstone herself within a wooden Indian box, meaning that Naomi's fiancé is innocent. At the end of the story, Naomi paints Mr. Quin in accordance with her own artistic and aesthetic principles. In this complicated and fascinating story, Christie sets the narrative abroad, situating her portrayals of femininity against a background of cultural displacement. As Alison Light has explained, Christie employs such settings to examine how characters respond when removed from their daily surroundings and known contexts, and confronted with cultural difference.[52] Moreover, in "The World's End," Christie depicts Naomi, a modern young woman, independent, travelling the world, driving a car, and pursuing her creative ambitions.[53] However, she is also depicted as harboring secret trauma and wounds that render her vulnerable. In "The World's End," the setting of Corsica enhances and problematizes the association of otherness with exile and marginalization, themes which are at the heart of this story.

The story's interrogation of femininity is presented in a series of confrontations between female characters. The Duchess of Leith, Satterthwaite's travel companion, has a loud and demanding personality and represents upper-class snobbishness and feeling of entitlement. This is most evident in her attitude towards Naomi, but can also be seen in her treatment of her maid. The Duchess displays a rather callous and dismissive stance towards her maid's wellbeing when the latter is taken ill on the boat journey.[54] The description foregrounds the oppression of working-class women and the disregard with which they are treated by the households and individuals they serve. Christie exposes this through the use of subversive humor. By mocking the Duchess' snobbish attitude and mannerisms, she portrays her as a figure of fun. However, she also hints at the humanity secretly harbored by the Duchess who wants to be seen publicly to dismiss her maid's illness but who brings her food when nobody is watching. This contradictory portrayal illustrates the unsustainable and damaging divisions between women caused by a class-ridden patriarchal society.

The Duchess's encounter with Naomi and her criticism of the latter's paintings serve to further foreground the contradictions of feminine identity, and class- and generational conflicts between women. This encounter also highlights the discriminatory and snobbish dismissal of their work endured by experimental women artists during his period.[55] The Duchess represents an older aristocratic class. She has financial means but needs a chaperone to travel with and lacks style.[56] In contrast, Naomi is young and developing a unique artistic vision. She is one of Christie's "bright young things, independent, adventurous women."[57] The conflict between these two female characters is framed by differing notions of artistry, appearance and class. Christie's descriptions of Naomi's physical appearance, intelligence and clothing draw attention to the character's bohemian style, while she sits alone in the hotel restaurant, suggesting social indifference or isolation. Recognizing her relation, the Duchess proclaims that Naomi is of modest means but inordinately proud, travels alone and generally resists conforming to conventional female stereotypes.[58] The stubbornly independent Naomi has also made controversial choices about who she mixes with. Again, the Duchess serves as the mouthpiece of conservative social disapproval of Naomi and her fiancé who is also an artist: "Mixed herself up with a most undesirable young man. One of that Chelsea crowd. Wrote plays or poems or something unhealthy."[59] However, in what could be seen as an act of compromise, Naomi's artistic involvement and potential threat to the establishment is lessened when she is portrayed as being consumed by depression over the false imprisonment of her fiancé.

In their confrontation over artistic standards, the Duchess once more serves as the mouthpiece of normative values, through her dismissive comments about female artistry and avant-garde experimentation. On seeing Naomi's paintings, the Duchess dismisses the abstract, experimental work, and addresses Naomi rudely, using the patronizing term "child." The Duchess concludes, "It seems quite easy to be an artist nowadays.... You just shovel on some paint."[60] She criticizes the paintings for their technique, and scorns their lack of adherence to realist representation and their garish and extreme use of color. The Duchess's implication is that these paintings and the use of thick paint and bold brush strokes are unfeminine. The Duchess goes so far as to complain that one of the paintings gives her "the creeps": the painting in question is in experimental style described as "queer vorticist" depicting a pear as "a swirling mass of evil, fleshy—festering."[61] Throughout the Duchess' tirade, Naomi remains composed and self-assured. With Naomi in "The World's End," Christie depicts a female artist struggling to be understood, at a time when women artists were marginalized from mainstream culture and their contribution to technical experimentation was diminished by that same culture. Echoing Virginia Woolf's portrayal of the painter Lily

Briscoe in her 1927 novel *To the Lighthouse*, whose art is also spoken of dismissively, Christie's portrayal of Naomi shows Christie critically engaging in cultural- and gender-political debates around women and creativity, and employing crime fiction as a form as a forum for the examination of these questions.[62] Importantly, Satterthwaite is on the edge of the social scene listening in on the Duchess and the actress. His intervention diffuses the confrontation between Naomi and the Duchess, as he effectively sides with the former. Christie uses Satterthwaite's character as an illustration of an audience that is open-minded enough to understand what Naomi is attempting to achieve in her art. When Satterthwaite the "connoisseur" with the "practised eyes" sees the merit and artistry in Naomi's paintings, he asks to purchase one of them, choosing one that combines vivid hues with a strict formal structure. Expressing his happiness at the purchase, Satterthwaite states that one day the painting will be worth a considerable sum of money.[63] This exchange portrays Satterthwaite as a sympathetic, non-predatory male who is able to see beyond the restrictive gender codes of the time, and who identifies with the female artist and is supportive of her endeavors.

Christie's Naomi is a complex and multifaceted woman who plays a central role in "The World's End," but who is not a victim of crime or a passive object. This move is signaled through the depiction of Naomi's mobility, and specifically her car. Naomi has travelled to Corsica to paint but also, the story suggests, in order to escape a stifling social scene back in Britain, and drives up to their destination in the Corsican mountains in the small car she has purchased. This portrayal presents an important image of self-reliance and modern femininity. Melissa Schaub has commented on this aspect of the modern woman, arguing that "the changes in women's personal freedom [can be seen in] their depictions of women in motion."[64] Naomi is precisely the kind of new female character that Christie explores in her work, which Makinen describes as "living 'otherwise,'" who acts like an "intrepid female adventurer,"[65] traveling alone and devoting herself to her art. Naomi has self-determination and artistic ambition; however, she is also defined by her relationship to her absent fiancé and the crime he is accused of having committed, and is confined by the narrative's insistence on the destructive dimension of her feelings for him. Naomi's engagement is a narrative ploy added to make her character more palatable and acceptable to a conventional mainstream readership because it insists on the centrality of the heterosexual romance plot for women. As Makinen says: "One of the main ways of making the women sympathetic and available to reader identification was to make them the subject of a romance element."[66] In this respect, Naomi is comparable to Woolf's characters who "demonstrate the lack of acceptance and the struggle to achieve self-sufficiency afflicting women outside the marriage plot."[67]

The portrayal of Naomi as a painter and independent traveler exemplifies Christie's efforts to resist one-dimensional characterization of women in fiction and culture. "The World's End" leaves us with the image of Naomi having produced a sketch of Mr. Quin, and seemingly experiencing a newfound optimism. This upbeat mood is caused not only by the revelation that fact her fiancé is innocent, but no doubt also by the encouragement and support she has received in her art from Satterthwaite. Naomi's determination to look forwards her future, and more specifically to stay true to her artistic vision, reflects Mary Evans's point about Christie's own positive view of the modern. Evans states that "throughout Christie's work ... is a robust articulation of the many optimistic possibilities of the modern. Christie is not a pessimist about any aspect of the modern ... she maintains optimism about human achievement and human relations."[68] "The World's End" presents a re-examination of feminine positions, highlighting possibilities for agency and creativity afforded to younger women of means and with connections, such as Naomi. Christie subtly embeds her story's subversive message regarding class and gender inequality and the arts within a mystery plot, couched by a heterosexual romance, and observed by Mr. Satterthwaite's "practiced eyes."

Seeing Differently

The stories I have examined here focus on the problems faced by young women, both upper-class and of more modest financial means, in negotiating a patriarchal culture which frequently threatens to marginalize, curtail, or harm them. Their differing responses to these pressures are evident in the stories' explorations of emotional excess and creativity as a site for resistance. I have also examined Christie's use of Mr. Satterthwaite as a male protagonist who sees differently, and who negotiates reality "with practised eyes," due to his fluid or ambiguous masculinity and peripheral position in the social gatherings described in the texts. In all three stories, the non-judgmental Satterthwaite provides a mediating, sympathetic male position in relation to the female characters, rather than a sexual menace or threat. Satterthwaite presents an alternative masculine position which mirrors the questioning of femininity and its construction in the *Mr. Quin* stories discussed here. In all three stories, Satterthwaite is depicted on the edge of social gatherings, observing conversations but identifying with those individuals occupying marginalized positions, typically women. In these stories, Mr. Satterthwaite, with his acute observational skills, becomes adept at noticing important details or pertinent aspects which are frequently overlooked and deemed insignificant by others. His observations not only prevent crime or solve crime, but importantly also enable him to provide a reassuring and empathetic presence for the young, isolated and troubled female characters depicted in the stories. Through his intuitive abilities and empathetic nature, Satterthwaite thus offers a counter-representation to the somewhat stereotypical masculinities often encountered in crime fiction, and to the invisibility of ageing characters in crime fiction and culture more broadly.[69]

As we have seen, a central preoccupation in the *Mr. Quin* stories is loss and its symbolic manifestations, such as the diminution or obliteration of identity and the self. This point is made by Patricia D. Maida and Nicholas B. Spornick in their discussion of the *Mr. Quin* stories. They have it that "death is the other focus of the stories, death in the form of murder or suicide."[70] These themes are of course central to crime fiction, but they also provide a link to "highbrow" modernist literary fiction and poetry in the 1920s and 1930s. Novels such as May Sinclair's *Life and Death of Harriett Frean* (1922) explore such ideas in various ways as part of a formal and thematic preoccupation with experimentation.[71] The erasure or loss of self takes a number of different forms in the *Mr. Quin* stories, but always has catastrophic consequences for the female characters. Isolated from other women and without the fortification of female friendships or alliances in a society which is often hostile and unsympathetic to their needs and desires, these female characters are portrayed as attempting in differing ways to resist patriarchal restrictions on women during the interwar period. Christie's portrayal of female characters in her *Mr. Quin* stories anticipate Gildersleeve's point about Christie's post–World War II work that "women, in this context, are at risk: whether they transgress the limits and traditional roles of the domestic sphere and become victims because they refuse or are refused the cloistering care of the Victorian family structure, or because they succumb to a postwar insistence on returning to an ordinary life that inevitably places women on the marriage market and at risk of making a hasty or unwise decision."[72] The crime short stories discussed here all focus on the severe and potentially deadly consequences for women of making the "wrong" choices, cautioning women against forming alliances with men which may lead to their victimization, and alluding to alternative means of defining themselves in the world.

This focus has enabled my chapter to place this overlooked short story collection within Christie's contemporary literary and cultural context. Considering Makinen's discussion of Christie's "violent women," it is interesting to note that in the stories examined here, it is the male characters that have the capacity for violence against others, echoing conventional crime fiction's gendered patterns of agency. In contrast, none of the female characters discussed here occupy the position of murderer or criminal in their respective narratives. The female characters examined here direct their violence inwards, resulting in either escapism (as is the case for Mabelle in "The Bird with the Broken Wing"), compromise (Gillian's decision to marry Charlie in "The

Face of Helen"; similarly, Madge and Roger in "The Bird with the Broken Wing"), or depression and suicidal impulses (Naomi in "The World's End"). These women are all young, from certain social class backgrounds, and without children, all of which impacts on their portrayal and the options available to them in the texts. Christie's short stories thus provide a unique insight into her representation of femininity, as well as of wider questions related to narrative, plot, and perspective. The *Mr. Quin* stories treat themes and topics that were pertinent to women's experience in the interwar years. Both "The Face of Helen" and "The Bird with the Broken Wing" hint at the possibilities and choices women faced in heterosexual relations at this time, and contain warnings to women against the ways in which patriarchal authority may seek to hurt them, should they transgress the boundaries of accepted and conventional conduct for upper-class women. In "The World's End," the crime plot revolving around unfair imprisonment serves to draw attention to the way in which characters are criminalized by society through their financial status. The story also examines how female artists experimenting with new formal and thematic strategies in their work are compartmentalized and trivialized. These issues were pertinent to Christie and other woman writers at the time, preoccupied with reimagining femininity and its representation by exploring narrative conventions without conforming to the requirement to depict marriage as a happy ending. Christie's crime fiction short stories in *The Mysterious Mr. Quin* promote explorations of gendered identities and agency and invite reflection on twenty-first century readings of the Christie canon. They help us to acknowledge and assess the questioning and experimental potential of Christie's fiction.

Notes

1. Agatha Christie, "The Face of Helen" in *The Mysterious Mr. Quin* (London: HarperCollins, 2003), p. 230.
2. See Makinen's essay in the present volume, for example.
3. Michael Cook, *Detective Fiction and the Ghost Story: The Haunted Text* (Basingstoke: Palgrave Macmillan, 2014), p. 89.
4. *Ibid.*
5. Patricia D. Maida and Nicholas B. Spornick assert that "Harley Quin and Mr. Satterthwaite continue to spark interest perhaps because they are so different from [Christie's] other detectives" (p. 121).
6. Cook, *Detective Fiction and the Ghost Story*, p. 95.
7. My discussion focuses on representations of femininity, rather than the relationship between Mr. Satterthwaite and Mr. Quin, or Mr. Quin's presence/absence within the stories.
8. Cook, *Detective Fiction and the Ghost Story*, p. 97.
9. Patricia D. Maida and Nicholas B. Spornick discuss the Mr. Quin stories from a different angle, focusing on the figure of Mr. Quin and the theme of love. They state that "love relationships and the reuniting of estranged but true lovers dominate this collection." See *Murder She Wrote: A Study of Agatha Christie's Detective Fiction* (Bowling Green: Bowling Green State University Popular Press), p. 124.

10. Melissa Schaub, *Middlebrow Feminism in Classic British Detective Fiction: The Female Gentleman* (Basingstoke: Palgrave Macmillan, 2013), p. 38.

11. This question is also examined by Virginia Woolf in her novel *Mrs. Dalloway* (1925).

12. Agatha Christie, "The World's End," *The Mysterious Mr. Quin* (London: HarperCollins, 2003), pp. 335–336. Here, the Duchess is rudely dismissive of Naomi's paintings, due to their experimental style and bold use of color and technique.

13. Elsewhere I have discussed the capacity of the crime short story to encourage and elicit textual experimentation and to challenge generic conventions and boundaries; see Beyer "Bags."

14. Cited in Cook, *Detective Fiction and the Ghost Story*, p. 90.

15. Cook, *Detective Fiction and the Ghost Story*, p. 91.

16. Mary Evans, *The Imagination of Evil: Detective Fiction and the Modern World* (London: Continuum, 2003), Ch.3.

17. Christie, "The Face of Helen," p. 234.

18. Sarah E. H. Moore, *Crime and the Media* (Basingstoke: Palgrave Macmillan, 2014), p. 245. See also Merja Makinen's incisive comments about Poirot as "ungovernable": *Agatha Christie: Investigating Femininity* (Basingstoke: Palgrave Macmillan, 2006), p. 39.

19. Christie, "The Face of Helen," p. 229.

20. *Ibid.*, p. 230.

21. Cook, *Detective Fiction and the Ghost Story*, p. 107.

22. Agatha Christie, Foreword to *The Mysterious Mr. Quin*.

23. Elizabeth Kowaleski-Wallace (ed.), *Encyclopedia of Feminist Literary Theory* (Abingdon: Routledge, 2009), p. 76.

24. Christie, "The Face of Helen," p. 233.

25. *Ibid.*, p. 234. Christopher Marlowe used the phrase "the face that launched a thousand ships" to describe Helen of Troy in his play. See Laurie Maguire, *Helen of Troy: From Homer to Hollywood* (Chichester: John Wiley & Sons, 2009), p. 159.

26. Christie, "The Face of Helen," p. 233.

27. *Ibid.*, p. 234.

28. *Ibid.*, pp. 242, 240.

29. *Ibid.*, p. 234.

30. *Ibid.*, p. 243.

31. *Ibid.*, p. 235.

32. Cathy Cole, *Private Dicks and Feisty Chicks: An Interrogation of Crime Fiction* (Fremantle: Curtin University Books, 2004), p. 154.

33. Christie, "The Face of Helen," p. 243.

34. *Ibid.*, pp. 234–235.

35. Evans, *The Imagination of Evil*, ch. 3.

36. Agatha Christie, "The Bird with the Broken Wing" in *The Mysterious Mr. Quin* (London: HarperCollins, 2003), p. 297. Katherine Mansfield's short story "Miss Brill" and its outsider protagonist provides an interesting parallel to the depiction of Mr. Satterthwaite, illustrating that Christie's work shared many thematic and textual commonalities with more "literary" fiction.

37. Alison Light, *Forever England: Femininity, Literature and Conservatism Between the Wars* (London: Palgrave, 2013), p. 80.

38. Christie, "The Bird with the Broken Wing," p. 300.

39. *Ibid.*

40. *Ibid.*, p. 323.

41. *Ibid.*, pp. 301–302.
42. *Ibid.*, p. 305.
43. Makinen, *Agatha Christie*, p. 111.
44. Christie, "The Bird with the Broken Wing," pp. 303–304.
45. *Ibid.*
46. *Ibid.*, p. 304.
47. Jessica Gildersleeve, "'We're All Strangers': Postwar Anxiety in Agatha Christie's *The Mousetrap*," *Clues: A Journal of Detection* 32.2, p. 116.
48. Christie, "The Bird with the Broken Wing," pp. 306–307.
49. Makinen, *Agatha Christie*, p. 81.
50. Ellen Moers, *Literary Women* (London: The Women's Press), pp. 245, 247.
51. Christie, "The World's End," p. 349.
52. Light, *Forever England*, p. 91.
53. Makinen (p. 6) also discusses the significance of cars in Christie's portrayals of female autonomy.
54. Christie, "The World's End," p. 332.
55. This is a topic also treated by Virginia Woolf in her artist's novel *To the Lighthouse* (1927).
56. Rosina Nunn is another interesting female artist figure in the story.
57. Makinen, *Agatha Christie*, p. 66.
58. Christie, "The World's End," p. 333.
59. *Ibid.*, p. 334.
60. *Ibid.*, pp. 335, 334.
61. *Ibid.*, p. 336.
62. As mentioned, Merja Makinen has done this topic justice in her contribution to the present volume.
63. Christie, "The World's End," pp. 337–338.
64. Schaub, *Middlebrow Feminism in Classic British Detective Fiction*, p. 41.
65. Makinen, *Agatha Christie*, p. 64.
66. *Ibid.*, p. 65.
67. Patricia Juliana Smith, "Gender in Women's Modernism" in Maren Tova Linett (ed.), *The Cambridge Companion to Modernist Women Writer* (Cambridge: Cambridge University Press), p. 91.
68. Evans, *The Imagination of Evil*, ch. 3.
69. See also Moore's fascinating discussion of Hercule Poirot as outsider character.
70. Maida and Spornick, *Murder She Wrote*, p. 125.
71. Makinen (p. 9) also mentions Sinclair as a contemporary of Christie's.
72. Gildersleeve, "We're All Strangers," p. 118.

Bibliography

Beyer, Charlotte. "'Bags Stuffed with the Offal of Their Own History': Crime Fiction and the Short Story in *Crimespotting: An Edinburgh Crime Collection*." *Short Fiction in Theory and Practice* 3.1, pp. 37–52.
Christie, Agatha. *An Autobiography* (1977). London: Harper, 2011.
_____. "The Bird with the Broken Wing" (1930). *The Mysterious Mr. Quin*. London: HarperCollins, 2003, pp. 297–328.
_____. "The Face of Helen" (1930). *The Mysterious Mr. Quin*. London: HarperCollins, 2003, pp. 229–257.

_____. "The World's End" (1930). *The Mysterious Mr. Quin*. London: HarperCollins, 2003, pp. 329–359.

Cole, Cathy. *Private Dicks and Feisty Chicks: An Interrogation of Crime Fiction*. Fremantle: Curtin University Books, 2004.

Cook, Michael. *Detective Fiction and the Ghost Story: The Haunted Text*. Basingstoke: Palgrave Macmillan, 2014.

Evans, Mary. *The Imagination of Evil: Detective Fiction and the Modern World*. London: Continuum, 2009. E-book.

Gildersleeve, Jessica. "'We're All Strangers': Postwar Anxiety in Agatha Christie's *The Mousetrap*." *Clues: A Journal of Detection* 32.2, pp. 115–123.

Goodman, Lizbeth. *Literature and Gender* (1996). London: Routledge, 2013.

Kowaleski-Wallace, Elizabeth (ed.). *Encyclopedia of Feminist Literary Theory* (1996). Abingdon: Routledge, 2009.

Liggins, Emma, Andrew Maunder and Ruth Robbins. *The British Short Story*. Basingstoke: Palgrave Macmillan, 2011.

Light, Alison. *Forever England: Femininity, Literature and Conservatism Between the Wars* (1991). Abingdon: Routledge, 2005.

Linett, Maren Tova (ed.). *The Cambridge Companion to Modernist Women Writers*. Cambridge: Cambridge University Press, 2010.

Maguire, Laurie. *Helen of Troy: From Homer to Hollywood*. Chichester: John Wiley & Sons, 2009.

Maida, Patricia D., and Nicholas B. Spornick. *Murder She Wrote: A Study of Agatha Christie's Detective Fiction*. Bowling Green: Bowling Green State University Popular Press, 1982.

Makinen, Merja. *Agatha Christie: Investigating Femininity*. Basingstoke: Palgrave Macmillan, 2006.

Moore, Sarah E. H. *Crime and the Media*. Basingstoke: Palgrave Macmillan, 2014.

Schaub, Melissa. *Middlebrow Feminism in Classic British Detective Fiction: The Female Gentleman*. Basingstoke: Palgrave Macmillan, 2013.

Sinclair, May. *Life and Death of Harriett Frean* (1922). Project Gutenberg, www.gutenberg.org.

Smith, Patricia Juliana. "Gender in Women's Modernism" in Maren Tova Linett (ed.), *The Cambridge Companion to Modernist Women Writers*, Cambridge: Cambridge University Press, 2010, pp. 78–94.

Woolf, Virginia. *Mrs. Dalloway*. London: Hogarth Press, 1925.

_____. *To the Lighthouse*. London: Hogarth Press, 1927.

"The sumptuous and the alluring"
Poirot's Women, Dragged Up and Dressed Down

J. C. Bernthal

> "To Hercule Poirot, she still represented the sumptuous and the alluring."
> —Agatha Christie, "The Capture of Cerberus"[1]

This essay joins a growing body of work that approaches Agatha Christie from a queer perspective. More precisely, it identifies what I have described elsewhere as "queer potential" in Christie's detective fiction.[2] That is to say, in this essay I consider spaces in Christie's writing where human identity itself appears undefinable; where there is no such thing as "truth" about a person, or a "normal" individual. From there, it is possible to read Christie, a writer well-known and much decried as a conservative novelist, queerly.

Assessing Christie's queerness, I am not merely looking for gay or lesbian characters in her several novels, short stories and play scripts. I am looking for queerness at the very heart of her conventional plots and characters. After considering the extent to which Christie's most popular detective, Hercule Poirot, can be considered a conventional hero, I will turn to his very heterosexual friend Captain Hastings, before considering the women in Poirot's life. Hastings' love life, and his friendship with Poirot, can be theorized with reference to the work of Eve Kosofsky Sedgwick, who has claimed that male-male friendships are always predicated on something erotic, and that men who fight over a woman are in fact enjoying something intense and emotional between themselves.[3]

Just as Sherlock Holmes respected one woman, a criminal who outsmarted him, Poirot also admires a single woman: he praises the Countess Vera Rossakoff, a flamboyant and unrepentant jewel thief, as "a woman in a thousand—no, a million!" and the question of their marriage is raised more than once.[4] Rossakoff is not a demure, conventional love interest; she is downright exuberant, taking great pride in her femininity. Reading this character as so overly feminine that she is a mockery of femininity itself means reading her role as Poirot's romantic interest—the proof of his heroic straightness—as part of a wider generic parody.

There are two other women in Poirot's life: his friend, the crime writer Ariadne Oliver and his machine-like secretary, Miss Lemon. Some work has been done on Oliver,[5] but Miss Lemon is relatively unchartered territory.[6] I would like to consider Lemon less as a character than as a comic device—as a woman, absurdly under-characterized, she is merely a part of Hercule Poirot's orderly modern(ist) world. However, on some occasions, the machine-like coldness slips and she fails to compute. Most ostensibly, she shocks her employer by making three errors in a single letter and then attributing her weakness to family problems. In such moments, Felicity Lemon illustrates the inadequacy of any homogenous description of even the dullest individual. How broad, after all, is the great detective's worldview if he has failed to consider the woman closest to him—his secretary—as a real person with sensitivities and relatives?

Finally, this essay considers how Rossakoff and Lemon have appeared in the popular television series *Agatha Christie's Poirot* (1989–2013). My first and most unorthodox claim is that on-screen Poirot is transformed into a subtly but conventional heterosexual hero; his eccentric chivalry is reformulated for the screen as less a foreign flourish than a response to falling in love with various women. Rossakoff appears on-screen as less autonomous and more sensitive than in the books—she depends on Poirot's manly protection. By her final appearance, in "The Labors of Hercules" (2013), the countess's unmediated pursuit of pleasure has led to bad parenting. In other words, Rossakoff has become a woman who, without Poirot's guiding authority, has descended into unacceptable femininity. Lemon, on the other hand, is mercifully spared the pain of becoming a love interest; as in the books, her attentions belong entirely to filing. However, the character on screen is, as it were, "rounded" and made more sympathetic to a 1990s and early twenty-first century audience than the literary Lemon. She is portrayed as naïve and maternal—in other words, as the only acceptable kind of non-sexualized woman in a man's world. In "rounding" the characters, dramatists invest deeply in binarized narratives of feminine worth, which appear satirized in the literature. Maternal or grotesque, virgin or whore, the characters on-screen are earnest products of a heteronormative misogynistic context. Perhaps Christie's literary texts are richer in queer potential than the television adaptations, despite the latter's democratic intentions.

Poirot and Hastings: A Rad Bromance

It would be difficult to find a "straighter" writer than Agatha Christie: Julian Symonds noted shortly after the novelist's death that "few feminists or radicals are likely to read her."[7] But that is simply not true. As intimated above, Christie has attracted attention from feminists, and from LGBTQ+ readers.[8] Moreover, since her first publication, Christie has enjoyed an almost universal fan-base. I would like to put Christie's success down in part at least to her under-acknowledged comic touch. While her books appear profoundly conventional, formulaic and the opposite of subversive, they are constantly making fun of the conventions to which they appeal.

Christie's detectives, beginning with Poirot, are at least mock-heroic. Traditional scholarship reads Christie as an author entirely faithful to Arthur Conan Doyle's Sherlock Holmes formula, distinguished by the soundness of her puzzles. However, building on Alison Light's suggestion that Christie exhibits "anti-Victorian and anti-nostalgic elements," several commentators have considered her prose "self-consciously ironic," and discussed Poirot as an "antiheroic feminised" critique of "male heroism."[9] The construction of acceptable maleness is a process clearly reflected in characters' interactions with Poirot, who is able to solve crimes precisely because nobody takes him seriously, as they would a fit young Englishman. Furthermore, Poirot's relationship to English masculinity is dependent on his relationship to Captain Hastings, described by Christie as a "stooge" with a patriotic military background.[10]

Christie acknowledged that she wrote "in the Sherlock Holmes tradition,"[11] but her context was not Conan Doyle's. Sherlock Holmes (first appearance, 1887) has become synonymous with national heroism in the late Victorian period. In "His Last Bow," which Conan Doyle penned some time after receiving his knighthood for services to propaganda, Holmes prepares himself, and the nation, for the Great War. When Christie's first novel, *The Mysterious Affair at Styles*, was published in 1920, Britain was recovering from the conflict. An enormous loss of life and the need for women to assume traditionally manly tasks with men displaced to the battlefield meant that, while war had formerly been idealized as something that "made men," it became seen as something that "could destroy as well as make men."[12]

An esoteric intellectual, Conan Doyle's Holmes seems detached from everything but his investigations. When his sidekick, Dr. Watson, admires a woman's beauty, Holmes says, "I did not observe."[13] Holmes is "not a whole-soul admirer of womankind," but he does occasionally theorize about how he would treat a wife. This is important: it permits readers to accept his relationship with Watson, unsuspicious of their live-in closeness. Watson, moreover, is a ladies' man, boasting of "an experience of women which extends over many nations and three separate continents," and frequently pointing out "attractive" or "beautiful" women.[14] However, these moments never dominate the text and Holmes's affection for Watson, while rarely mentioned, is afforded more actual space when it does feature.[15] Such a vehement gaze at women insists upon straight, or more precisely non-homosexual, desire. Watson's objectification of women is necessary in the context of his affection for Holmes, and it licenses the latter's celibate misogyny, enacting an "intimate prohibition" that, for queer theorist Eve Kosofsky Sedgwick, characterizes "homosexual panic."[16]

In some respects, Poirot is an anti–Holmes. He is introduced in *Styles* a few paragraphs after Captain Hastings has confessed to "a secret hankering to be a detective" like "Sherlock Holmes." Hastings is puzzled by Poirot's "extraordinary" appearance, his height, his effeminacy, and the fact that he used to be one of the most respected policemen in Europe.[17] Poirot is, notably, Belgian, rather than French: he takes pride in correcting people on this count. Charles Brownson notes that Poirot's Belgian-not-French status makes him, racially, "twice an outsider."[18] We may take this further, and suggest that it more deeply "others" Poirot as a hero. After all, French men were thought to be highly masculine and sexually assertive, with Robert Graves and others telling of French brothels on the front line during the war. It was French virility, not Belgian neutrality, that featured in British medical reports and American magazine editorials expressing concerns over the state of European masculinity. Making Poirot Belgian rather than French, Christie presents a less-than-threatening kind of foreign heroism, while also exploiting racial stereotypes. As a foreign but questionably manly hero, Poirot stands outside of, but also confirms, British masculine security. On a generic level, as the stock-detective with an unfamiliar but competent methodology, he similarly proves an inauthentic figurehead for the status quo he upholds.

Holmes's "ignorance [is] as remarkable as his knowledge": he does not know, for instance, that the earth orbits the sun, an ignorance he defends because it means there is more room in his brain for important information. Indeed, having learnt about the earth's rotation, Holmes endeavors "to forget it," discriminating knowledge before he can process it.[19] On the contrary, Poirot weaves a tapestry out of overlooked clues. He solves his first case by observing that "the objects on the mantelpiece" are out of order and later identifies that a suspect who claims to have pricked herself on a rose is lying because the rose in question was thornless.[20] The ability to notice people's eating habits or conversational quirks is something he has picked up from women, because "women ... see everything, they notice the little detail that escapes the mere man."[21] The details which Poirot appreciates are domestic and as Stephen Knight notes, "classically, and stereotypically female."[22] They are also overlooked by Poirot's rivals. The kind of generic masculinity to which Christie responds, then, labels things too trivial to be of importance if they do not fit a pet theory. With Poirot's openness to feminine codes of knowledge, detective fiction's veracity is both undermined and opened up.

And then there is the sidekick. As Christie's version of Watson, Hastings responds to his prototype's masculinity. Poirot often complains that Hastings "prostate[s him]self before all [women] who are good-looking" while "psychologically ... know[ing] nothing whatever about them."[23] The almost arbitrary silliness of Hastings' gaze towards women is emphasized from the outset: in *Styles*, he falls madly in love with two unsuitable women. A few pages into the second novel he has already assessed every woman as a potential love interest, prompting Poirot to exclaim: "Already you have seen a goddess!"[24]

Like a number of heterosexual men, Hastings is strangely attracted to the male friend who so confidently eschews rituals which absorb Hastings himself. In the Sedgwickian sense, homosexual panic has been inevitable in patriarchal societies, which have encouraged "certain intense male bonds ... not readily distinguishable from the most reprobated bonds."[25] The urge to find a female body to fall in love with qualifies and validates as un-perverted the intensity of affection between Hastings and his friend (or teacher, to whom he is a disciple). By *The Big Four* (1927), Hastings has married but left his wife in Argentina, with no communication, because he felt like living with Poirot. While over the course of the book, he grows to let Poirot touch him—"I ... did not attempt to evade the embrace with which he overwhelmed me"[26]—he qualifies this closeness by falling in love with every auburn-haired woman he meets. Hastings' wife, known as "Cinderella" because he sometimes forgets her name, is at one point believed to have been kidnapped, which upsets her husband—but he never goes to see how she is. By *Curtain: Poirot's Last Case*, Hastings' wife has died and Hastings has joined Poirot, who feeds him cocoa, tucks him into bed and is known to Hastings' daughter as "Uncle Hercule." The close friendship between Poirot and Hastings rests on a parodic version of Holmes and Watson's sexual coding. However, reading Hastings as an insecurely heterosexual figure helps us interpret the character's parodic generic function in the context of masculinity's frustrations and the limitations of human desire.

"What a woman!" The Countess Rossakoff

Small men, Christie writes, are bound to find "big, flamboyant women" attractive.[27] She is explaining Poirot's fondness for a dubious Russian Countess, Vera Rossakoff. If the dandified Poirot is Christie's response to Holmes, Rossakoff is a response to Irene Adler. Appearing in one story, Adler is one of Conan Doyle's most popular characters, being the only woman his detective, Holmes, admires. A fairly androgynous jewel thief and blackmailer, she outwits Holmes by dressing as a boy in "A Scandal in Bohemia." She earns his respect, permission to flee justice with a lover and the accolade "*the woman*," distinguishing her from the rest of her sex but also, of course, making her a figurehead for palatable womanliness in the series.[28]

Also a jewel thief, Rossakoff is excessive—more "foreign" than Poirot—and she represents a heightened femininity that is performed rather than innate. That is to say, she enjoys dressing up, insisting that women should "try to please," and is adamant that "to be content with what Nature has given you ... is *stupid!*"[29] Whereas Conan Doyle regretted not having injected humor into his fiction, Christie's portrayal of Poirot's "flamboyant" object of desire, as we shall see, is evidently comical.[30] By exaggerating Rossakoff's ornaments of femininity, and her feminine appeal to Poirot, Christie is able to mock a range of conventions, from femininity to class prejudice and the character's narrative function as Poirot's Adler.

Noting Christie's adjectives for Rossakoff, "*voluptuous, lush, exotic,* and *highly coloured*," Earl F. Bargainnier has observed that the orderly "Poirot's taste in women is the exact opposite of that in furnishings." This, he concludes, is why Rossakoff does not return after only a few appearances: she does not fit into Poirot's world.[31] Bargannier's analysis insightfully draws attention towards the burlesque, unruly, extroverted nature of Rossakoff's character and bearing. However, her incongruence with the rest of Poirot's tastes is hardly an authorial mistake that Christie tried to undo by removing the character: the remarks quoted above about "small men" enjoying the company of "big, flamboyant women" appear in almost as many titles as Rossakoff herself. In this sense—if only in this sense—Christie presents Poirot's attraction to Rossakoff as a deviation from his usual primness that is entirely consistent. The character's "voluptuous" and "exotic" nature stands for over-the-top femininity. As Poirot himself routinely fails as a masculine hero, the type of woman who attracts him has to be more feminine than he is, lest he also be considered a failed heterosexual. As a result, however, Rossakoff's performance of femininity is so heightened that it becomes self-parodic; a drag act, as shall be discussed. Like other prominent authors of the classical whodunit, Christie disapproved of detectives' need for a "female interest."[32] By making Rossakoff forcefully feminine and incongruent with Poirot's other interests, Christie draws attention towards the mechanical insincerity of sexual attraction in popular literature.

Rossakoff is introduced in "The Double Clue," a 1923 short story. Jewels have been stolen, and Poirot believes the most likely suspect to be a Russian countess about whom little is known: she may be an imposter, he reasons.[33] However, after meeting Rossakoff, he revises his opinion. Although Poirot usually visits suspects, Rossakoff invades his space by calling on him and Hastings at home. She is introduced as

> a whirlwind in human form [who] invaded our privacy, bringing with her a swirl of sables (it was as cold as only an English June day could be) and a hat rampant with slaughtered ospreys. Countess Vera Rossakoff was a somewhat disturbing personality.[34]

As presented, the woman is something more than human, her intimidating "personality" initially presented through reference to her clothes and subsequently in terms of her vocal "flood of volubility" and the "exotic scent" she leaves upon sweeping out of the room.[35]

Like a male drag artist, Rossakoff takes normal feminine signifiers to discordant excess. She does not simply have a sable coat, but "a swirl of sables" which connects with her body, as the swirling makes it part of the "whirlwind in human form" that Hastings claims she is. Even her hat is personified when it is described as "rampant," and not just with feathers but with "slaughtered ospreys": Christie, who had a passion for sable coats and was no campaigner for animal rights, draws attention to life and action in relation to traditionally static objects of clothing. Killed animals here contribute to the countess's vitality and quality of life: Christie presents one living body constructed from corpses. The coat also prompts Hastings' aside, a clichéd remark about English weather, so as an object it introduces an introspective gaze from the narrator asserting his gendered and national identity. On Rossakoff, bodies are theatrical properties, creating "disturbing" power.

Rossakoff's intimidating presence and the emphasis on clothes in establishing her character represent extremes of exotic confidence and artistic allure akin to those in a drag performance. A male drag artist who exaggerates the ornaments of femininity thereby emphasizes her own maleness beneath the dress, so drag can "mock traditional femininity and heterosexuality."[36] For a male-to-female drag act to be successful, the spectator must be convinced that beneath the woman's clothes sit men's genitals: part of the performance is the recognition of "the man beneath the skirt," untwining sex and gender, exposing femininity as mere artifice.[37] Drag takes the performative aspects of gender to hyperbolic excess, undermining the spectacle of gender itself. Gail Hawkes claims that

> if "drag" is verbal shorthand for the performative use of gendered dress codes to subvert the hegemonic twining of gender and sexuality, then we can speak in this sense, of dress as performance, of women "dragging up as women," or of men "dragging up as men."[38]

Robert Tyler suggests that the actress "[Greta] Garbo 'got in drag' whenever she took some heavy glamour part." Acting, for Tyler, is "all *impersonation*, whether the sex underneath is true or not."[39] To an extent, Rossakoff's whole character can be considered a "heavy glamour part." With her exaggerated performance, Rossakoff exerts power over men and draws attention to the elements of her identity that allow this.

Before meeting her, Poirot is able to suggest that Rossakoff may be not a real countess but one of many "immigrants": "Any woman can call herself a Russian countess."[40] After their first meeting, he comments on her "real enough" sable: "Could a spurious countess have real furs? My little joke, Hastings.... No, she is truly Russian, I fancy."[41] The clothes are real so the woman is real. This may be a "joke" but Poirot insists that Rossakoff is "truly Russian" whereas before he had doubted that she was truly a countess. Poirot has to twist his premise to reach the desired conclusion. In fact, Rossakoff is described with the same language used of contemporary burlesque and drag artists.[42] The female impersonator Bert Savoy, who died the year "The Double Clue" was published, was described by one contemporary critic as "flamboyant, loud, bawdy" and "swish." "He would wear jewelry of an exaggerated size."[43] The "overt sexuality" of his female persona was emphasized by the exaggerated nature of his corset, wig and draping gowns. This is equally a description of Rossakoff, the woman whose "very flamboyance attract[s] Poirot," whose "magnificent shoulders" are carried with "a magnificent gesture."[44] Rossakoff here must necessarily be an exotic fantasy: for the notoriously bourgeois Poirot, this means being an aristocrat. Poirot discounts his suspicion that Rossakoff might not be a real countess without admitting to the fact that she seems inauthentic. Rossakoff's *femme du monde* femininity is only attractive insofar as it is caricatured.

The two eccentrics' paths cross a few times in short stories, and Poirot frequently recalls the countess, usually when judging young women unfavorably against her standard: in *Hickory Dickory Dock* (1958), for instance, he makes the against-the-grain observation that "girls of today" do not wear enough make-up, his mind "dart[ing] to the memory of the Countess Vera Rossakoff. What exotic splendour there, even in decay!"[45] Certainly, the last time Poirot and Rossakoff meet, the latter objects with rigor to "girls" who "do not even try" to attract men, and in response Poirot admires her "heavy Titian tresses" and "corset laced tight"; "it was undeniable that she, at least, was still trying and trying hard!"[46] By now, she owns an underground nightclub, appropriately named Hell. Poirot sees her in Hell and they never meet again.

Rossakoff, then, is remembered as forbidden fruit, ripe in decay. She appeals to Poirot, proud polisher of the bachelor button, as an unreal and entirely artificial woman. To paraphrase the influential gender theorist Judith Butler, it is only via a stylized performance of woman-ness that Rossakoff is welcomed into the macho world of the detective novel. This is the Holmesian model, in parody.

Miss Lemon, the Mechanical Woman

Having left the countess in Hell, Poirot sends her a lavish bouquet of flowers. His secretary, Miss Lemon, is tantalized. Usually a grim and efficient typist, whose sole aim in life is to invent a filing system, she sets down her work. "Her filing system was forgotten," we learn. "All her feminine instincts were aroused." She wonders whether, "at his age," Poirot could really be interested in marriage.[47] These "feminine instincts" would shock the detective. There are few women in Poirot's life, and his secretary's sex is something he apparently fails to register.

Lemon is one of Christie's cross-over characters, in that she features in Poirot adventures and in lesser-known stories about the statistician J. Parker Pyne. The secretary—certainly the woman secretary—is not a Holmesian trope, and Poirot's efficient servants reflect his status as a modern man in a fast-moving urban world. After all, as Poirot reflects at the beginning of *Hickory Dickory Dock*,

> With George, his perfect manservant, and Miss Lemon, his perfect secretary, order and method ruled supreme in his life. Now that crumpets were baked square as well as round, he had nothing about which to complain.[48]

It comes as a shock, then, when Poirot's "precision instrument" of a secretary—"so completely machine made"—makes three mistakes in a simple typing job because she is worried about her sister. "Poirot," the reader learns, "had never conceived of Miss Lemon's having a sister. Or, for that matter, having a father, mother, or even grandparents."[49]

Miss Lemon is, fundamentally, a modern product. In one story, Poirot considers her as "composed entirely of angles," thereby "satisf[ying his] demand for symmetry." Indeed, as he observes again, "she was a human machine—an instrument of precision"; "he had never considered [her] as a woman."[50] Poirot likes Lemon, whose forename, Felicity, is only revealed fleetingly in *Hickory Dickory Dock*, because of her lack of imagination. When he does consider his secretary "as a woman" in "The Mystery of the Spanish Chest" (1960), he laments her lack of "voluptuous curves," comparing her unfavorably to "a certain Russian countess. But," he concludes, "that was long ago now."[51] The old demands of the crime fiction genre have disappeared and the ideal woman of the 1930s is not only unlikely but also unhuman.

This all ties in with contemporary debates about human identity becoming "mechanized" in the modern world. In Elizabeth Bowen's novel *To the North* (1932), cars tear through cities while their drivers sit still, mechanically operating switches and pedals; critics have long noticed a tension in Jean Rhys's modernist prose between women's sense of "responsive, covert inner self and [the] mechanical external one" required to succeed in society.[52] Miss

Lemon, this precise and perfect angled machine, keeps proving her inhumanity with exceptions to the rule; speculating on romance, mistyping, having a sister. How perfect is this paragon of modern womanhood? Even the supreme Lemon fails to hold true to form, and therefore the fashionable construction is flawed. The tension between the "responsive" interior and the "mechanical" exterior is loquacious in its apparent absence from the text.

Miss Lemon is a character whose role in each narrative is to remind readers that she is a non-character; a real-not-real woman. Part of her failure to warrant attention as a woman lies in her ugliness. The words "hideous" and "ugly" always surround her. As an author, Christie distrusts women who are very ugly as much as she distrusts the very beautiful. Her heroines are young and "plain"—there is a mobility in their plainness; they can make themselves up according to whichever witness they are trying to manipulate. "It is really a hard life," says Anne Beddingfeld, the protagonist of an early novel. "Men will not be nice to you if you are not good-looking, and women will not be nice to you if you are."[53] Women stand out in Poirot's symmetrically modern, ironically generic world only if they are extravagantly feminine or outstandingly unfeminine; "sumptuous and … alluring" or "ugly and efficient." The books adopt a conservative, even misogynistic, worldview—but perhaps the "c" is back-to-front.

On Television

There have been several attempts to translate Agatha Christie's fictional world to the screen. Both Lemon and Rossakoff have appeared as minor characters in short-lived projects such as *The Agatha Christie Hour* (London Weekend Television, 1982) and *Murder on the Orient Express* (Daniel H. Blatt, 2001). However, both have become major supporting characters in the highly successful television series *Agatha Christie's Poirot*. Having explored Christie's presentation of Poirot and the women in his life from a queer perspective, I will now consider how these characters and their relationships have translated to the screen. For many, "Agatha Christie" in the twenty-first century is the sum of her media success: the merest glance at Christie's official website or Facebook page reveals that television adaptations have been elevated to the status of canon.

In the early 1990s, Poirot became an unlikely "sex symbol" among middle-aged television viewers.[54] Perhaps in response to this interest, despite his prissy accent and dainty mannerisms, this Poirot becomes surprisingly virile and conventional over the course of the series. He even considers marriage in several episodes, always to "nice English girls."[55] In "Cards on the Table" (2005), he is able to identify a homosexual murderer because the latter never "tried [his] luck" with a beautiful woman, whom Poirot considers "irresistible": the straight Poirot sees something suspicious, and ultimately unethical, in a man who does not share his sexual appetite.

Poirot's heterosexuality is made explicit from the third season when he has a romance with Vera Rossakoff in "The Double Clue." In his memoirs, David Suchet, the star of *Poirot*, describes Rossakoff as "the one woman with whom Poirot falls in love."[56] Suchet compares Rossakoff to Conan Doyle's Irene Adler, but concludes that, unlike Adler, Rossakoff "does not outwit [Poirot]. Instead, he allows her to get away with her crimes."[57] Playing into the cultural myth that Christie molded her characters around plots, and that therefore finer points of character are less important than the finer points of the puzzle, Suchet here considers Rossakoff as submissively feminine. In Suchet's reading, Rossakoff depends on Poirot's love and authority to "get away with her crimes," and—like Poirot—Suchet does not question anything else about the character: he does not entertain the notion that Rossakoff's whole identity, or at least her aristocratic femininity, is a performance. The character, as portrayed by Kika Markham in the relevant episode of *Poirot*, has no memorable characteristics. In the short story, Rossakoff is feminine, aristocratic and foreign to the point of comic implausibility, but there is no suggestion of artifice in the television character, and no other character discusses Rossakoff's dubious title or "strong personality."

In the adaptation, Rossakoff seems to be less a clearly-defined character in her own right than a factor in the development of Poirot's character: she exists insofar as she provides Poirot with heterosexual romance and heterosexual heartbreak. The most flamboyant stereotypes Christie draws upon to sketch the character do not translate to the screen, but other stereotypes, about the passivity and understated beauty of attractive femininity, do. Markham described her character as one charged, like a conventional wife, with "want[ing] to change" Poirot.[58] Her motivations are not really explored, though, and Suchet quotes Poirot from the screenplay: "You are the most remarkable, the most unique woman I have ever met [but m]arriage is not for me."[59]

Suchet compares the final scene to *Brief Encounter* (1945): "The end of the film has him effectively saying goodbye to any chance of love, and … condemned to remain wrapped forever in his own loneliness."[60] For Suchet, Rossakoff is significant only to draw out Poirot's "deep regret at never having truly experienced love."[61] There is nothing playful and less still irreverent in the relationship—it accords with a reassurance Suchet frequently made in promotional interviews about *Poirot*: that he is, "Lord knows, emphatically not a 'luvvie.'"[62] Decisions in adaptation and Suchet's performance establish Poirot as a heterosexual figure, rewriting the satire that underscores his relationship with the Countess in Christie's prose.

A very different Rossakoff appears in the final season of *Poirot*, played by Orla Brady. Now a kleptomaniac instead of a jewel thief, and an alcoholic, this new Rossakoff is certainly at the center of comedy. However, the joke is on her: she is a bad mother, who has not settled down with a good husband but bundled her daughter all over the world, creating an unstable life that has driven the latter to serious crime. This Rossakoff still lives for pleasure and is deeply invested in her appearance—when Poirot comments, "You look well," she responds, "I want to look like a goddess; one of the better ones"— but she is trying to please herself and not male admirers, a set of priorities that causes Poirot and others to wince. Indeed, she is not too bothered to have missed out on passion with Poirot ("A love like ours could have burned down this city," she remarks, disinterested. "Such a waste," before passing through a doorway into a bright light). Of course, for most twenty-first century viewers, a woman who lives for pleasure and strives to look good because she wants to rather than to satisfy the male gaze is a very good thing indeed. As an individual, there can be no doubt that the twenty-first century Rossakoff is a more inspiring figure than those of the books and the early series. However, as a character in a fictional world, this character is judged whereas Rossakoff's generic function as a woman, and not the woman herself, is mocked in the literary texts. *Agatha Christie's Poirot* features two Rossakoffs, each a staple of that Freudian binary: Madonna/whore.[63]

Finally, there is Miss Lemon, a character of such little substance that she could not exist on the screen without artistic liberties being taken. Moreover, an extreme product of the interwar period, Miss Lemon is uninteresting to contemporary viewers. Portrayed by Pauline Moran in the television series, Felicity Lemon is more than a secretary to Poirot: she acts as a friend and surrogate mother, chiding him over his diet, exchanging gifts, playing word games over ice-cream, taking part in a séance and even hypnotizing Captain Hastings. The character is undeniably more rounded; she is very definitely now a real person, and a likable one at that. There is something genuinely subversive in the creation of a strong recurring woman character who is not defined by any relationship and who never has a romantic subplot of any kind. However, she is consigned to the role of matron; although clearly younger than all the male leads, Miss Lemon appears as a multi-purpose mother figure who rarely leaves her small office and is not allowed any more significance in the actual events than Christie's literary character. Pauline Moran, playing Miss Lemon in the series, gets significantly less screen time per episode than minor recurring characters such as Inspector Japp (Philip Jackson). When she is an angled and mechanical furnishing in Poirot's satirically modern apartment, Lemon's limited narrative significance makes sense; when she is a rounded and likeable character, it does not.

Like Suchet, Moran has discussed the need to stay "faithful" to "the books" and "the Canon" when appearing in *Poirot*.⁶⁴ Although she never quite claims to have grounded her character—whose interest in astrology reflects her own—in the literary texts, Moran like other cast members has promoted the television series as a visual version of the books; an authentic slice of "Agatha Christie." In publicity, the television series has been continuously positioned as "authentic" with reference to an implied author. This conjured Agatha Christie is conservative, strait-laced and robustly heterosexual. Her world is one in which men look at women, the good women adapt to the male gaze and the bad women stare back.

Where does this lead us, by way of conclusion? Agatha Christie has a reputation for simple, nostalgic conservatism—but to what extent is this fueled by the conservative nostalgia of television adaptations and fan communities? When it comes to gender, there is something lukewarm in the books' clear-cut perspectives. We cannot dismiss Christie as a purveyor of cozy ephemera, demanding no more thought than a cryptic crossword. Other essays in this volume have questioned the good and evil binary in Christie; I suggest that masculinity and femininity are also far from secure as opposite constructions, and the codification of human desire is presented as arbitrary. Reading Christie queerly means reading her as an ironic master of the mystery genre and an engaged social commentator.

NOTES

1. Agatha Christie, "The Capture of Cerberus" in *Hercule Poirot: The Complete Short Stories* (London: Harper, 2008), pp. 844–864 (p. 846).
2. See J.C. Bernthal, *Queering Agatha Christie* (Basingstoke, Palgrave Macmillan, forthcoming).
3. Eve Kosofsky Sedgwick, *Between Men: English Literature and Male Homosocial Desire* (New York: Columbia University Press, 1985).
4. Agatha Christie, *The Big Four* (London: HarperCollins, 1993), p. 211; "The Capture of Cerberus," p. 864.
5. See especially Merja Makinen, *Agatha Christie: Investigating Femininity* (Basingstoke: Palgrave Macmillan), pp. 48–52.
6. An exception, of course, is Meg Boulton's contribution to the present volume.
7. Quoted in Bernthal, *Queering Agatha Christie*.
8. See, for instance, Marty S. Knepper, "Agatha Christie: Feminist," *The Armchair Detective* 16 (1983), pp. 398–406; Dennis Altman, *The End of the Homosexual?* (St. Lucia: University of Queensland Press, 2013), pp. 129–132.
9. Susan Rowland, *From Agatha Christie to Ruth Rendell* (Basingstoke: Palgrave Macmillan, 2001), pp. 51, 21, 38.
10. Agatha Christie, *An Autobiography* (London: Harper, 2011), p. 282.
11. *Ibid.*
12. Jessica Meyer, *Men of War: Masculinity and the First World War in Britain* (Basingstoke: Palgrave Macmillan, 2009), p. 5.
13. Arthur Conan Doyle, "The Sign of Four" in *The Penguin Complete Sherlock Holmes* (London: Penguin, 2009), pp. 87–161 (p. 96).

14. Arthur Conan Doyle, "The Sign of Four," pp. 95–96.

15. When Holmes fears that a gunshot has injured Watson: "Then my friend's wiry arms were round me.... It was worth a wound—it was worth many wounds—to know the depth of loyalty and love which lay behind that cold mask." Holmes goes on to "rip [Watson's] trousers up with a pocket knife" to investigate, and swear that if Watson had been damaged he would have killed the attackers. Arthur Conan Doyle, "The Adventure of the Three Garridebs" in *The Penguin Complete Sherlock Holmes* (London: Penguin, 2009), pp. 1044–1055 (p. 1053).

16. Eve Kosofsky Sedgwick, *Epistemology of the Closet*, updated ed. (Berkeley: University of California Press, 2008), p. 162.

17. Agatha Christie, *The Mysterious Affair at Styles* (London: HarperCollins, 1993), pp. 11, 23. I have written about Poirot's masculinity and nationalism more extensively in "'Every Healthy Englishman Longed to Kick Him': Masculinity and Nationalism in Agatha Christie's *Cards on the Table*," *Clues: A Journal of Detection* 32.2 (2014), pp. 103–114.

18. Charles Brownson, *The Figure of the Detective: A Literary History and Analysis* (Jefferson: McFarland, 2014), p. 60.

19. Arthur Conan Doyle, "A Study in Scarlet" in *The Penguin Complete Sherlock Holmes* (London: Penguin, 2009), pp. 13–87 (p. 21).

20. Christie, *The Mysterious Affair at Styles*, p. 217; *Sad Cypress* (London: Collins, 1940).

21. Christie, *The Big Four*, pp. 207, 161.

22. Stephen Knight, *Crime Fiction Since 1800: Detection, Death, Diversity* (Basingstoke: Palgrave Macmillan, 2010), p. 90.

23. Agatha Christie, "The Cornish Mystery" in *Poirot's Early Cases* (London: Harper, 2002), pp. 57–80 (p. 73).

24. Agatha Christie, *The Murder on the Links* (London: Bodley Head, 1923), p. 16.

25. Sedgwick, *Epistemology of the Closet*, p. 185.

26. Christie, *The Big Four*, p. 252.

27. Ibid., p. 211.

28. For a rich discussion of Adler's gender ambiguity, and her significance in a macho genre, see Marjorie Garber, *Vested Interests: Cross-Dressing and Cultural Anxiety* (New York: Routledge, 1994), pp. 191–196.

29. Christie, "The Capture of Cerberus," p. 848. Emphasis in original.

30. Arthur Conan Doyle, *Memories and Adventures: An Autobiography* (London: Wordsworth, 2007), p. 108; Agatha Christie, "The Double Clue" in *Hercule Poirot: The Complete Short Stories* (London: Harper, 2008), pp. 282–290 (p. 286).

31. Earl F. Bargainnier, *The Gentle Art of Murder: The Detective Fiction of Agatha Christie* (Bowling Green: Bowling Green University Popular Press), pp. 53–54. Emphasis in original.

32. Agatha Christie, "Mystery Writers in England" in *Ask a Policeman* (London: HarperCollins, 2012), pp. xiii-xx (p. xi).

33. Christie, "The Double Clue," p. 285.

34. Ibid., p. 286.

35. Ibid., p. 287.

36. Leila J. Rupp and Verta Taylor, *Drag Queens at the 801 Cabaret* (Chicago: University of Chicago Press, 2003), 136.

37. Roger Baker, *Drag: A History of Female Impersonation in the Performing Arts* (New York: Cassell, 1994), p. 157.

38. Quoted in Moya Lloyd, *Beyond Identity Politics: Feminism, Power and Politics* (London: Sage, 2005), p. 136.
39. Quoted in *Ibid.*, p. 108. Emphasis original.
40. Christie, "The Double Clue," p. 285.
41. *Ibid.*, p. 286.
42. For Christie's fondness of pantomime dames and female impersonators, see *Autobiography*, p. 140.
43. J. D. Doyle, "More Bert Savoy" in *Queer Music Heritage* (June 2004), accessed May 1, 2014, www.queermusicheritage.us.
44. Christie, *The Big Four*, pp. 188–189.
45. Agatha Christie, "The Mystery of the Spanish Chest" in *Hercule Poirot: The Complete Short Stories* (London: Harper, 2008), pp. 421–455 (p. 421).
46. Christie, "The Capture of Cerberus," p. 850.
47. *Ibid.*, p. 864.
48. Agatha Christie, *Hickory Dickory Dock* (Glasgow: Fontana, 1988), p. 5.
49. *Ibid.*, pp. 5–6.
50. Christie, "The Mystery of the Spanish Chest," p. 421.
51. *Ibid.* The story, written in 1960, is an expanded version of another story, first published in 1932.
52. Elizabeth Abel, quoted in Nancy R. Harrison, *Jean Rhys and the Novel as Women's Text* (Chapel Hill: University of North Carolina Press, 1988), p. 118.
53. Agatha Christie, *The Man in the Brown Suit* (London: Pan, 1973), p. 13.
54. Peter Haining, *Agatha Christie's Poirot* (Boxtree: LWT, 1995), p. 19.
55. David Suchet quoted in *Ibid.*, p. 19.
56. David Suchet and Geoffrey Wansell, *Poirot and Me* (London: Headline, 2013), p. 113.
57. *Ibid.*
58. Quoted in Haining, *Agatha Christie Poirot*, 19.
59. Quoted in Suchet and Wansell, *Poirot and Me*, pp. 113–114.
60. *Ibid.*, p. 114.
61. *Ibid.*, p. 62.
62. Quoted in Phil Penfold, "A Passion for Poirot," *Yours* (April 2004), p. 6.
63. Sigmund Freud, "On the Universal Tendency to Debasement in the Sphere of Love" (1912), *Complete Works of Sigmund Freud*, vol. 11 (London: Vintage, 2001), pp. 177–190.
64. Pauline Moran, "Poirot and Me," *Guardian* (November 10, 2013), accessed January 1, 2015, www.theguardian.com/tv-and-radio/2013/nov/10/pauline-moran-poirot-tv.

Bibliography

Agatha Christie's Poirot. Television series, Granada and ITV Studios, 1989–2013.
Altman, Dennis. *The End of the Homosexual?* St. Lucia: University of Queensland Press, 2013.
Baker, Roger. *Drag: A History of Female Impersonation in the Performing Arts* New York: Cassel, 1994.
Bargainnier, Earl F. *The Gentle Art of Murder: The Detective Fiction of Agatha Christie.* Bowling Green: Bowling Green University Popular Press.
Bernthal, J. C. "'Every Healthy Englishman Longed to Kick Him': Masculinity and Nationalism in Agatha Christie's *Cards on the Table*." *Clues: A Journal of Detection* 32.2 (2014), pp. 103–114.

___. *Queering Agatha Christie: Revisiting the Golden Age of Defective Fiction.* Basingstoke: Palgrave Macmillan, forthcoming.
Brownson, Charles. *The Figure of the Detective: A Literary History and Analysis.* Jefferson: McFarland, 2014
Christie, Agatha. *An Autobiography* (1977). London: Harper, 2011.
___. *The Big Four* (1927). London: HarperCollins, 1993.
___. "The Capture of Cerberus" (1947). *Hercule Poirot: The Complete Short Stories.* London: Harper, 2008, pp. 844–864.
___. "The Cornish Mystery" (1923). *Poirot's Early Cases.* London: Harper, 2002, pp. 57–80.
___. "The Double Clue" (1923). *Hercule Poirot: The Complete Short Stories.* London: Harper, 2008, pp. 282–290.
___. *Hickory Dickory Dock* (1955). Glasgow: Fontana, 1988.
___. *The Murder on the Links.* London: Bodley Head, 1923.
___. *The Mysterious Affair at Styles* (1920). London: HarperCollins, 1993.
___. "The Mystery of the Spanish Chest" (1960). *Hercule Poirot: The Complete Short Stories.* London: Harper, 2008, pp. 421–455.
___. "Mystery Writers in England." *Ask a Policeman.* London: HarperCollins, 2012, pp. xiii-xx.
___. *Sad Cypress.* London: Collins, 1940.
Conan Doyle, Arthur. "The Adventure of the Three Garridebs" (1924). *The Penguin Complete Sherlock Holmes* London: Penguin, 2009, pp. 1044–1055.
___. *Memories and Adventures: An Autobiography* (1924). London: Wordsworth, 2007.
___. "The Sign of Four" (1890). *The Penguin Complete Sherlock Holmes.* London: Penguin, 2009, pp. 87–161.
___. "A Study in Scarlet" (1887). *The Penguin Complete Sherlock Holmes.* London: Penguin, 2009, pp. 13–87.
Doyle, J. D. "More Bert Savoy." *Queer Music Heritage* (June 2004), www.queermusicheritage.us.
Freud, Sigmund. "On the Universal Tendency to Debasement in the Sphere of Love" (1912). *Complete Works of Sigmund Freud*, vol. 11. London: Vintage, 2001, pp. 177–190.
Garber, Marjorie. *Vested Interests: Cross-Dressing and Cultural Anxiety.* New York: Routledge, 1994.
Haining, Peter. *Agatha Christie's Poirot.* Boxtree: LWT, 1995.
Harrison, Nancy R. *Jean Rhys and the Novel as Women's Text.* Chapel Hill: University of North Carolina Press, 1988.
Knepper, Marty S. "Agatha Christie: Feminist." *The Armchair Detective* 16 (1983), pp. 398–406.
Knight, Stephen. *Crime Fiction Since 1800: Detection, Death, Diversity.* Basingstoke: Palgrave Macmillan, 2010.
Lloyd, Moya. *Beyond Identity Politics: Feminism, Power and Politics.* London: Sage, 2005.
Makinen, Merja. *Agatha Christie: Investigating Femininity.* Basingstoke: Palgrave Macmillan, 2006.
Meyer, Jessica. *Men of War: Masculinity and the First World War in Britain.* Basingstoke: Palgrave Macmillan, 2009.
Moran, Pauline. "Poirot and Me." *Guardian* (November 10, 2013).
Penfold, Phil. "A Passion for Poirot." *Yours* (April 2004), pp. 5–7.

Rowland, Susan. *From Agatha Christie to Ruth Rendell*. Basingstoke: Palgrave Macmillan, 2001.
Rupp, Leila J., and Verta Taylor. *Drag Queens at the 801 Cabaret*. Chicago: University of Chicago Press, 2003.
Sedgwick, Eve Kosofsky. *Between Men: English Literature and Male Homosocial Desire*. New York: Columbia University Press, 1985.
_____. *Epistemology of the Closet* (1990), updated ed. Berkeley: University of California Press, 2008.
Suchet, David, and Geoffrey Wansell. *Poirot and Me*. London: Headline, 2013.

"The Encyclopedic Palace of the World"
Miss Lemon's Filing System as Cabinet of Curiosities and the Repository of Human Knowledge in Agatha Christie's Poirot

Meg Boulton

The discussion in this essay is one of collected knowledge, visual signifiers and cultural memory surrounding the totemic loci of Miss Lemon and her filing system, as well as the cabinet that houses it as it is glimpsed through Christie's work, and through subsequent adaptations of her novels for television. The discussion focuses on the role of Miss Lemon's filing cabinet (and on that of its creator), suggesting that it/they are a pivotal element in the visual presentation of accumulated knowledge and the deductive process as displayed to the viewer in the television series of *Agatha Christie's Poirot*. This series of adaptations (broadcast between 8 January 1989 and 13 November 2013, first aired by LWT and later produced by ITV Studios), are so much part of the public engagement with Agatha Christie's work that for many they *are* Christie, although it must be said that the adaptations *en masse* are frequently divisive among fans and scholars of Christie's work. Despite such differences of opinion surrounding the treatment of individual episodes across the adaptations, the (tele)visual versions of Christie's books have become immersed in the popular consciousness surrounding the author, dictating the way her plots, characters and settings play out in our imaginations, and affecting intertexts with the narrative space of the novels that perform a role somewhere between palimpsest and interstice; inserting familiar characters into scenarios and narratives not originally penned by Christie, while reproducing aspects of her famous stories.

The on-screen adaptations present a lush, vivid world that surrounds Poirot, his companions and his adversaries, providing those viewing the episodes with an immersive and hyper-saturated encounter with Poirot: with his world; with the places he goes; the people he sees; the criminals he encounters; the cases he solves. We, in a privileged viewing position, see his geographies and his psycho-geographies; witness his professional and private lives as they unfold; case by case, year by year.

While the early adaptations created under the aegis of Clive Exton (the primary scriptwriter and the series story consultant) and Brian Eastman (who produced the first eight seasons from the pilot until 2001, when the series underwent a marked shift in tone), are, for the most part, largely faithful to the novels (as distinct from the later, highly filmic adaptations created by Michele Buck and Damien Timmer), there *are* departures from Christie's text within the televised versions that may not sit entirely happily for those primarily concerned with ideas of verisimilitude, the privileging of the original and authorial intention.[1] Changes include dramatists writing the characters of Captain Hastings and Miss Lemon (played by Hugh Fraser and Pauline Moran) into several cases in which they do not feature as written by Christie. This was an act of insertion intended to give Poirot the stability of an on-screen "family," as Exton explained during an interview for the *Poirot* episode of the *Super Sleuths* documentary directed by Janette Clucas in 2006:

> I do think, for a television series, you need a basic family unit, whether it's a family or not; people who interact with each other. Also, it's very useful, for a not very clever writer like me, to have somebody for Poirot to confide in.[2]

As well as writing in Hastings, Miss Lemon and Philip Jackson's Chief Inspector Japp to the first eight seasons of the adaptations, Exton and Eastman deepened their characters, adding elements of human interest, hobbies and backstories unseen in Christies novels, reminding those who both read and watch her that the televised world of Poirot is a creative act of adaptation from the original. Yet, along with the acknowledgment that the television adaptations are just that, *adaptations*, it must also be recognized that the adaptations of *Agatha Christie's Poirot* present extraordinarily fertile ground for analysis of the way in which Christie's ideas lend themselves to a graphic (re)casting and (tele)visual identity, (if allowed to exist as separate and distinct entities to the novels and thus worthy of consideration in their own right); being intriguing (re)presentations of Christie's works that exist within an extraordinarily rich and detailed visual environment. It is, in part, the depth and detail of this environment that enables the type of discussion produced here—as the created, imagined spaces that are presented and produced by the creators of the televised versions of Christie, particularly those of Poirot's apartment in the early adaptations, not only provide a continuous backdrop for the staging of the deductive narrative but also provide a plethora of nuanced shifts and subtleties that substantiate and support the narrative of the drama as it plays out on-screen.

Indeed, it is the space of Poirot's apartment that forms the epicenter of this discussion, since, as has long been recognized, the house (like domestic space more generally) is a potent space of memory; an active component of identity and self.[3] As noted by Gaston Bachelard, in his seminal work on the phenomenology of the interior, *The Poetics of Space* "inhabited space transcends geometric space,"[4] and certainly, the space created in the adaptations of Christie is *inhabited*—opulently envisioned; full of period detail, saturated with objects and cultural ephemera. These spaces are entirely inhabited, and it is, in part, the richness of the detail of the interiors in the adaptations that facilitates the relationship between the viewer and the characters on-screen; surrounding them with lived spaces and personal objects; giving them a place, making them a world. This type of object-orientated resonance is demonstrated again and again in the visual choices made by the creators of *Agatha Christie's Poirot*, typified in the domestic spaces and objects with which they choose to surround their protagonists; which, to some extent come to visually codify them, emulating and echoing their patterns of behavior for a long-term audience, viewing across seasons. In part the sustained visual analysis of the object-spaces that flood the world of the detective, as applied here, is aided by Eastman's decision to fix the stories in 1936, effectively halting time and stemming the chronology created by Christie herself, whose later mysteries play out against the ultra-modernity of the 1960s.[5] The stopped time of the mid–1930s seen on-screen provides a glamorous chronological constant, allowing a stable visual vocabulary to emerge across the series and thus ensuring tiny developments in costume or object gain significance in their own right, speaking volumes about the nuances of character and plot.

The Woman Behind the System

The focus of this paper is largely on Miss Lemon, Poirot's formidable and elusive secretary—who also appears in a secretarial role in Christie's *Parker Pyne* series—as well as the filing system she creates, which takes up a large amount of the visual "space" throughout the adaptations; ostensibly corralled within an outer-office, but continually glimpsed through the liminal threshold spaces of corridors, doorways and the glass partition window that divides Miss Lemon's office from the main living space in the apartment (which also functions as Poirot's office) as the episodes unfold. In his discussion of domestic space Bachelard states that "the house furnishes us dispersed images and a body of images at the same time,"[6] which could equally be said of the filing system that functions as record and regulator for Poirot's world. It is a once a fragmented image, spread across the series in facets, glimpsed in half-shots, presented as background *and* shown as the fundamental aspect of the administrative machine that keeps the fictive world in order, a continuous presence that is both aspect and extension of its creator and of the detective whose intellect it reflects, records and monumentalizes. Miss Lemon herself is a figure who appears relatively infrequently in the literary texts, but despite her elusiveness is understood to be otherwise indispensable to Poirot. She is woven into the fabric of the television adaptations, where she is given a far weightier presence, involved in detection, actively enabling Poirot's patterns of metal deduction both in and out of the office.

In the mystery novel *Hickory Dickory Dock* (1958), Christie centralizes Miss Lemon, making her the agent through which the mystery unfolding around her sister is introduced to Poirot. Here she is described as a "hideous and efficient woman.... For all practical purposes, that is to say, she was not a woman at all. She was a machine the perfect secretary." We are told that "Miss Lemon's Heel of Achilles had always been her imagination. She had none. On questions of fact she was invincible. On questions of surmise she was lost."[7] We are informed that she "was sublimely incurious by nature,"[8] and that she was "the most efficient woman that ever lived."[9] These descriptions of her match those given in "How Does Your Garden Grow?" where we are told that "she enjoyed typing, paying bills, filing papers and entering up engagements. To be asked to imagine herself in hypothetical situations bored her very much but she accepted it as a disagreeable part of a duty."[10]

This, then, is the woman behind the system; the formidable and machine-like mind that created the overarching cabinet that becomes the visual epitome of triumphant deduction across the series. Identifying, catching and "collecting" criminals could be said to be a leitmotif in Christie's oeuvre for her fictive detectives and readers alike, and this is perhaps most coherently demonstrated to her audience through the visual device of Miss Lemon's system, which is presented in tantalizing fragments to the reader/viewer of the novels and their subsequent adaptations; being, like Lemon herself, vastly more present in the television adaptations than in the books, where it is introduced in absentia, existing more as an abstract concept in Miss Lemon's mind than as anything with an object-oriented reality. As readers, we are told, for example, that "her real passion in life was the perfection of a filing system besides which all other systems would sink into oblivion. She dreamed of such a system at night."[11] It is through such narrative fragments that we become aware of the filing system, encountered, as it is, through Miss Lemon's abstracted and gleeful imaginings of her patented system as a possibility, as potential. Nonetheless, its intangible presence is there to be read in her all-consuming passion for filing and systematizing the paper-portfolio of Poirot's deductive admin; a passion once described by the meticulous Christie scholar and archivist John Curran as "seriously sad!"[12] Certainly it is *serious*, as despite its slightly nebulous and abstract presence in the novels, on-screen the filing system is a ubiquitous presence, filling a room with its ranks of ordered cabinets and containing a vast miscellany of detail about past cases. The burnished wood, brass handles and neatly labeled identification cards on the drawers of the cabinet are a visual reminder of cases past and cases to come; containing all the minutiae and scope of the Poirot-verse within its cataloged confines.

This encyclopedic structure arguably finds its origin in the exotic collections and Linnaean taxonomies that fill and govern the rare and wonderful specimens of enlightenment era curiosity cabinets and *wunderkammer* of early modern Europe.[13] Felicity Lemon's filing system, "besides which all other filing systems will sink into oblivion,"[14] and the on-going on-screen evolution of her all-encompassing card catalog and the cabinet which houses it, is not only central to the ordering of Poirot's methodical world and indeed to Poirot himself, acting as both an identifying and signifying feature of the detective/stories, but may be thought of as the inheritor of these early collections. The (self-)contained encyclopedic system (which remains an abstract in the novels but is extant and immediate in Poirot's on-screen world, present though its collective identities as being the material realization of Poirot's consciousness, the product of Miss Lemon's material record and as it exists in the viewer's imagination) asks questions of who is privy to what; of how knowledge is controlled and ordered; of how the taxonomization of societal behaviors may abet the deductive process and how the ordering of chaos into a cataloged and controlled cabinet may provide a greater control in the face of murder and mayhem. But, as will be argued here, it also holds the key to how the modern viewer engages with the presentation of Christie's cases and narratives as a visual construct somewhere between the imaginary world on screen and the suspended real world of the viewer.

The catalog and its containing cabinet, presented on-screen variously as object, concept and iconic image relates to the wider phenomenology of the interior presented by Christie in her books and is further developed by those translating her narratives into a visual medium in terms of the psychological spaces and clandestine human histories it simultaneously conceals and reveals. As noted, one of the functions of Miss Lemon's system is to provide a comprehensive archive of the detective's past, while simultaneously offering insight into future human behaviors—several times throughout the series, for example, we see Poirot and his companions use the system to inform current investigations. As a repository of knowledge, the cabinet is an inanimate presence throughout the adaptations that effectively bears witness to the detectives' interior world, to his current endeavors and to his past victories; illustrating his prowess as a detective and holding him to a continuum of deductive genius embodied by this tangible monument to his previous cases. Thus the catalog is a thing that both imposes and composes order; continually offering possible connections between disparate ideas and absent facts through the data held within its compartments, continually generating new knowledge for author and audience alike. As such, this discussion of a contained and functioning encyclopedic entity that preserves the past while it continues to evolve, generating a surfeit of information through the actions of its curator and amanuensis as well as those of its autocratic subject, that continually intersects with the present must be set into a wider discussion of space and containment on-screen in the Christie adaptations. This, in turn, creates further points for consideration, such as how the visual arrangement of space, the manifestation of knowledge and the visualization of deductive processes and of criminal agency alike engage with our perceptions of (and preoccupations with) Christie, as well as with her narratives and protagonists, the rational and the irrational as they appear in this fictive world.

For practical reasons, as noted above, this discussion focuses on the "early years" episodes of *Agatha Christie's Poirot*, as shown on ITV under the direction of Exton and Eastman, as although some of the narrative arcs become less true to Christie's originals in the post–2001 seasons, the less frequent appearances of Miss Lemon and Hastings *is* more in keeping with the textual originals. In addition to the disappearance of Poirot's secretary and his companion in the later seasons, the filing cabinet that is such a prevalent part of the early episodes also disappeared when Poirot's flat underwent a revamp in 2005; when he seemingly moved to another apartment in Whitehaven Mansions. This move came complete with a change in decor and with a loss of the outer office that had been occupied by Miss Lemon and her cabinet-creation, disrupting the role of the cabinet within the television series and leaving a gap in continuity—as the series, until this shift, had self-identified its cross-referential chronology as embodied by the case-by-case nexus of information contained within the filing cabinet, which is so central to the visual identity and overarching narrative of the early adaptations.

To set this discussion (and Miss Lemon's Cabinet) in a wider context, it is important to consider the ideas of collecting and curating so tied up with the hording of the rare and the wonderful in the enlightenment era collections, which, in their complete and complex networks form a visual embodiment of the early modern epistemology of knowledge through their contents, their creation and their controlled display; at once pre-figuration and echoic narrative of Miss Lemon's fictional creation.

To have a confessional moment, having grown up immersed in both the television series and the novels and short stories, Poirot (for me, and many others), is hard-wired "comfort reading/watching." Over the last decade or so I have lost count of the number of times I have watched the series, or re-read the books, a continual background to other things, other topics. Spaces, structures and collections (of various forms) all play a role in my wider research so it is perhaps not surprising that somewhere in all these hours of watching I was subconsciously drawn to Miss Lemon's superlative system. *Things*, for want of a better term, in boxes and cabinets are something I find academically irresistible, and all the while watching Suchet's portrayal of Poirot's "gray cells" in action I was becoming increasingly fond of the cabinet, as and when it had its moments on screen. Having established that, and having such *a priori* knowledge that Miss Lemon (and her patented system) are a significant part of the first twelve years of the Poirot productions, when I first came to research this chapter, I was slightly surprised by how ever-present the cabinet is across the early adaptations, functioning, almost, as an extra character operating alongside Poirot and his companions. As stated, this visual presentation of the cabinet is at odds with the original literary texts, where it is mentioned tantalizingly and then dropped out of sight. Here, though, in *Agatha Christie's Poirot*, it is visually pervasive and Miss Lemon, her files and the cabinet which houses her system are prominent parts of encountering these narratives on-screen, acting as bracket and background to the more dynamic elements of the plot.

"A multiplicity of frames"

Visual examples of the manner and method in which Miss Lemon's filing cabinet (and the system it contains) shapes, echoes, evolves and symbolizes Christie's plots and characters will be considered in more detail below, but before addressing specific examples it is fruitful to consider analogous examples of systemic curating, collecting and containing information which is so much a part of the "modern moment" captured and presented in *Agatha Christie's Poirot*. Curiosity cabinets and *Wunderkammer*, acknowledged forerunners of the modern museum, present encyclopedic systems that mirror that of Miss Lemon's cabinet; all are types of composite epistemological collections that are located in fixed spatial environments, which are intrinsic to the identity of the collections they contain. The resemblances between the cabinet/system of Poirot and the Curiosity cabinet occur both in the manner they perform, and in the manner they are most usually presented. Cabinets of curiosities were encyclopedic collections of objects whose categorical boundaries were, in pre-modern Europe, yet to be fully defined. Modern re-readings of these objects have subsequently designated them as belonging primarily to the field of natural history (albeit often a history that has since proved false—such as the ubiquitous narwhale tusk/unicorn horn conflation found throughout early collections), geology, ethnography, archaeology, religious or historical relics, works of art (including cabinet paintings, which form a meta-narrative of the cabinet, presenting a microcosmic point of mirrored presentation where the cabinet encounters a version of itself within its collection, and thus must confront itself as a conceptual object), and various antiquities or scientific curios.

The spaces of these early collections were widely regarded as microcosms or theatres of the world, conveying, through symbolic iconographies, abbreviated visual language and the potency of universalizing and totalitarian acquisition, a coherent and persuasive demonstration of their owner's symbolic control of the world through the mastery of these contained replicas, which presented indoor, controlled and miniaturized reproductions of all creation and all understood knowledge; held and displayed in a known, mapped, contained space. While the specific items in any one curiosity cabinet or *wunderkammer* vary depending on the tastes, times and interests of the collector in general, there could be said to be three compulsory categories of inclusion for compiling and showcasing a curiosity cabinet: *naturalia* (products of nature), *arteficialia* (or *artefacta*, the products of man), and *scientifica* (the testaments of man's ability to dominate nature, such as astrolabes, clocks, automatons, and scientific instruments). These theoretical underpinnings to the Curiosity cabinet may also be seen in the rationale behind Miss Lemon's cabinet, with *its* specific taxonomic system of knowledge. This correlation becomes possible if, for example, we read the people concerned with Poirot's case histories as being analogous to *naturalia*, the products of nature; the crimes committed as synonymous with the idea of *artefacta*, the products of man; and the deductive process itself as *scientifica*—all then may be said to have a place in the microcosmic world of the cabinet: whereby human history, activity and psychology is collected, ordered, confined and displayed.[15]

Patrick Mauriès has described the space of the Curiosity Cabinet as "find[ing] its *raison d'être* in a multiplicity of frames, niches, boxes, drawers and cases, in appropriating to itself the chaos of the world and imposing upon it systems—however arbitrary—of symmetries and hierarchies."[16] This rationale of a confined, contained miniature that functions as a microcosm of the world, as expressed through its container and as demonstrated through the Curiosity cabinet, is again echoed in Miss Lemon's system, which organizes the information generated by Poirot's professional activity (which is, of course, also the psycho-geographic boundary of the world created by Christie for her audience). Indeed, in the 1989 televised version of "The Adventure of Johnny Waverly," Miss Lemon describes her system thus:

>MISS LEMON: It's nearly complete, you see. My system.
>HERCULE POIROT: Ah.

> MISS LEMON: Every one of your cases classified and cross-referenced five different ways.
> HERCULE POIROT: Five?
> MISS LEMON: Oh, yes. In this cabinet, names of witnesses; in this, name of perpetrator, if known. Victim's trade or profession. Type of case: abduction, addiction, adultery—see also under marriage, bigamy—see also under marriage, bombs.
> HERCULE POIROT: See also under marriage?[17]

So described, a vivid idea of the scale and scope of Miss Lemon's cabinet of curiosities forms; even as a purely conceptual entity, as in the original literary texts, the system has a monumentality that echoes its complex and shifting visual arrangement as found in the adaptations—where it changes shape throughout its on-screen life, reflecting the events of the series, the narrative of the cases and the actions of the characters. The reflection of the wider encyclopedic collections of curiosity cabinets is also found in the fictive *presence* of the arranged system of data; in its being housed in a separate space in Poirot's apartment and in the symbolic presence of the knowledge and memories it houses, as well as in the systematic exactitude with which it is composed. Alone, the comprehensive litany of types of criminal activity listed by Miss Lemon is impressive, but it is the ease and effortlessness of the cross-referencing mechanisms set within her system that most completely illustrate the complexities of the system (a system capable of housing the myriad nuances of vast swathes of information associated with both criminal and detective alike), that begin to highlight the sophistries of Miss Lemon's system. Moreover, Poirot's teasing response of "see also under marriage" speaks to his relationship to the system, as will be expounded below.

Alongside the Curiosity cabinets recalled by Miss Lemon's filing system, a further analogous example of an equally comprehensive social machine for thinking is found in Marino Auriti's *Encyclopedic Palace of the World*, created in the 1950s and currently housed in the American Folk Art Museum, New York. The model was conceived by Auriti as an imaginary museum, a building to "hold all the works of man in whatever field, discoveries made and those which may follow ... [It wa]s an entirely new concept in museums designed to house humankind's greatest achievements, 'everything from the wheel to the satellite.'"[18] A scale model of a building Auriti dreamed would eventually be constructed in Washington D. C., the *Encyclopedic Palace* is comprised of seven tiers of lathe-turned skyscraper, made of mixed media, including various woods, metal, plastic (including hair combs), celluloid, and topped by a television antennae. The model took about three years to build and is on a scale of 1:200, which means that if it were actually built, the palace would stand 136 stories and 2,322 feet, which would have made it the tallest building in the world at the time Auriti imagined it.[19] From its relative obscurity as a quasi-lost cultural object (akin to the largely vanished wunderkammer of early modern Europe), the *Encyclopedic Palace of the World* was reclaimed by the 55th Venice Biennale in 2013, which used Auriti's piece as its curatorial rationale envisioned by Massimiliano Gioni, and indeed, for its title—*Il Palazzo Enciclopedico*. Gioni termed his vision for the Biennale an exhibition on obsessions and the transformational power of imagination; acknowledging its homage to Marino Auriti's imagined architectural utopian encyclopedia, complete with its tiny celluloid windows with its hand-drawn mullions and tiny balustrades made of hair combs, elevating ephemeral everyday objects to art and possessing an imagined scope that far outweighs its scale.[20]

Now, encyclopedic systems for thinking and for containing (all) knowledge are not new; nor were they as Auriti was designing his *Encyclopedic Palace*, but such models have been prominently returned to popular consciousness of late by projects such as last years' Biennale or, more recently, by the BBC's *Sherlock*—wherein Sherlock Holmes' Mind Palace is presented as a highly visual encyclopedic structure which, like Miss Lemon's filing system in its on-screen incarnation, provides an immersive encounter with the invisible mechanics of the deductive process for the viewer. The method of loci,[21] also called the memory palace, is a mnemonic device introduced in the classical world and, in short, is a method of memory enhancement which uses visualization to organize and recall information; an imaginary filing system if you will. As part of this technique the subject memorizes the layout of a familiar piece of architecture—a place, a building, the arrangement of shops on a street, or any similar geographical entity which is composed of a number of discrete loci. If one wishes to remember an item or, indeed, a set of items, the person using the system literally "walks" through these loci and commits an item to each one by forming a linked bond between the item and a/ny distinguishing feature of that locus. Retrieval of remembered items is subsequently achieved by "(re)walking" through the loci, allowing the associative bond between visualized locus and memory-object to produce the memory. The Sherlockian Memory Palace, as played out on-screen in the adaptations enables the viewer to locate themselves within the narrative of deduction; we are, at times, physically placed into Holmes's Memory Palace as it meanders and unfurls across the screen. Although the on-screen presence of this encyclopedic system is showier and more visceral than the analogous processes shown in Poirot where a slow blink or a satisfied smile communicate the ending of deductive reasoning for the Belgian detective, the memory palace and the encyclopedic cabinet have several things in common. If (in an unlikely, but nonetheless appealing, hypothetical scenario) the two methods of visualizing a deductive process on-screen were conflated by the producers of both shows, then surely Christie's viewers would have taken an imaginary walk through Miss Lemon's filing cabinet.

From these considerations of encyclopedic systems in wider cultural, literary and televisual contexts, we can turn to address the various presentations of Miss Lemon's own encyclopedic system within the Poirot adaptations. From the outset, it is noteworthy that while the filing cabinet that houses the system is almost always present during *any* interior shot of the apartment, it is not a static background presence—the cabinet evolves over the course of the episodes, a mutable point of shifting, fluid movement and change. Such phenomena of flux are seen in the various points of its use, in its compilation, creation and ordering. Over the course of the episodes, we often see Miss Lemon actively involved in the process of creating, revising or curating it. It grows; it expands; additional cabinets are added to the original system of shelving; on an almost permanent basis various loose files and papers surround it, waiting to be incorporated into the system; and, once, it is rehoused, stored and then rearranged in its entirety having been retrieved from storage following Poirot's brief and unsuccessful retirement.

Ownership of the system and its overarching cabinet is a tricky thing to locate. Clearly the taxonomical system of ordering belongs to Miss Lemon, indeed she and it are often conflated on-screen for the viewer. During the course of the episodes, we frequently see her immersed in it, surrounded by it. We see it constantly in the process of creation in the background of the detective stories, evolving under her authority. Miss Lemon is seen continually typing, as we witness her generating more paper, more parts for admission to the system as it expands across seasons. Her protectiveness of it is fierce, as exemplified by her reaction to Hastings' disastrous attempts to use the system in her absence in the 1991 adaptation of "How Does Your Garden Grow?" adapted for television by Andrew Marshall and directed by Brian Farnham.

This type of authoritative, authorial control is also demonstrated in her engagements with the moving firm who are returning the system to its proper place in *Lord Edgware Dies*, adapted for television by Anthony Horowitz and again directed by Farnham, in 2000. Indeed, such is the ferocity of her reaction when the removal men, who have already disordered the system in the liminal and vulnerable moment of its fragmented and fragile state of transportation outside the protective confines of cabinet-container, drop the carefully arranged and cataloged boxes that hold the disparate components of the cabinet (and thus the encyclopedic system), that it creates a comedic effect. However amusing, in that moment, her ownership of the encyclopedic system is complete. Once disaster (i.e., the dropping of a box or two of files during their transportation before the cabinet is recreated as a functioning systemic whole) is averted, her barely suppressed, slightly maniacal glee at the need to reorder the system is as amusing as it is all encompassing, demonstrating the (inter)relationship between Miss Lemon and the cabinet. The system, as it stands, must be continually updated or it will cease to function as an active and useful member of the team; becoming instead obsolete, cold. In that moment, the cabinet and the information it holds teeters in its object-identity; at risk of transforming into something other; at risk, in other words, of becoming solely an archive, rather than an encyclopedic system that performs with something between memorial and active agency.

Evolution and Disappearance of the Cabinet

A fundamental aspect of the cabinet's identity, however, is that as much as it reflects Miss Lemon, the filing cabinet and its contents also reflect Poirot himself. While Hastings' engagement with it is fraught and marginalized, Poirot does not directly engage with it, yet it is clear that it is linked to him; indeed in many ways, being his the product of his psychological output and representing his metal cosmology, it *is* him. In the presentation of Poirot and cabinet on-screen we see a clear link between the two; in moving through his apartment and his day, whether alone or engaging with others, he often situates himself in direct relation to it—sitting or standing opposite, facing it—it is frequently in his sight line, forming a visual counterpoint to his totemic intellectual presence in the space of his apartment, serving to recall and present his past successes as he wrestles with (and inevitably solves) his current problem/s. It bears repeating that the cabinet functions as both a figure of the past and a harbinger of the future; a colossus of information, a quiet, galvanic presence that forms a visual parallel to Poirot's deductive processes, endlessly housing and ordering information while life goes on around it.

Also of interest, and perhaps somewhat less expected than the (visual) relationship between Poirot and the encyclopedic system, are the multiple instances in which the as-yet-unrevealed perpetrator of the crime locates themselves in proximity to the cabinet. They unwittingly place themselves in relation to it, divided from it by the glass window into the outer office; yet always, obviously, in close relation to it, often, indeed caught between it and the figure of Poirot himself, thus forming a spatial, deductive binary around the perpetrator. This placement of Poirot and cabinet foreshadows the eventual outcome of the investigation, as despite the machinations of the criminal-antagonists, and their conviction that they will outwit and out-think Poirot, evading detection, their (self-)placement between the detective and his encyclopedic other (the reflection of his intellect, preserved in the space of the cabinet) intimates their ultimate downfall; and their inevitable cataloging and containment within the very cabinet that forms a seemingly neutral background to their crimes; merging with the other crimes and criminals it contains. This placement is seen over and over again; with Marcus Waverly in the 1989 adaptation of "The Adventure of Johnny Waverley," Nigel Chapman in the 1995 adaptation of *Hickory Dickory Dock*, Mr. Graves in the 1993 adaptation of "The Adventure of the Italian Nobleman" and Miss Jane Plenderleith in the 1989 adaptation of "Murder in the Mews" all locating themselves in relation to the cabinet when visiting Poirot at his apartment, to name but a few.

Throughout the adaptations, the filing cabinet is frequently juxtaposed visually with the inferior systems of others, perhaps most notably that of Scotland Yard's new (and highly prized) forensic division. This comparison consistently highlights the superiority of Miss Lemon's system, resulting in some really delightful moments in the television series (if size mattered, for instance, the police force would be in trouble!). The Yard's filing system, as portrayed, is composed of one in-tray and one filing cabinet, as opposed to the expansive stretches of space devoted to Miss Lemon's cataloguing of Poirot's cases, housed in their glorious cabinet. Indeed, the juxtaposition of the superiority of Miss Lemon's system as set against the modern scientific advancements of the police force provides one of my very favorite tableau in the series, where, in the 1989 adaptation of "Four and Twenty Blackbirds," the mystery is solved onstage in a theatre by Poirot with the entire forensic body of Scotland Yard "staged" to "act" as a convincing scientific backdrop of the "modern method" to his denouement of Lorrimer as the murderer; the modern method, frozen in the act of falling short of the encyclopedic system.

As demonstrated by this theatrical foray, far from being a static, monolithic immovable machine—which one might expect, given the scale and scope of its cabinet—Miss Lemon's system in fact acts as a sort of web or nexus within the visual field of the Poirot-verse—engaging with the world and with similar systems of information. In *Lord Edgware Dies* and in *Hickory Dickory Dock* the cabinet and its contents are instrumental in solving the crime, in the televised versions of these stories. Once, through one of its subsections on specialist London jewelers which helps to reveal the true narrative behind the gold box in Carlotta Adams' death; and, perhaps more remarkably, in *Hickory Dickory Dock*, through a symbiotic relationship with another cabinet of curiosity-esque space—the London Transport Lost Property office (and through the presence of its portable counterpart as constructed onscreen in the Hickory Road hostel by Poirot and Miss Lemon to assist in the dénouement of the crime).

When the cabinet is seen outside the confines of Poirot's apartment (either as a curtailed chalk-board presence or as part of a network communicating with the similar encyclopedic space of the London Lost Property office) it is always shown accompanied by, or as performing through the agency of its creator Miss Lemon—as the relationship between the two is almost entirely symbiotic. As mentioned above, when at work in Poirot's apartment, she is often shown either surrounded by component parts of the system or portrayed in the act of generating further information to be incorporated into its drawers and compartments. There is an interesting piece of visual staging that occurs throughout the episodes of the first eight seasons that affirms her relationship to the cabinet. When giving a wide shot of the cabinet as background from Poirot's living room into the outer-office where Miss Lemon works we are repeatedly presented with an image of Miss Lemon, seen through glass, sitting at her typewriter, in the act of generating future data for confinement in the cabinet, which forms a backdrop to whichever scene is playing out. In the little changing space of the apartment, in front of the window which links the space of living room and the office beyond, which frames the scene of Miss Lemon and the cabinet is a glass table, upon which resides a bowl of ceramic fruit. Taken together, this repeated scene is a rather extraordinary one, the presence of the perpetual fruit effectively transforming the image of the cabinet and Miss Lemon at work into a Still Life[22]; framed and frozen by the window. This act of transformation, with its strong visual references to the artistic tradition of Still Life painting, with its endemic (and problematic) belief that the subject of the work "*exists*" as discussed by Bryson,[23] and its ideas of memory and morality, the real and the realized all seem to be particularly apposite frameworks to contemplate the role of Miss Lemon and her superlative system. She is both real and unreal, a fictional character given a yet more fictional presence as she is written into narratives she was never meant to occupy. Her encyclopedic system is an entity with both symbolic and actual resonances across the series, weaving in and out of narratives, engaging and engaged with by character and viewer alike; yet, in its perpetual presence and continual evolution it is a presence that serves to monumentalize and enable the deductive process, but also to memorialize it.

Memory, here, is significant, because as Christie tells us in the opening line to *Lord Edgware Dies*, "the memory of the public is short."[24] As such, in closing, I wish to address the curiously spatial nature of the cabinet in relationship to its audience, as opposed to the characters that surround it. For the viewer, the cabinet and its system are at once pivotal and liminal—providing points of encounter and tension throughout the viewing of these episodes; but also capable of providing spaces of forgetting. Placed, as noted, in an anti-chamber to Poirot's living room, accessed in the apartment through two threshold points the cabinet is both centralized and marginalized, an object acting as both foreground and background. Indeed, in its on-screen presentation, it is most-often seen through a glass window—an aspect which almost transforms the cabinet into a curiosity in its own right. In closing, I would like to draw attention to one of the most frustrating aspects of Miss Lemon's Cabinet—in that, due to a network change and a stylistic shift in the construction of *Agatha Christie's Poirot*, it vanishes from the viewer's gaze. Having spent around 32 episodes becoming ever more convinced of the cabinet's centrality to Poirot's identity and deductive method, and its role in memorializing and monumentalizing his intellectual achievements, it vanishes from the screen alongside its creator, surviving only as a memory for its viewers.

However, such is the power of the cabinet and the system that it sustains, that it lives on past this imposed invisibility. Having been ever-present, indeed, omnipresent, the cabinet takes up residence in those watching (and re-watching) the adaptations. In recognizing and considering Christie's cases, in discussing them, in making cross-connections across the narratives, as it does, and in observing their minutiae, *we*, as viewing audience, become part of the Encyclopedic Palace of Knowledge created by Miss Lemon; as, despite its on-screen absence, it continues to function, in the collective mind of the viewer, as both memorial and memory palace. Thus, even in absentia, the cabinet and the encyclopedic system it contains remain a vital part of encountering the televised universe of Poirot; as real as Christie's characters themselves; a remembered curiosity that functions as symbolic signifier for our own collecting of Christie as readers and viewers of her work.

Notes

1. See R. Barthes, "Death of the Author" and "From Work to Text" in *Image-Music-Text* (Waukegan: Fontana Press, 1993), pp. 142–148 and 155–164, respectively; see also M. Foucault, *Language Counter-Memory Practice: Selected Essays and Interviews*, D. F. Bouchard (ed.) (Ithaca: Cornell University Press 1980), pp. 113–38 and Sean Burke, *The Death and Return of the Author: Criticism and Subjectivity in Barthes, Foucault, and Derrida* (Edinburgh: Edinburgh University Press, 1998).

2. Clive Exton as interviewed by Janette Clucas in the documentary *Super Sleuths* (Season 1, Episode 1).

3. For further reading see Gaston Bachelard, *The Poetics of Space* (Boston: Beacon Press, 1994).

4. Bachelard, *The Poetics of Space*, p. vii.

5. Peter Haining, *Agatha Christie's Poirot* (London: Boxtree and LWT), p. 14.

6. Bachelard, *The Poetics of Space*, p. 3.

7. Agatha Christie, *Hickory Dickory Dock* (Glasgow: Fontana, 1981), p. 9.

8. *Ibid.*, p. 28.

9. *Ibid.*, p. 30.

10. Agatha Christie, "How Does Your Garden Grow?" in *The Regatta Mystery and Other Stories* (New York: Avon, 1939), p. 65.

11. *Ibid.*, p. 51.

12. Curran's comment on the nature of Miss Lemon's obsession with filing was given in an interview for ITV's series *The People's Detective*, which aired in 2010. Many thanks to Eirik Dragsund for help locating this quotation, who writes the blog *Investigating Poirot*, where it first came to my attention in the entry *The Big Three:*

Hastings, Miss Lemon and Japp (December 20, 2012), accessed May 3, 2015, www.investigatingpoirot.blogspot.co.uk.

    13. For a comprehensive introductory text to these collections see Patrick Mauriès' *Cabinets of Curiosities* (London: Thames and Hudson, 2002).

    14. Christie, "How Does Your Garden Grow?" p. 51.

    15. Mauriès, *Cabinets of Curiosities*, pp. 23–25.

    16. *Ibid.*, p. 12.

    17. Renny Rye (dir.), "The Adventure of Johnny Waverly," *Agatha Christie's Poirot*, 1.3, dramatized by Clive Exton (London Weekend Television, 1989).

    18. V. Rousseau, "*Encyclopedic Palace*" [sic.] exhibition label for *Self-Taught Genius: Treasures from the American Folk Art Museum*, curated by S. C. Hollander and V. Rousseau (New York: American Folk Art Museum, 2014).

    19. *Ibid.*

    20. See Massimiliano Gioni et al. (eds.), *Il Palazzo Enciclopedico (The Encyclopedic Palace), The 55th Exhibition catalog of the Venice Biennale* (Venice: Marsilio Editori, 2013).

    21. For an introduction to this see Edward Hollis, *The Memory Palace: A Book of Lost Interiors* (London: Portobello Books, 2013), especially pp. 14–21.

    22. For further information see Norman Bryson, *Looking at the Overlooked: Four Essays on Still Life Painting* (London: Reaktion, 1990). See also Erika Langmuir, *A Closer Look: Still Life* (London: National Gallery, 2010).

    23. Bryson, *Looking at the Overlooked*, pp. 7–15, particularly p. 7.

    24. Agatha Christie, *Lord Edgware Dies* (London: HarperCollins, 2007), p. 9.

Bibliography

Agatha Christie's Poirot. Television series, Granada and ITV Studios, 1989–2013.
Bachelard, Gaston. *The Poetics of Space*. Boston: Beacon Press, 1994.
Barthes, Roland. "Death of the Author" and "From Work to Text." *Image-Music-Text* (1979). Waukegan: Fontana, 1993.
Bryson, Norman. *Looking at the Overlooked Four Essays on Still Life Painting*. London: Reaktion, 1990.
Burke, Sean. *The Death and Return of the Author: Criticism and Subjectivity in Barthes, Foucault, and Derrida*. Edinburgh: Edinburgh University Press, 1998.
Christie, Agatha. *Hickory Dickory Dock* (1957). Glasgow: Fontana, 1981.
_____. "How Does Your Garden Grow?" (1935). *The Regatta Mystery and Other Stories*. New York: Avon Publications, 1939.
_____. *Lord Edgware Dies* (1934). London: HarperCollins, 2007.
_____. *The Man in the Brown Suit* (1924). London: Pan, 1973.
Foucault, Michel. *Language Counter-Memory Practice: Selected Essays and Interviews*. Ed. D. F. Bouchard. Ithaca: Cornell University Press, 1980.
Gioni, Massimiliano, et al. *Il Palazzo Enciclopedico* (The Encyclopedic Palace). The 55th Exhibition catalog of the Venice Biennal, Venice, Marsilio Editori, 2013.
Haining, Peter. *Agatha Christie's Poirot*. London: Boxtree and LWT, 1995.
Hollis, Edward. *The Memory Palace A Book of Lost Interiors*. London: Portobello Books, 2013.
Langmuir, Erika. *A Closer Look Still Life*. London: National Gallery, 2010.
Mauriès, Patrick. *Cabinets of Curiosities*. London: Thames and Hudson, 2002.

"One must actually take facts as they are"
Information Value and Information Behavior in the Miss Marple Novels

MICHELLE M. KAZMER

> "There are many ways we prefer to look at things. But one must actually take facts as they are, must one not?"
> —Agatha Christie, *The Murder at the Vicarage*[1]

One perspective not often brought to the study of detective fiction is that from the field of information science. Among other topics, information science is concerned with information behavior, or how people behave with respect to information: needing, seeking, accidentally encountering, avoiding, evaluating, storing and so forth. Examining the solving of a mystery as an information behavior has potential for insights into the genre and into our twenty-first century readings of detective fiction. Current audiences are accustomed to modern information technology and the information behaviors afforded by it: amateur sleuths hack computer systems or professional detectives analyze trace evidence for DNA. Highly technologized contemporary information environments leave us to ask: in what ways do the manipulation of information value, and the sophistication of the information behaviors, in novels written by Agatha Christie in the early to mid-twentieth century, continue to enthrall readers in the twenty-first?

Within the information science discipline, many scholars have conducted research that focuses on information behavior and information value in real-life contexts; another important research stream focuses on the use and recommendation of fiction for entertainment. It is much less common to see information behavior theories applied to helping us understand the construction of fictional narratives and actions.[2] Theorizing the solving of a mystery as an information behavior has potential for insights into the detective fiction genre overall. This approach can also increase our understanding of how information value is co-constructed in real-life contexts by focusing on how mystery authors' narratives succeed in convincing, holding the attention of, and occasionally fooling, real-world readers.

The analysis presented here is an extension of my work in studying shared knowledge practices and how those are shaped by the contexts in which they occur.[3] For this analysis, I chose the theoretical approach afforded by information worlds theory. The theory of information worlds was created by Gary Burnett and Paul Jaeger, and published in 2008.[4] In creating information worlds theory, Burnett and Jaeger drew on two existing conceptual frameworks. The first was Elfreda Chatman's "Small Worlds," where information behaviors occur within local, largely homogeneous social settings.[5] The second was Jurgen Habermas's "Lifeworld," the sum total of all information resources and norms culture-wide.[6] Burnett and Jaeger sought to resolve this big/small dichotomy to examine information *within* individual worlds as well as interactions *across* multiple worlds. Information worlds theory includes four concepts: social norms, social types, information value, and information behavior. Social norms are the shared understanding of rightness and wrongness in observable social behaviors; social types are the shared perceptions of individuals' roles in the context of the information world. The social norms, social types and social worlds as viewed through economic/political/sociological lenses have already been heavily studied for early detective fiction.

The concepts of information value and information behavior are open for analysis, specifically as they help us learn about how amateur detectives—and particularly women—function in the worlds constructed by and for them in the literature. Information value is defined as the shared understanding of what is worth attention and what information is meaningful within an information world. Information behavior is the full range of normative behaviors related to information. Information behavior includes such concepts as information needs, seeking, use, avoidance, rationing and management. People in various situations need information, and they may or may not be aware of those needs. Faced with an information need people may seek information actively, such as by searching a website, or passively encountering information during daily activities, for example, reading billboard advertisements while driving. People use information to inform decisions, to build knowledge or to influence the actions of others. They may avoid undesirable information, and withhold or ration information they give to others. Acquired or created information is managed: organized, stored/archived, preserved or discarded. Within this chapter, the two concepts of information behavior and information value are used to examine the twelve Miss Marple novels.[7] The analysis demonstrates that Miss Marple lives within sophisticated information worlds that are shaped not only by contextually-determined social norms and social values, but by information-oriented behavior and co-creation of information value. Applying these concepts to the Marple novels indicates several aspects of Miss Marple's praxis that are susceptible to information worlds analysis.[8] This essay focuses on three: access, tactics and value.

Access

A central problem with fictional amateur detectives (as opposed to a government detective affiliated with the police or even a professional or a "licensed" consulting detective) is how the author can write them legitimately into the plot and offer them access to a mystery that is, strictly speaking, none of their personal or professional concern. From an information behavior perspective, this problem is reframed as how to secure the detective access to an information world. For Christie, in the Marple novels, the specific problem is how to get Miss Marple to a place where she can access information, make her own judgments as to its value, analyze the information and present her conclusions in a way that is valued by those in a position to act upon them.

In twenty-first century detective fiction the same access problems exist, although they are often framed in terms of technology access. The amateur sleuth has to break into a computer system to get a DNA or autopsy report, or has to figure out how to kludge together some kind of wireless network in the face of jammers set up by the enemy or the police (who are often the same). For Miss Marple, while the technologies may be simpler, the information access problems are not necessarily more tractable. Before using tactics (below), she has to get to the right place (a hotel, a house, a town) and to do so requires leveraging her social position. From a social perspective, Miss Marple gets embedded structurally via her interpersonal relationships with the clergy or with individuals (almost always men) who have law enforcement power or substantial money. Miss Marple's presence is not sufficient to provide access; solving a mystery, and meeting her ethical imperative of seeing the culprit brought to justice (by causing or taking action), requires access to information.

Social and physical access facilitates information access, but even access to information is not enough—one has to be able to act upon information, manipulate it, and be able to convince others to act upon it. For example, in *The Body in the Library* (1942), once Miss Marple is placed in a nearby hotel and in view of people who can help her, she can then engage in dialogue with the former Commissioner of Scotland Yard, Sir Henry Clithering, who can act legitimately upon her deductions and provide access to a network of individuals who can provide information of high value. Miss Marple begins her probe into this mystery via a typical self-devaluing statement, saying, "It's rather embarrassing for me, because, of course, I am no use at all."[9] Sir Henry Clithering responds by interrogating the possibility that the people in this mystery will remind her of people she has already known, by asking, "No ideas? No village parallels?" Miss Marple then launches the rest of their interaction proper by offering the first move in an information-seeking process, saying, "I don't know very much about it all yet."[10] A significant shift with respect to information seeking happens here: through the remainder of that chapter section, Marple does most of the talking; she is not seeking information *from* Sir Henry Clithering. Clithering has, as he phrases it, called Marple into consultation, and his contribution is actually to provide access to the people to whom Marple is subsequently able to speak in Chapter 9— Adelaide Jefferson and Mark Gaskell—who provide key information needed for her to solve the murders.

In *The Body in the Library*, there is little difficulty in getting Miss Marple into physical proximity to the location where most of the information activity about the murders is conducted (that is, not necessarily where the murders happened or the bodies were found, but where the key people are staying), because that location is a relatively public space (a hotel). A hotel-as-public-space is found in other Marple novels, such as *At Bertram's Hotel* and *A Caribbean Mystery*. In these cases, as in *The Body in the Library*, the question of access is of gaining access to the information world itself, because physical access to the setting is not overly difficult (and any difficulties of financial access are solved generously and graciously by Miss Marple's successful author nephew, Raymond West).

Some of the novels demonstrate a very different access problem, that of how to get Marple into a closed (country house) setting before she can focus on using information tactics to solve the mystery. *A Pocket Full of Rye* (1953) contains such an example of Marple gaining access to a very firmly bounded information world. In it she uses her age, gender, religion and social position, combined with the natural upheaval of a household that has been home to three murders, to insinuate herself not only into the mystery but into the house. This is described in Chapter 13, when she arrives unannounced at Yewtree Lodge after the third murder: "So charming, so innocent, such a fluffy and pink and white old lady was Miss Marple that she gained admittance to what was now practically a fortress in a state of siege."[11]

Marple's reason for putting all of these tools at her disposal into play is that she had prior personal knowledge of one of the victims—the victim whose role as a parlormaid rendered her the most powerless of the victims.

Marple announces her arrival on the doorstep of Yewtree Lodge by saying, "I have come ... to speak about the poor girl who was killed. Gladys Martin." The butler immediately admits her to the house, where she engages in dialogue with a member of the household and is rapidly shepherded to Inspector Neele, the law enforcement representative on the premises in charge of the murder case. He uses his own knowledge of human nature to inform his decision to take Miss Marple into his confidence right away ("Miss Marple would be useful to him. She was upright, of unimpeachable rectitude and she had, like most old ladies, time on her hands and an old maid's nose for scenting bits of gossip"),[12] but later readers learn that he has also relied on a typical test of Miss Marple's bona fides—verifying her worth with a powerful member of law enforcement—when he tells her: "I've heard something about you at the Yard.... It seems you're fairly well-known there."[13] She responds in kind by admitting her long-standing friendship with Sir Henry Clithering. This information-world access problem resolved, Miss Marple and Inspector Neele proceed to share, sift, and organize information together to solve the mystery.[14]

Tactics

Gaining access to an information world is a necessary condition for engaging in the information practices needed to solve a mystery, but it is not a sufficient condition. Social and physical access facilitates information access, but simply having access to information is not enough—one has to be able to act upon information, manipulate it, and be able to convince others to act upon it. Once Miss Marple has established her bona fides with the right people (such as Sir Henry Clithering; although establishment of that relationship occurs primarily in the short stories, the relationship is leveraged in the novels), those people's descriptions of her represent high value on her, the information she provides, and her information behaviors. This is in contrast with the descriptions of Miss Marple by people who have not yet seen her and who tend to continue to refer to her as an "old pussy" who is "nosy."[15] In other words, the uninitiated tend to consider Miss Marple an unsophisticated person who seeks information, but in a way that is morally questionable and of limited value because of her gender, her age and where she lives. Clithering, the retired head of Scotland Yard who is familiar with her skills, poses the alternative view, saying, "She's just the finest detective God ever made. Natural genius cultivated in a suitable soil."[16] That "suitable soil" is exactly the small village in which she lives. Miss Marple argues for her use of the village as a source of knowledge about life by saying, "Nothing, I believe, is so full of life under the microscope as a drop of water from a stagnant pool."[17] Far from being an information-poor context, St. Mary Mead is unexpectedly information rich.

To solve each mystery, once she has gained access through physical location and through reputation, Miss Marple needs to act in various specific ways with respect to information. She needs to engage in a suite of information behaviors, most of which can be framed as "tactics," because they are goal-focused and part of a larger—usually unexplicated, although not hidden, as part of Christie's method for playing fair while keeping the solution from being too obvious to the reader—strategy of attack.

When readers of the novels meet Miss Marple in *The Murder at the Vicarage* (1930), they soon encounter the conflict between her oft-repeated description of her own information world as being limited and simple—"Living alone, as I do, in a rather out-of-the-way part of the world"—and the complexity of her information behavior. One example of this complexity is her recognition of the need to ration information strategically when dealing with Inspector Slack: her tactic is complex rationing, in which she controls the amount, method and timing of disclosures, rather than a much more simplistic technique of withholding everything.[18]

In addition to controlling her information sharing, Marple uses tactics to confirm and elicit information, tactics well known in the literature and to readers. A common one is the bluff or trap, usually sprung using another person as a cat's paw. A significant complexity in the use of this tactic is that Miss Marple carefully assesses from whom the false information that serves as the bait of the bluff or trap is likely to be believed. One example of this complexity is her choice of Megan, an unsophisticated twenty-year-old woman with no apparent qualifications as a blackmailer or as a detective's assistant, to set a "blackmail" trap in *The Moving Finger* (1943). When the protagonist and narrator of *The Moving Finger* accuses Miss Marple of "roping in Megan" to this trap, which all along he claimed was far too dangerous an activity for Megan, Miss Marple tells him sternly:

> There was no evidence against this very clever and unscrupulous man. I needed someone to help me, someone of high courage and good brains.... Yes, it was dangerous, but we are not put into this world, Mr. Burton, to avoid danger when an innocent fellow-creature's life is at stake.[19]

Having decided that Megan was the correct person to deliver the blackmail information most plausibly, Miss Marple is not to be dissuaded by risk. Similarly, in *The Murder at the Vicarage*, the "false warning" trap Marple creates for the murderers is sprung by a village doctor, whom she chooses as being the most plausible deliverer of the false warning. Dr. Haydock has, earlier in the book, spoken openly of his sympathy for a medicalized view of crime, speculating that the tendency to murder or theft may be glandular and in that case should be cured rather than punished (judicially and socially).[20] When Miss Marple plans to trap the murderers by having a false warning delivered to them that will stimulate their flight (an explicit indicator of guilt), she therefore selects Haydock as the most plausible information carrier, saying, "the warning should come from somebody who is known to have rather unusual views on these matters. Dr. Haydock's conversation would lead anyone to suppose that he might view such a thing as murder from an unusual angle."[21] Because the doctor could plausibly be believed to be sharing true information that would facilitate the murderers' escape, he is the perfect person to ensure their capture.

While much of Miss Marple's information is acquired through everyday conversation and through her day-to-day lived experience, she also explicitly engages in information *seeking* tactics. Three of these will be discussed here. First is her use of what a modern reader would think of as an *information source*; Miss Marple's personal use of *formal* information sources is relatively rare, and thus is noteworthy when it happens. For example, in *The Mirror Crack'd from Side to Side* (1962), she pursues "her own methods of research," requesting old film magazines from the proprietor of the local hairdressing parlor to help her understand the social world of film stars.[22] In *4.50 from Paddington* (1957), Miss Marple reaches out to Leonard Clement (the now-grown son of the vicar who lives next door to Miss Marple) for a railway map, using it to discover a likely dumping place for a dead body.[23]

Miss Marple also uses *informal* information sources, which include personal exchanges in which she is explicitly seeking information via questions, as well as artifacts that are not formal information sources.[24] An example of such an artifact is found in *A Murder Is Announced* (1950), when Miss Marple refers to Miss Blacklock's old correspondence to help solve a riddle of identity and subsequently a murder. Asking questions is considered a normal part of Miss Marple's social role, and therefore is an information behavior she can perform without raising undue suspicion about her motives (even if she annoys people in the process, they are unlikely to be suspicious). As Inspector Neele muses to himself in *A Pocket Full of Rye*,

> She'd get things out of servants and out of the women of the Fortescue family perhaps, that he and his policemen would never get. Talk, conjecture, reminiscences, repetitions of things said and done, out of it all she would pick the salient facts.[25]

Miss Marple herself repeatedly points out that it would be considered less normal if she *didn't* ask questions in an inquisitive way. In *Sleeping Murder* (1976) she explains to the young married protagonists Gwenda and Giles that she has learned so much about the past surrounding the victim by "gossiping a little. In shops—and waiting for buses. Old ladies are supposed to be inquisitive."²⁶ Similarly, she reassures Inspector Craddock in *A Murder Is Announced* that she will be safer (despite being in assumed proximity to an as-yet-unidentified murderer) if she asks questions of the people she meets, saying, "we old women always do snoop. It would be very odd and much more noticeable if I didn't."²⁷ Leveraging this ability to ask personal questions of practically everyone she meets allows Marple to elicit the information she needs in order to compare the situation at hand with a parallel experience from St. Mary Mead, or to share with the relevant law enforcement representative to build a more complete picture of the crime.

Lastly, Miss Marple uses physical tactics to seek information. Although her age generally prevents her from engaging in very vigorous or dangerous physical endeavors, she is not loath to perambulate herself in the service of justice. This is seen throughout the twelve novels, from the earliest to the latest. *The Murder at the Vicarage* finds her outside, ostensibly birdwatching while using her binoculars to gain information by spying on Gladys Cram. Later in that book, she is impelled by her curiosity at having received a wrong-number telephone call to venture abroad in the middle of the night to find out if she "couldn't do something"²⁸: "something" turns out to be identifying the murderer(s), saving an innocent man from being wrongly convicted or allowed to die, and designing the trap through which the murderer(s) would be caught. She spends her own money and embarks on two extra train journeys in *4.50 From Paddington* in an effort to locate the likeliest spot for the disposal of the murder victim.

One of the most memorable of Miss Marple's very physical excursions in search of information is her broken-heeled-shoe trek in *A Caribbean Mystery* (1964). Desiring to observe the surreptitious actions of Arthur Jackson in the cabin of his employer, Mr. Rafiel, she produces

> a pair of shoes the heel of one of which she had recently caught on a hook by the door. It was now in a slightly precarious state and Miss Marple adroitly rendered it even more precarious by attention with a nail file.²⁹

Carrying this engineered shoe as a prop, "with all the care of a Big Game Hunter approaching upwind of a herd of antelope, Miss Marple gently circumnavigate[s] Mr. Rafiel's bungalow."³⁰ She lies down on the ground, waiting to see if Jackson has heard her and ready with her broken heel excuse should he appear. He does not, and, "shielding herself slightly with a festoon of creeper she peer[s] inside."³¹

Marple engages in a variety of information behaviors, including seeking information from formal and informal sources, using physical tactics to seek information, and developing complex techniques for providing information to others. For information to be useful, or considered useful, or acted upon, it also needs to be considered valuable within the information world in which it is being deployed. Miss Marple and Agatha Christie work together to characterize, describe and manipulate information value for the characters within the novels and for the reader.

Value

Marple often signifies the disclosure of valuable information by undervaluing herself, prefacing her disclosure by saying things such as "I know that I am very often rather foolish and don't take in things as I should."[32] She then provides information that others value because it is based on her sound logic (for example, the flawed timing of the Colonel's note in *The Murder at the Vicarage*) or on tangible physical evidence (such as Lawrence Redding's rock which is not the correct type for her rock garden, or the wilted plant in the Vicar's study). Although Miss Marple consistently presents her evidence and logic using devaluing language, her information behaviors are not only complex. They also intentionally produce information that will be valued and thus acted upon by people who need it and have the power, directly or by proxy, to protect the innocent and convict the guilty.

In the earlier section on "access," I argued that Miss Marple has to rely on people in authority to facilitate her access to information settings; similarly, because she is a private individual, she must convince someone with law enforcement authority that her information has value. Only once they are convinced will they be willing to act. In general Miss Marple relies on one key player figuring out for himself (he being a man who has the needed authority or power) that her reasoning and conclusions are almost always accurate, rather than she actively seeking to prove her worth. This one key player who satisfied himself of her value—often Sir Henry Clithering, as noted earlier—then justifies Marple to others who may question her skills. In some cases, such justification is not sufficient, and Marple is explicitly tested.

Inspector Craddock explicitly "tests" Marple soon after the first murder in *A Murder Is Announced*. As Sir Henry Clithering's godson, Craddock has already been told that Miss Marple is a worthy ally, but, as a competent detective, Craddock is determined to verify this information himself. Craddock tests Marple during their first meeting by saying, "The truth of the matter is that the facts are indisputable. Whatever conflicting details these people give, they all saw one thing." Miss Marple responds by pointing out, "gently" we are told, that "they couldn't—actually—have seen anything at all" because they were all in a dark room with a single bright light being shined into their eyes.[33] In response Craddock increases his assessment of the value of her potential contributions, thinking to himself, "She'd got it! She was sharp, after all. He was testing her by that speech of his, but she hadn't fallen for it."[34]

Another way Miss Marple helps shape others' valuing of the information they find is by encouraging skepticism. She frequently reminds people that they need to question the value of all the information around them, but particularly information they get from other people. It is not that she places no value on information provided by people, but again (as with her use of the rationing tactic mentioned earlier), her approach is more nuanced than binary (by binary I mean a choice of assigning no value or having absolute trust). So, while Miss Marple rarely uses formal information sources, and makes extensive use of information she gets from other people, she treats that information with high skepticism and processes it using logic and her prior knowledge of how humans act in specific situations or in response to specific stimuli. She frequently reminds others that they should apply more skepticism in their valuations of information. In *The Body in the Library*, Miss Marple summarizes this process of information valuing to Mrs. Bantry: "The trouble in this case is that everybody has been much too *credulous* and *believing*," she states. "You simply cannot *afford* to believe everything that people tell you. When there's anything fishy about, I never believe anyone at all! You see, I know human nature so well."[35]

Similarly, in *Sleeping Murder*, Marple uses her concerns about the naïveté of the protagonists (young Gwenda and Giles, mentioned above) to justify gaining access to the information world surrounding their mystery. Of Gwenda and Giles, she says, "I'm worried about those two. They're very young and inexperienced and much too trusting and credulous. I feel I ought to be there to look after them."[36] Having gained access to this information world (on "doctor's orders") Miss Marple frequently reminds the protagonists *and thus the reader* to apply skepticism to any information that comes from people. By the end of the book, she has repeated this exhortation so many times that she even reveals a hint of exasperation, saying, "My dear Giles, you've fallen into the trap again—the trap of believing *what is said to you*."[37]

Marple's skepticism over information provided through what people say is foregrounded in *They Do It with Mirrors*, where it is apparently placed in direct contradiction with her friend and host Carrie Louise Serrocold's inherent trusting nature. Miss Marple says of her old friend, "Carrie Louise is *not* an ordinary woman. She lives by her trust, by her belief in human nature."[38] While in *Sleeping Murder* the need for skepticism is stressed repeatedly, in *They Do It with Mirrors*, Marple's tendency toward skepticism is repeatedly contrasted with Mrs. Serrocold's trusting nature. In the end, however, Serrocold's trust and belief in what she thought and felt provide Marple with the most effective direction for her own skepticism; Marple realizes that, rather than her normal tactic of not believing what she was *told*, she needs in this case to disbelieve what she *saw*. Marple explains towards the end:

> Everyone kept saying how Carrie Louise lived in another world from this and was out of touch with reality. But actually, Carrie Louise, it was reality you were in touch with, and not the illusion. You are never deceived by illusion like most of us are. When I suddenly realized that, I saw that I must go by what *you* thought and felt.[39]

She goes on to say, "So therefore, if I was to go by you, all the things that *seemed* to be true were only illusions."[40] Even a reader familiar enough with Marple to exercise a healthy skepticism of information provided by others can be fooled by this subtle twist.

The Moving Finger provides an extended example of information value that includes aspects of skepticism, authority, and truth.[41] The plot of *The Moving Finger* is organized around a specific information type—the malicious anonymous letter—that is in one way of very low value, because it is despised, detested, and reviled, yet is in some ways that actually "count," of very high value. By "ways that actually count," I mean value assessments that influence people's beliefs and actions. Information does not have to be true to have value in the sense that it influences thoughts and actions. False information can also have high value in the sense that it influences people to behave or act badly; the value here is not in the truth, but in the impact on actions.

Within the novel, one character (Mrs. Dane Calthrop, who also serves as Miss Marple's means of access to this information world; as the vicar's wife and Miss Marple's friend, she invites Marple to stay in her home specifically to help solve the mystery) points out that the information contained within the anonymous letters is factually inaccurate—but false information can have high value and influence people's behavior strongly. The malicious letters in *The Moving Finger*, or rather the information contained within them, influence people's beliefs and actions in specific ways. Boyfriends are made to feel (unjustly) suspicious of girlfriends; a brother and sister are made to feel (inaccurately) unwelcome in town; a secretary and a maid change employers to avoid (non-existent) scandals.

Mrs. Dane Calthrop has pointed out that the anonymous letters are not true and have no face value as information; but the information contained in them still has high negative value as evaluated by its influence on thought and action. At this point Marple engages in the second prong of the double bluff and reveals that in reality, the letters also do not actually carry the high negative value that pretends to undergird them. Not only do the letters and their contents have no information value that derives from truth, they also have no true intentional value; there is no true malicious intent behind the letters because they are all just a distractor. Or, while there is malicious intent behind the sending of the letters, it has nothing to do with the information contained in the letters (true or false) or its perceived value by their recipients. They are serving exclusively as a distractor, and their complicated low/high information value is distracting the characters in the novel and the reader from a far more mundane act of evil: a man's murder of his wife.

Marple explains the letters' role as a distractor using a phrase ("no smoke without fire") that is a motif of the novel: "If you disregard the smoke and come to the fire," she suggests, "you know where you are. You just come down to the actual facts of what happened. And putting aside the letters, just one thing happened—Mrs. Symington died."[42] The plot twist revealed when Marple solves the mystery is an information value twist. Once Miss Marple (and the other characters, and the reader) disregard the smoke and come to the fire—that is, focus on the information whose value is associated with real motivations—only then can justice be achieved.

This essay has focused on a small yet rich sub-set of the Christie corpus, the twelve Miss Marple novels. Using information worlds theory, and specifically the concepts of information behavior and information value, I examined three aspects of Miss Marple's praxis: access, tactics, and value. In each case, the hard work put in by Agatha Christie and by Miss Marple is shown to be more nuanced than might be expected, and indicates how information sources and information behavior operate in complex ways in these information worlds. Miss Marple, as a woman, often uses typically feminine self-devaluating language and relies on men to gain access to information worlds and to support the perceived value of her information—to make it "actionable." This analysis has demonstrated that the information tactics she employs are smart, sophisticated and effective.

My hope is that the reader, having read this essay, will in the future encounter detective fiction in part by looking at information worlds, how the fictional detectives are constrained by their information worlds and how they gain access to information worlds. Information behaviors and tactics used in detective fiction are complex and rely on the readers' shared and usually tacit understanding of information value, which can be manipulated by the author through the characters' actions and dialogue as well as through narrative. Both formal and informal information sources are discovered, referred to, evaluated, and applied in detective novels; the use of modern information technology to support storage, access and delivery of sources does not matter so much as the information behaviors and valuations that are applied to them. Information behavior in detective fiction is not just finding the facts and then solving the murder. It is a much more complex story of access, tactics and manipulating information value.

Notes

1. Agatha Christie, *The Murder at the Vicarage* (London: HarperCollins, 2005), p. 56.

2. For exceptions, see Rhiannon Gainor, "The Relevant Clues: Information Behavior and Assessment in Classic Detective Fiction," presented at the annual conference of the Canadian Association for Information Science, Fredericton, Canada, June 2–4, 2011; Deborah Hicks and Caroline Whippey, "'Everyone Forgets that Knowledge Is the Ultimate Weapon': Information Seeking Practices in *Buffy the Vampire Slayer*," presented at the annual conference of the Canadian Association for Information Science, Waterloo, Canada, May 31, 2012; Don. L. Latham and Jonathan M. Hollister, "The Games People Play: Information and Media Literacies in the Hunger Games Trilogy," *Children's Literature in Education* 45 (2014), pp. 33–46.

3. Recent work includes Michelle M. Kazmer, et al., "Information Use Environments of African-American Dementia Caregivers Over the Course of Cognitive-Behavioral Therapy for Depression," *Library & Information Science Research* 35.3 (2013), pp. 191–199; Michelle M. Kazmer, et al., "Distributed Knowledge in an Online Patient Support Community: Authority and Discovery," *Journal of the Association for Information Science and Technology* 65.7 (2014), pp. 1319–1334.

4. Gary Burnett and Paul R. Jaeger, "Small Worlds, Lifeworlds, and Information: The Ramifications of the Information Behavior of Social Groups in Public Policy and the Public Sphere" *Information Research* 13.2 (2008), paper 346.

5. Elfreda A. Chatman, "Life in a Small World: Applicability of Gratification Theory to Information-Seeking Behavior," *Journal of the American Society for Information Science* 42 (1991), pp. 438–449; "A Theory of Life in the Round," *Journal of the American Society for Information Science* 50.3 (1999), pp. 207–217.

6. Jurgen Habermas, *The Theory of Communicative Action* (Boston: Beacon Press, 1984).

7. These are the Marple novels with the date of first publication: *The Murder at the Vicarage* (1930); *The Body in the Library* (1942); *The Moving Finger* (1943); *A Murder is Announced* (1950); *They Do It with Mirrors* (1952); *A Pocket Full of Rye* (1953); *4.50 from Paddington* (1957); *The Mirror Crack'd from Side to Side* (1962); *A Caribbean Mystery* (1964); *At Bertram's Hotel* (1965); *Nemesis* (1971); *Sleeping Murder* (1976, but written decades earlier).

8. The word "praxis" is not a focus of this essay, but it was selected intentionally because of Miss Marple's insistence on action. Her middle-of-the-night raid on Mr. Rafael in *A Caribbean Mystery* (New York: Dodd, Mead, 1965, pp. 226–227) has all the key elements of Miss Marple-ness—a surprise attack, a knitted scarf, an insistence on action, and the ostensible devaluing of her own ideas—in one tidy package: "Miss Marple, standing there in the moonlight, her head encased in a fluffy scarf of pale pink wool" says, "I think we may have to act quickly. Very quickly. I have been foolish. Extremely foolish. I ought to have known from the very beginning what all this was about. It was so simple."

9. Agatha Christie, *The Body in the Library* (London: HarperCollins), p. 77.

10. *Ibid.*

11. Agatha Christie, *A Pocket Full of Rye* (London: HarperCollins, 2006), p. 82.

12. *Ibid.*, p. 87.

13. *Ibid.*, p. 165.

14. Among the Marple novels this one is unusual: at the end of the narrative,

the reader, Miss Marple, and Inspector Neele all know who the culprit is, but an arrest has not occurred.

15. Agatha Christie, *Nemesis* (New York: HarperCollins, 2013), ch. 3, section 3; Agatha Christie, *At Bertram's Hotel* (New York: Black Dog & Leventhal, 2007), p. 11; Christie, *The Body in the Library*, p. 140.

16. Agatha Christie, *A Murder Is Announced* (New York: Black Dog & Leventhal, 2006), p. 47.

17. Christie, *The Murder at the Vicarage*, p. 168.

18. In *The Murder at the Vicarage*, another female character, Lettice Protheroe, engages in strategic information rationing. Like Miss Marple, she is more interested in an accurate outcome than in providing strictly "true" information during the rationing process (p. 184).

19. Agatha Christie, *The Moving Finger* (New York: HarperCollins, 2013), ch. 13.

20. Christie, *The Murder at the Vicarage*, p. 112.

21. *Ibid.*, p. 247.

22. Agatha Christie, *The Mirror Crack'd from Side to Side* (New York: HarperCollins, 2013), ch. 13.

23. Agatha Christie, *4.50 from Paddington* (New York: Black Dog & Leventhal, 2007), p. 30.

24. See Donald O. Case, *Looking For Information: A Survey of Research on Information Seeking, Needs, and Behavior*, 3d ed. (Bingley: Emerald, 2012).

25. Christie, *A Pocket Full of Rye*, p. 87.

26. Agatha Christie, *Sleeping Murder* (New York: HarperCollins, 2013), ch. 11.

27. Christie, *A Murder Is Announced*, p. 127.

28. Christie, *The Murder at the Vicarage*, p. 237.

29. Christie, *A Caribbean Mystery*, p. 184.

30. *Ibid.*

31. *Ibid.*, p. 185. Ellipsis original.

32. Christie, *The Murder at the Vicarage*, p. 54. See related literature: Pamela McKenzie and Philippa Spoel, "Borrowed Voices: Conversational Storytelling in Midwifery Healthcare Visits," *Canadian Journal for Studies in Discourse and Writing* 25.1 (2014); R. Savolainen, "Asking and Sharing Information in the Blogosphere: The Case of Slimming Blogs," *Library & Information Science Research* 33.1 (2011), pp. 73–79.

33. Christie, *A Murder Is Announced*, p. 102.

34. *Ibid.* In *A Pocket Full of Rye*, Inspector Neele similarly tests Miss Marple by making a false assertion about the order of two of the murders to see if she will correct him. She does.

35. Christie, *The Body in the Library*, p. 127. Emphasis original.

36. Christie, *Sleeping Murder*, ch. 25.

37. *Ibid.* Emphasis original.

38. Agatha Christie, *They Do It with Mirrors* (London: HarperCollins, 2013), ch. 11.

39. *Ibid.*, ch. 23.

40. *Ibid.* Emphasis original.

41. "Truth" is a contentious characteristic of "information," and rightly so. See Case, *Looking for Information*, pp. 67–68.

42. Christie, *The Moving Finger*.

Bibliography

Burnett, Gary, and Paul R. Jaeger. *Information Worlds: Social Context, Technology, and Information Behavior in the Age of the Internet.* New York: Routledge, 2010.

_____. "Small Worlds, Lifeworlds, and Information: The Ramifications of the Information Behavior of Social Groups in Public Policy and the Public Sphere." *Information Research* 13.2 (2008), paper 346. http://InformationR.net/ir/13-2/paper346.html

Burnett, Kathleen, Mega M. Subramaniam, and Amelia N. Gibson. "Latinas Cross the IT Border: Understanding Gender as a Boundary Object Between Information Worlds," *First Monday* 14.9 (2009). http://firstmonday.org/ojs/index.php/fm/article/view/2581/2286

Case, Donald O. *Looking for Information: A Survey of Research on Information Seeking, Needs, and Behavior I* (2002), 3d ed. Bingley: Emerald, 2012.

Chatman, Elfreda A. "Life in a Small World: Applicability of Gratification Theory to Information-seeking Behavior." *Journal of the American Society for Information Science* 42 (1991), pp. 438–449.

_____. "A Theory of Life in the Round." *Journal of the American Society for Information Science* 50.3 (1999), pp. 207–217.

Christie, Agatha. *At Bertram's Hotel* (1965). New York: Black Dog & Leventhal, 2007.

_____. *The Body in the Library* (1942). London: HarperCollins, 2005.

_____. *A Caribbean Mystery* (1964). New York: Dodd, Mead, 1965.

_____. *4.50 from Paddington* (1957). New York: Black Dog & Leventhal, 2007.

_____. *The Mirror Crack'd from Side to Side* (1962). New York: HarperCollins, 2013. E-book.

_____. *The Moving Finger* (1943). New York: HarperCollins, 2013. E-book.

_____. *The Murder at the Vicarage* (1930). London: HarperCollins, 2005.

_____. *A Murder Is Announced* (1950). New York: Black Dog & Leventhal, 2006.

_____. *Nemesis* (1971). New York: HarperCollins, 2013. E-book.

_____. *A Pocket Full of Rye* (1953). London: HarperCollins, 2006.

_____. *Sleeping Murder* (1976). New York: HarperCollins, 2013. E-book.

_____. *They Do It with Mirrors* (1952). New York: HarperCollins, 2013. E-book.

Gainor, Rhiannon. "The Relevant Clues: Information Behavior and Assessment in Classic Detective Fiction." Presented at the annual conference of the Canadian Association for Information Science, Fredericton, June 2–4, 2011. www.cais-acsi.ca/ojs/index.php/cais/article/view/264

Habermas, Jurgen. *The Theory of Communicative Action.* Boston: Beacon Press, 1984.

Hicks, Deborah, and Caroline Whippey. "'Everyone Forgets That Knowledge Is the Ultimate Weapon': Information Seeking Practices in *Buffy the Vampire Slayer.*" Presented at the annual conference of the Canadian Association for Information Science, Waterloo, May 31–June 2, 2011. www.cais-acsi.ca/ojs/index.php/cais/article/view/639

Kazmer, Michelle M., Robert L. Glueckauf, Jinxuan Ma, and Kathleen Burnett. "Information Use Environments of African-American Dementia Caregivers Over the Course of Cognitive-behavioral Therapy for Depression." *Library & Information Science Research* 35.3 (2013), pp. 191–199.

Kazmer, Michelle M., et al. "Distributed Knowledge in an Online Patient Support Community: Authority and Discovery." *Journal of the Association for Information Science and Technology* 65.7 (2014), pp. 1319–1334.

Latham, Don, and Jonathan M. Hollister. "The Games People Play: Information and

Media Literacies in the Hunger Games Trilogy." *Children's Literature in Education* 45 (2014), pp. 33–46.
McKenzie, Pamela, and Philippa Spoel. "Borrowed Voices: Conversational Storytelling in Midwifery Healthcare Visits." *Canadian Journal for Studies in Discourse and Writing* 25.1 (2014). www.cjsdw.com/index.php/cjsdw/article/view/36
Savolainen, Reijo. "Asking and Sharing Information in the Blogosphere: The Case of Slimming Blogs." *Library & Information Science Research* 33.1 (2011), pp. 73–79.

And Then There Were Many
Agatha Christie in Hungarian Translation

Brigitta Hudácskó

Trivia lists on book publishing seldom fail to point out that Agatha Christie is one of the highest-selling authors, internationally, of all time. It should come as no surprise then, that she has been—and still is—one the most popular crime fiction authors, with a long and varied history of publication and translation, in Hungary. If we examine the history of the Hungarian publishing market during the course of the past century, however, Christie's apparent popularity is not necessarily such a pre-determined success story as it may seem.

During and after the years of World War II, up to the democratic turn of 1989, the publication of Western literature in general, and genre fiction specifically, was strongly discouraged and sanctioned by various political and cultural measures in Hungary. Of course, the extent and rigor of these sanctions changed over time, and these changes had direct effects on publishing (and translation) policies and practices.

The objective of this essay is twofold: after giving an introduction to the history of Hungarian publishing in the second half of the twentieth century, I would like to examine the progression of Agatha Christie translations, with a focus on the translation of realia and similar culture-specific items. The key word in my investigation is *foreignness*—meaning both the cultural foreignness of the crime genre on the Hungarian literary horizon and possible instances of linguistic foreignness apparent in the texts themselves.

The Case of the Missing Genre

Agatha Christie has been a relatively constant presence on the Hungarian literary scene since the 1930s. While other Golden Age writers were only sporadically translated, if at all, "hardboiled" fiction has also been popular, so we can safely claim that crime fiction in general has had an established readership in Hungary for decades.[1] Despite this, the critical reception of translated or original popular literature in Hungarian had little if anything to say about detective fiction, prior to the twenty-first century.[2] Despite the long history of reading detective fiction in Hungary and the relatively steady—in the recent decades ever increasing—enthusiasm for it, the production of original Hungarian works in the crime genre has never really matched the audience's eagerness. There have been attempts, of course, but not many of these authors—who symptomatically often published under English pseudonyms—have managed to garner significant attention, and the critical reception of both Hungarian and international crime fiction has traditionally been lackluster.[3] There are always unknown factors behind a genre's success or failure at any given time or in a certain cultural setting, but some facts can be established with relative certainty in the case of Hungarian crime fiction. The most significant of these known factors probably is that historical developments did not always look favorably upon genre fiction. The first Hungarian translations of Agatha Christie novels appeared in 1930,[4] but a few years later the financial and cultural circumstances generated by the events of World War II hindered the publication of popular fiction and from the 1940s, under the communist regime, crime fiction was strongly discouraged. In his volume on the Hungarian publishing industry of the time, István Bart examines translation politics as a part of cultural politics, and points out that "[translation politics] effect the social standing of individual languages and may even affect the successful enforcement of human rights, especially when these policies are practiced by the state."[5] Of course, cultural and translation policies are not only of national importance, nor are they merely state-regulated: in *Is That a Fish in Your Ear?*, David Bellos discusses the global flows in translation, as well as central and peripheral languages, touching upon the relationship between language and the empire:

> A truly dominant language that has a great army and a well-filled treasury behind it ... is the one tongue from which you do not ever need to translate. People just learn it, because without it their prospects are blocked. English does not dominate the world in the way that Latin did, because it is massively translated into vernaculars. Translation is the *opposite* of empire.[6]

Bellos also points out that the Union of Soviet Socialist Republics (USSR) was formed on explicitly anti-imperialist grounds, which, among most other areas of life, influenced translation politics within Soviet Russia and in other countries of the Eastern block. However, "only translation could serve as a public alibi for what was in most other ways a classic instance of imperial expansion."[7] These "anti-imperialistic imperial efforts" had severe effects on the translation politics of socialist countries, Hungary included.

Suppressed, Supported, Suffered: Hungarian Publishing Up to 1989

In his overview of Hungarian publishing policies after World War II, Bart discusses how communist and socialist cultural policies were formed with the specific conviction and purpose in mind that literary representations have a direct effect on the reality represented and they also have a role in forming the audience's mindsets, meaning that literature was both an end and the means to this end for policy-makers of the time. The governing power, the Hungarian Socialist Workers' Party, was clear in its concerns regarding Western literature. In a directive issued in 1958, they expressed a fear that

> if there is no party and state control, there is no socialist culture either, and in that case the reactionary bourgeois views can spread freely; and when the socialist consciousness weakens, breaking down the socialist economic-social bases will also become easier.[8]

In a directive from 1965, the party condemned mass culture as cultural garbage:

> Each view that is capable of conserving such individualism, which presents the old relationship between society and the individual and disregards the needs and opportunities of the developing socialist community, is harmful for society and may also lead to painful conflicts within the individual's life.[9]

The party directives were put into effect via the Publishing Directorate, which was founded in 1954. From that point on it laid down not only what was and was not desirable in literature in general, but among other responsibilities, it supervised and directed Hungarian publishing and book distribution, made annual plans for the national publishing industry, allocated the paper supplies and supervised libraries up until 1989; in short, it functioned as a ministry of publishing of sorts.[10] The Directorate had several implicit behests but only one explicit guiding principle: publishing policies should at all times serve the interests of current foreign policies.[11] This principle hardly made financial sense, as the political interests of the time favored works of Soviet literature, while the audience was less enthusiastic about these developments and would rather pay more for popular literature—which is exactly what happened.

To balance out the impossible cultural and political ambitions envisioned by the Directorate, the institution of "subsidy" was introduced in the publishing industry[12]: at its most basic, the subsidy system meant that successful, popular books had to be sold for a higher price, the profit was subsequently channeled back to less prosperous publishers, ensuring that titles garnering meager public interest could still be published and perpetuating a seemingly endless cycle of financial insensibility. The subsidy system was also needed in times of paper shortage, when directives commanded publishers to cut back on Western literature and put a stop entirely to bestsellers.[13] A well-known, albeit unofficial, contemporary slogan described the cultural politics of the time as the period of the three Ss, *suppressed, supported, suffered*, meaning that certain cultural products were obviously supported, such as Soviet literature, others outright banned, while the regime suffered the existence of cultural products of a third category: undesirable, albeit less harmful popular works, which could bring in profit to subsidize the production of further supported works.

The Case of Detective Fiction Under Socialism

Detective fiction clearly belonged to the third, "suffered" category: the social and cultural background to these stories was clearly unwelcome, but the significant public interest and the profit produced by this interest could not be disregarded. The case of detective fiction was quite simple: from the 1970s more and more very successful crime titles appeared on the market, so a counter measure was introduced. From that point on, only two publishing houses, Európa and Magvető were allowed to produce detective fiction, five titles each per year, with 90,000 copies per title, while other publishing houses worked within such thematic limitations and with so scarce paper supplies that they could not even consider publishing detective fiction.[14] To get a better understanding of the hostility towards the genre, let us look at the opinion of a contemporary cultural influencer, which points out several supposedly unacceptable tendencies characteristic of crime fiction. The well-known cultural researcher, philosopher and university professor, Andor Maróti, who published and lectured widely on questions of education and culture, published an essay in 1961 titled "The Irrelevancy of the Adventure Novel."[15] In this essay—which could serve as an explanation for the decades-long hiatus in the publishing of crime fiction—Maróti details in what ways the genre-specific requirements of the adventure story (which, in his understanding, also included the genre of crime fiction) are incompatible with contemporary socialist values and cultural norms. In his view, the genre of crime fiction requires excitement, thrilling situations, black and white, flat characters and an extraordinarily brave hero, and the adventures serve as mere tools or plot devices to show off the hero's amazing qualities which help him conquer the most astonishing difficulties and the most cunning villains. However, this kind of hero-centric, individualistic attitude had no reason for existence or relevance at that time in the given social and cultural discourse, which strongly discouraged both endeavors motivated by individualistic ethics and the allegedly cheap thrills provided by adventure stories, favoring instead narratives of more educational value.[16]

Although Maróti's characterization rings truer for the dime novel than for Golden Age crime fiction, there are two points worth closer examination here. First of all, it seems like a valid argument that the individualistic ethics present in Western detective fiction had hardly any tradition in Hungary, and, on the other hand, the law-enforcement agencies did not share the respect and moral prestige that we can observe in multiple crime stories featuring the Scotland Yard officials. If anything, law-enforcement was often the butt of jokes in crime narratives and in everyday discourse—and not in the way as the Scotland Yard is occasionally depicted as slightly incapable in the fiction of Arthur Conan Doyle or Agatha Christie. In certain cases in these stories, the police merely lack the means which would enable them to solve specific crimes, while the liminal status of Sherlock Holmes, Poirot or Miss Marple makes it possible for amateur detectives to reach better results. For example, Holmes has access to his Irregulars who collect insider information for him, while Poirot and especially Miss Marple are able to casually socialize with those involved in a criminal case, which would be impossible for the police, although, of course, not because of their incompetency. In the specific cultural context in question there is a history of downright incompetent policemen in Hungarian fiction and especially on television, which is probably a reminder of and a jab at all the atrocities Hungarian citizens had to suffer at the hands of the corrupt law-enforcement agencies during the communist and socialist times, and even earlier than that[17]: the dishonorable status of the police officer was not entirely the product of communism, as even a 1928 source mentions the impossibility of a police officer becoming the hero of an adventure novel, since "the secret police is the most despised agency of Hungarian political life. When authors introduce a 'mole' into their stories, its only function is to serve as a villain."[18] Bálint Varga, on his quest to explore the beginnings of Hungarian crime fiction, also points out the dubious situation of the police officer all through history: during the time when Hungary was part of the Austro-Hungarian Monarchy the institution of the detective was established, which of course did not necessarily equal the role of the informer, but the collective consciousness certainly equated the two. So Hungarian authors first could not feature police officers because these officials did not exist (up until the second half of the nineteenth century), and when they finally emerged, their questionable activities did not make them attractive or popular subjects of fiction.[19]

However, it was not only the unwelcome presence of the policeman that hindered the emergence of Hungarian crime fiction: the ever-present indicators of the British class system in Golden Age novels were entirely alien in an allegedly classless socialist society, with its entirely different social registers and formulae. The "everything rotten to the core" sentiment of hard-boiled crime fiction might have appeared more familiar to the reader (and, moreover, to the author) of the time, but this approach would not have been suffered under any circumstances by the authorities governing Hungarian cultural politics.

However, the very coziness of the Golden Age detective story seemed homely, and its non-threatening foreignness made it possible for Agatha Christie to establish herself on the Hungarian market. Between 1930 and 1944, twenty-three of her novels were published, but after 1945—and the discursive turn the end of the war brought about—classic British detective fiction was marginalized. For Christie, specifically, it meant that between 1945 and 1960 only three of her novels were published, and only after 1960 did a so-called "Agatha Christie renaissance" begin, which is still going strong even today. In technical terms it means that most of Christie's works are in print at all times, and not only in the form of reprinted earlier editions, but also new editions. With these, new translations are published each year. The progression of these editions clearly reflect the reception crime fiction has received in Hungary, and also the double critical standard which we can, on occasions, still notice when it comes to detective and/or popular fiction.

Even though some of Agatha Christie's works have been published by lesser known houses or by those who have since gone out of business, such as HungaPrint, her main publisher in Hungary is Európa Kiadó, probably the biggest and certainly the most prestigious of Hungarian publishing houses. On the one hand, the approach of the smaller publishing houses reflected a general opinion—that of the reading public and that of academia—that detective fiction should be forgotten as quickly as the momentary pleasure it provides. These books were published in paperback, on cheap paper, with notoriously negligent—and presumably quick—translations. At the same time, though, Európa took an entirely different approach when they started publishing Christie in hardback.[20] Their more considered translations indicate an attempt to launch Christie into the canon of serious literature in Hungary.

At this point we should take a look at Christie's position in the Hungarian literary canon. In international criticism she is generally regarded as a "middlebrow" author, but this category has been historically missing from the Hungarian tradition, leading to a number of different approaches in publication. Európa, for instance, has done a lot to present Christie as one of their highbrow authors, but, surprisingly, from 2010 to 2011 the publishing house collaborated with *Népszabadság*, a leading Hungarian daily paper, to launch a series of twenty-five Christie titles, which one could buy with the paper every fortnight. This edition came out in paperback, on cheap recycled paper, effectively writing Christie back into the dime novel tradition, into the masses of popular authors.

This move may seem as a destruction of idols, especially coming from a house which had previously taken great pains to canonize Christie. However, some context is useful: in the same offer, on weeks when the Christie volumes were not on sale, one could buy the works of the most popular crime fiction/humor/adventure writer Jenő Rejtő, who is still hardly recognized by academia—despite his immense popularity—and who was almost without exception published in the typical yellow paperback style. We could interpret this gesture as one devaluating Christie, as she had been dragged down from her pedestal as a serious writer; but maybe the fact that her works were being published alongside the critically under-appreciated Rejtő oeuvre elevated the status of the latter. By the same token, I would argue that Christie was democratized once again—once more available to the reading public. This publishing maneuver amply illustrates the still somewhat dubious Hungarian attitude towards crime fiction and Christie's unique position within it.

Translating (and) Foreignness: Hercule Poirot's Christmas

Bellos defines "translating down" as an instance of translating "toward a vernacular with a smaller audience than the source, or toward one with less cultural, economic, or religious prestige, or one not used as a vehicular tongue."[21] Translating crime fiction from English to Hungarian is certainly an instance of translating down, and even though it has been established previously that English does not necessarily function as a truly dominant language, in general practice it will require substantially less effort from the translator to familiarize the target language audience with the cultural reality of English than in the case of "translating up" *to* English from a peripheral language. However, if we consider the specific case of translating Agatha Christie to Hungarian during socialism, we can understand this familiarizing process as hindered or altered variously, due to the lack of or restricted access to cultural resources (both on the side of the translator and on that of the reading public), changing publishing policies, and changes in national ideology, which affected each edition differently.

Furthermore, translating popular fiction is always a complex issue: from the publisher's point of view as well, popular fiction is often considered momentary both regarding the cultural reality it depicts and in its perceived literary shelf-life, and if there are limited funds to be distributed, it is not always the first priority, when it comes to assigning time and manpower to— and there is always the pressure of time to publish a piece while it is still in the center of public attention. Time is of the essence for the translator as well, as s/he must be aware of the social and cultural reality of the book in question to be able to render the pieces of realia and do it against the clock, of course. These issues all factor in to various degrees in Hungarian translations of Christie novels, as well as in the translations of the novel chosen for investigation.

For the purposes of this essay I have examined three Hungarian translations of *Hercule Poirot's Christmas*. Between them, these texts touch upon practically all of the problems mentioned so far, as well as providing a typical example of the evolutionary process of Hungarian Christie editions. The first Hungarian edition, appearing shortly after the original English publication in 1939, was translated by the critically acclaimed fiction writer, Lola Kosáryné Réz, with the title *Valaki csenget ...* ("Someone Rings the Bell..."). A revised translation by Katalin Csanády appeared in 1975, and was later used by several different publishing houses in a range of editions. Finally, as part of Európa's extensive efforts to celebrate the 120th anniversary of Christie's birth by retranslating and republishing a number of her works, it was rendered again, by Judit Gálvölgyi, in 2012. An exhaustive linguistic and/or statistical analysis of words changed and lexical or cultural items mistreated in each of these texts is beyond the scope of the present chapter, but examining a number of symptomatic *loci* in the text may tell us a lot about the fate of cultural items in translation and about the evolution of Christie translation as well. In the focus of this short case study stand instances of cultural or linguistic foreignness—*foreign* in any sense of the word—and the treatment of foreignness in the three Hungarian translations.

Considering *foreignness*, we might invoke Umberto Eco who, in his volume *Mouse or Rat: Translation as Negotiation*, discusses two basic approaches toward cross-cultural translation: one of these is "foreignizing," where the translator strives to make the reader aware of the foreign and mediated nature of the text. The other is domesticating, where all possible attempts are made to bring the text closer to home and make is sound familiar to the target language audience.[22]

Whether they prefer foreignizing or domesticating, one of the issues translators of fiction face is the question of dialects and accents, just as in *Hercule Poirot's Christmas*: the novel contains two instances of foreigners speaking English and their unique usage is marked in the text. The first is the detective Hercule Poirot, with his consciously overcomplicated and circumstantial phrases and French interjections. The second, the Spanish Pilar Estravados, who speaks fluent English, but with a slight accent. Translating these speakers' dialogue can be problematic, since Hungarian is not a language that easily lends itself to dialectic use—and even if it did, the problem of "foreign-soundingness" poses its own set of difficulties. In the English original one can get a feel for Pilar's foreignness by the grammatically correct, but slightly off-kilter structures she uses. For example: "My mother was English. That is why I talk English so well" and "I drove in a car all across the country and there was much destruction. And I saw a bomb drop and it blew up a car."[23] These remarks appear in the very first scene where readers encounter Pilar on a train. Rendering Pilar's idiolect in Hungarian poses considerable difficulty, since Hungarian is a language with few regional dialects that are generally recognizable, and even to those who can discern them, there are hardly any cultural connotations attached to dialect beyond geographic region. Hungarian, then, is by no means a language that easily lends itself to expressing different accents and dialects, especially when they are supposed to connote foreigners speaking the language.

In this instance, however, the problem does not arise from an accent or a dialect itself, but from an idiolect, a unique—and here slightly nonstandard—personal use of language, which manifests itself both on the level of vocabulary and in the sentence structure. In Pilar's case, her idiolect is mostly characterized by avoiding contracted forms ("You are not English, no?"; "That is so, is it not?"; "No, I do not love you") and by frequently using "yes" and "no" instead of proper tag questions.[24] For the Hungarian translator, this may appear problematic, since—due to the agglutinative nature of the language—contracted forms do not exist in Hungarian, and instead of context-dependent tag questions Hungarian uses the word "ugye" in every instance this grammatical structure is applied. Still, rendering this idiolectic usage should not be impossible in Hungarian, but interestingly—perhaps worryingly—none of the translations manages to capture it, and Pilar speaks perfect Hungarian—or, on occasion in Csanády's translation, she expresses herself not only perfectly but more exquisitely than the idiolectic characteristics present in the original English text would allow. The decision not to render a character's idiolect in translation may be explained away in such cases when individual language use is of no or little significance in the whole of the text, and its lack does not diminish the enjoyment or interpretation. In the case of Pilar Estravados, however, this does not seem to be case: Pilar is supposed to be a daughter of an English mother and a Spanish father, she was raised as bilingual, therefore she may speak English with native proficiency. After all, she herself says, "I am really very English indeed."[25] Later, however, it turns out that Pilar is not who she is supposed to be: she is a Spanish citizen, who merely travelled together with the late Pilar, and after the girl's death, she claim her identity and presented herself as Pilar to the girl's family. Therefore we could regard her language use as a clue betraying her true identity—and in this case, the loss of the idiolect in translation does hinder interpretation, as the Hungarian reader is denied a significant clue pertaining to the mystery.

Bellos discusses the issue of the inherent "foreign-soundingness" of translated texts, and quotes the philosopher Jean d'Alambert, who says that "the way foreigners speak [French] is the model for a good translation," as this way the target text contains "the added flavor of a homeland created by its foreign colouring."[26] In the case of *Hercule Poirot's Christmas*, however, the question is not only whether or not the translated text should sound foreign to the reader as it is, but also what happens to those utterances that already bear a certain "foreign-soundingness" in the original. We have already seen in Pilar's case that this "added flavor" is lost here, and we can witness the same phenomena in the translation of Poirot's circuitous style as well. Poirot likes to emphasize his foreignness in his phrasing as well, and not only with the application of French interjections: for instance, in his interrogations he makes a habit of using statements as questions, such as "You had been telephoning?" or "You had been away a long time?" or "You came for a short visit—or a long one?"[27] Once again, while not shockingly ungrammatical, his utterances are stylistically marked. Translating these sentences poses further problems, as there is no specific word order for the interrogative in Hungarian—and word order in general is more flexible than in English—so the translator needs to find another way to circumnavigate Poirot's speech patterns. Another characteristic feature of Poirot's language use is raising (usually) the subject of the sentence to the level of a fragmented clause or even individual sentence, such as "The bullet wound, the cut throat, the crushed-in skull? It is there your preference lies?"[28] or "So this case, it will make a big stir?"[29] While the solution of the issue regarding the interrogative word order may be problematic, rendering the emphasized subjects in Hungarian should be straightforward. Yet, all three translators seem to have decided against this: the questions are rendered as questions, or—on rare occasions—as mere statements. Along with the neglect of characters' "foreign-soundingness," this indicates that translators have carried the "domesticating" approach so far that Christie's characters have become more familiar—and more easily digestible—to Hungarian readers than they appear in the English original. In Poirot's case, however, the French interjections act as saving graces in the text, as they remain untouched (Gálvölgyi's version even provides the Hungarian translation of the French expressions), while in Pilar's case hardly anything remains to indicate her idiolect.

However, Pilar and Poirot are not the only characters with hints of foreignness to them: there is also Stephen Lee, a son of the victim, who has just returned from South Africa, meaning that there are occasional pieces of South African realia about him, and on occasions he finds himself searching for the correct word to use in a conversation. One the very first page on the novel readers experience him musing about the people at the station: "People! Incessant, innumerable people! And all so—so—what was the word?—so *drab*-looking! So alike, so horribly alike!"[30] Interestingly, the word "drab" becomes "szürke," that is, "grey" in both Csanády's and Gálvölgyi's version, thus Stephen's search for the correct word seems unmotivated as he appears to settle for a less expressive adjective. We can see more progress in the treatment of realia in his case, however: where the first translation has him reminiscing about the "veldt," a word referring to certain wide open rural spaces of Southern Africa, the 1975 version renders it as "préri" (prairie), while the 2012 version leaves it as "veldt," which, though not as easily understandable in Hungarian as "préri," manages to capture the South African allusion, while also retaining some of the original words, is in accordance with Bellos' suggestions for "foreign-soundingness."

While the choice of "préri" to substitute "veldt" may appear debatable, it is a less intrusive maneuver than the one we encounter in Lola Kosáryné Réz's earliest translation. Edit Dömötör in her analysis of the aesthetic and structuralist interpretation of crime in Hungarian popular literature points out that Kosáryné Réz augments her translation with an interpretative description at the end of the novel, when the identity of the culprit is revealed.[31] The murderer turns out to be Superintendent Sugden, who has so far led the official investigation and he ends the final confrontation with the following furious utterance, referring to the murder of Simeon Lee: "God rot his soul in hell! I'm glad I did it!" which exclamation concludes Part Six.[32] The following excerpt is a direct translation of Réz's Hungarian version:

> There was a deadly silence. Then Sugden suddenly jumped up. He hit the table with his fist and cried in an inhuman voice:
> "I'm glad I did it! I'm glad!"
> He ran into the others, while his eyes were rolling back into his head. With great difficulty, he was finally contained. By the evening, he was already locked up in a lunatic asylum, heavily medicated, sitting on a hospital bed and looking in front of himself with a distorted smile on his face.[33]

The liberties taken by the translator here clearly go beyond the decisions suggested by any foreignizing or domesticating approach, by presenting the murderer as a madman instead of an intellectual killer carrying out a coldly planned crime. While it was a common translational and editorial practice at the time to remove such elements of novels—especially in the case of popular fiction—which did not move the plot forward, this extension of the original ending does not seem to be in accord with contemporary translation practices.

We can find the reason for this maneuver once again in the cultural atmosphere of the era: the idea of depicting the common criminal as a hero who bravely confronts authority was revolting, as a criminal obviously has no other aim than his/her personal (and financial) advancement. Depicting the criminal as an intellectual being, who has planned out his/her deed with a cold head and did not act out of mere moral depravity in a moment of murderous passion would—according to the cultural influencers of the era—glorify the criminal, which would suggest a distorted—and probably also glorified—image of crime to the audience.[34] The intellectual element is therefore removed from the crime, and the criminal loses his/her glamor and becomes "common." Translation often aided and abetted this initiative and helped depict the murderer as a madman instead of a coldly calculating, intellectually driven entity.[35] This gesture, however, can be viewed as one entirely opposing other translational acts which brings the text closer to the reader: by presenting the murderer as a mentally ill person, the translation alienates the reader and hinders feelings of excessive sympathy with criminals—which is, of course, in accordance with the above mentioned cultural directives of the era. The two other translations, fortunately, were no longer influenced by such cultural initiatives, and they render the final words of Sugden in a literal translation of the original passage, with no additions whatsoever.

While the present investigation has allowed only a glimpse into the history of Agatha Christie's presence on the Hungarian literary scene, it has shed light on the effect of cultural politics on translation practices and on the production and consumption of detective fiction. While even during the time of socialism there were not any direct authoritative instructions regarding translation practices, merely general directives concerning publishing policies, these directives had a severe influence on everyday translating practices, with—sometimes deliberate, sometimes accidental—consequences on not only what could or could not be published, but also how the published and translated works could be interpreted. Even though her works have also been affected by various political maneuvers, Agatha Christie still appears to be an exception in the Hungarian history of crime fiction publishing: despite all historical and cultural disturbances, her works managed to remain not only popular and in print, but constantly revised in better editions as well, finally granting her a place in the Hungarian highbrow canon.

Notes

1. Crime fiction was first mostly considered a subgenre of adventure fiction, and adventure fiction has a more established history in Hungarian literature. Cf. Edit Dömötör, *"Az eltitkolt gonosztettet a szél is kifúvja?": A magyar bűnügyi irodalom ismeretelméleti megközelítése* (Budapest: E. Dömötör, 2011).

2. This is not to say, of course, that there has been no critical attention paid to detective fiction at all. The attempts have been few and far between, but one of them, for example, is Tibor Keszthelyi's *A detektívtörténet anatómiája* [The Anatomy of the Detective Story] (Budapest: Magvető, 1979).

3. The twenty-first century, however, has brought about several changes: on the one hand, two distinct and highly successful crime writers appeared on the scene, both writing historical fiction: Katalin Baráth, whose novels could be compared to those in the middlebrow tradition, and Vilmos Kondor, whose *Budapest Noir* has been published in several languages, English included (London: Harper, 2012). On the other hand, several academic volumes have been published on crime fiction, such as volumes written or edited by Krisztián Benyovszky: *Bevezetés a krimi olvasásába* [Introduction to Reading Crime Fiction] (Dunaská Streda: Lilium Aurum, 2007) or *A jelek szerint: a detektívtörténet és közép-európai emléknyomai* [The Clues Suggest: The Detective Story and Its Traces in Central Europe] (Bratislava: Kalligram, 2003).

4. Titles translated in 1930 included *The Big Four* (Légrády Brothers), *The Secret Adversary*, *The Murder of Roger Ackroyd*, and *The Murder on the Links*. The last three were published by Palladis, in a series called "Pengős regények" [Penny novels].

5. István Bart, *Világirodalom és könyvkiadás a Kádár-korszakban* (Budapest: Osiris Kiadó, 2002), p. 9.

6. David Bellos, *Is That a Fish in Your Ear? Translation and the Meaning of Everything* (New York: Faber and Faber, 2011), p. 205. Emphasis original.

7. *Ibid.*, p. 206.

8. Bart, *Világirodalom és könyvkiadás a Kádár-korszakban*, p. 22. Translation mine.

9. *Ibid.*, p. 26. Translation mine.

10. *Ibid.*, p. 17.

11. *Ibid.*, p. 14.

12. *Ibid.*, p. 23.

13. *Ibid.*, p. 25.

14. *Ibid.*, p. 28.

15. The Hungarian title of the essay is "A kalandregény időszerűtlensége," which directly translates to "The Ill-Timed Nature of the Adventure Novel." However, my translation of the title captures the themes of the essay more precisely.

16. Dömötör, *Az eltitkolt gonosztettet a szél is kifúvja?*, p. 75.

17. An example of this phenomenon may be Hungary's (so far) only attempt to produce its own martial arts themed cop show, inspired by films of Bruce Lee and Jackie Chan. Although it was cancelled several years ago, the show *Linda* (1983–89) has reached an iconic status and is still widely popular with Hungarian audiences, probably because of its very oddity which makes it stand out from the not too lengthy line of Hungarian crime series on television. As Renáta Zsámba notes in her analysis of *Linda*, the eponymous protagonist of the series and the show itself do not fit the Hungarian tradition because the individualist ethics featured in the series had had no roots in the socialist culture. In a similar vein, the titular character, the young and tomboyish Linda appeared to be the only competent police officer among all her older male colleagues (despite her being only a trainee), while the majority of the senior officers were untalented, idiotic characters, who spent their time eating out or drinking beer. This kind of characterization of authority figures clearly indicates a softening in ideological and representative discipline.

18. Dömötör, *Az eltitkolt gonosztettet a szél is kifúvja?*, p. 79.

19. Bálint Varga, "Nyomozás az első magyar krimi után" in K. Benyovszky and

P. H. Nagy (eds.), *Lepipálva: Tanulmányok a krimiről* (Dunajská Streda: Lilium Aurum, 2009), p. 65.

20. Even at the time of writing (2015) one can rarely find a hardback crime novel on the Hungarian market, whether translated or original. It is interesting, however, that Sophie Hannah's *The Monogram Murders* immediately received the "Christie treatment," as it came out in hardback at Európa Kiadó, while Hannah's previous novels have been published by another house, in paperback format.

21. Bellos, *Is That a Fish in Your Ear?*, p. 167.

22. Umberto Eco, *Mouse or Rat: Translation as Negotiation* (London: Phoenix, 2004), pp. 84–104. The introduction of these approaches can by no means considered novel, as choosing either the "foreignizing" or the domesticating path is an approach consciously or unconsciously, but always applied by translators and is discussed in theoretical texts on translation. As for the specific case of English-Hungarian translation, the issue is introduced and debated in volumes by Kinga Klaudy and Judy Szöllősy.

23. Agatha Christie, *Hercule Poirot's Christmas*, in *Murder on the Orient Express—Cards on the Table—Five Little Pigs—Hercule Poirot's Christmas* (London: Diamond Books, 1991), p. 338.

24. *Ibid.*, pp. 338, 339, 364.

25. *Ibid.*, p. 413.

26. Bellos, *Is That a Fish in Your Ear?*, p. 45.

27. Christie, *Hercule Poirot's Christmas*, pp. 398–399.

28. *Ibid.*, p. 379.

29. *Ibid.*, p. 381.

30. *Ibid.*, p. 335. Emphasis original.

31. Dömötör, *Az eltitkolt gonosztettet a szél is kifúvja?*, p. 99.

32. Christie, *Hercule Poirot's Christmas*, p. 489.

33. Agatha Christie, *Valaki csenget...*, trans. Lola Kosáryné Réz (Budapest: Pengős regények, 1939), p. 206. Translation mine.

34. Dömötör, *Az eltitkolt gonosztettet a szél is kifúvja?*, p. 98.

35. Something similar occurs in the translation of *Murder Is Easy* (1939), which first appeared in Hungarian in 1940 (trans. Éva Moharné Dobó). The Hungarian title was *A gyűlölet őrültje* ["Crazed by Hatred"], merging legal and medical discourse and emphasizing the "ill" nature of the murderer. Later editions, however, bear the title *Gyilkolni könnyű*, a direct translation of the original.

BIBLIOGRAPHY

Bart, István. *Világirodalom és könyvkiadás a Kádár-korszakban*. Budapest: Osiris Kiadó, 2002.

Bellos, David. *Is That a Fish in Your Ear? Translation and the Meaning of Everything*. New York: Faber and Faber, 2011.

Christie, Agatha. *Hercule Poirot karácsonya* (1939). Trans. Judit Gálvölgyi. Budapest: Európa Kiadó, 2012.

_____, *Hercule Poirot's Christmas* (1939). *Murder on the Orient Express—Cards on the Table—Five Little Pigs—Hercule Poirot's Christmas*. London: Diamond Books, 1991, pp. 333–492.

_____. *Poirot karácsonya* (1939). Trans. Katalin Csanády (1975). Budapest: Európa Kiadó, 2011.

_____. *Valaki csenget...* (1939). Trans. Lola Kosáryné Réz. Budapest: Pengős regények, 1939.

Dömötör, Edit. *"Az eltitkolt gonosztettet a szél is kifúvja?"*: *A magyar bűnügyi irodalom ismeretelméleti megközelítése*. Budapest: E. Dömötör, 2011.
Eco, Umberto. *Mouse or Rat: Translation as Negotiation* (2003). London: Phoenix, 2004.
Varga, Bálint. "Nyomozás az első magyar krimi után" in K. Benyovszky and P. H. Nagy (eds.), *Lepipálva: Tanulmányok a krimiről*. Dunaská Streda: Lilium Aurum, 2009, pp. 49–82.
Zsámba, Renáta. "Szocialista krimi kapitalista díszletekkel: Linda és a nyolcvanas évek." *Korunk*, March 2014, pp. 18–25.

Mother of Invention
Agatha Christie, the Middlebrow Detective Novel and Kerry Greenwood's Postcolonial Tribute Series

Jilly Lippmann

Agatha Christie casts a long shadow over the genre of mystery and detective fiction, but she has yet to be seriously considered in terms of her influence on and engagement with other aspects of literary culture. This chapter introduces three overlapping frames of interpretation for Christie's fiction (postcolonial, feminist and middlebrow) by showcasing how they converge in the work of contemporary Australian crime writer, Kerry Greenwood, whom Christie has influenced. In particular, this chapter will show how Kerry Greenwood's popular *Phryne Fisher* mystery series (1989 to present) produces a creative tribute to the Grand Dame of Crime, and as such, invites fresh consideration of Christie's work.

A best-selling and award-winning author who writes across many genres (and whose fiction, like Christie's, has been adapted for television), Greenwood has won a lifetime achievement award from the Sisters in Crime society and the Ned Kelly Award for Crime Writing. Greenwood's series is based on the investigations of a twenty-eight-year-old flapper-like detective: Phryne Fisher. Beginning in 1928 and including credible vignettes of interwar Melbourne city life, Greenwood's work not only engages with history through fiction, but also showcases her fascination with history and crime. Her choice of historical period coincides with the year writer Anthony Berkeley proposed a regular meeting with Dorothy Sayers, G.K. Chesterton and Agatha Christie, who then went on to establish the famous "Detection Club," which developed rules to establish what should be deemed "fair play" in detective fiction.[1] This coincidence can be read as a coded tribute to the golden age of detection.

However, despite having won global audiences and wide acclaim only a small number of critics have engaged with Greenwood's fiction. In the face of this lack of critical engagement despite (or perhaps because of) the popularity of her novels, issues of reception can be productively bought to bear on her work. This essay argues that Greenwood's work is not merely superficial popular fiction, but that it also offers an ambivalent criticism of late colonial society. Part fantasy postcolonial revisionism and part colonial critique, Greenwood's series can be understood as displaying both a playful frivolity as well as an educative register. As such, ambivalence is not only thematic but also formal, extending to her engagement with the middlebrow. Consequently, new readings of Agatha Christie will emerge here as much as (and through) new readings of Kerry Greenwood's series.

"Writing Back" to the Golden Age?

Though postcolonial readings of Christie's fiction are rare, the critic Sue Ryan-Fazilleau has pointed out that Greenwood's fiction provides a postcolonial interpretation and response to Christie's oeuvre. Ryan-Fazilleau proposes that the first novel, *Cocaine Blues* (1989), for example, "invites the reader to compare Greenwood's and Agatha Christie's crime fiction,"[2] and that the novel might be understood as a satire on Christie's technique, which takes up the stock tropes of English detective fiction to subvert them, in a kind of postcolonial "writing back."[3] For instance, Ryan-Fazilieau points out that the clever and highly sexualized Phryne solves the crime in the first pages of *Cocaine Blues*, rather than taking the whole novel to laboriously unlock the puzzle clue by clue. After solving the crime with her characteristically *feminine éclat*, Phryne then promptly departs from England (the place predominantly represented in Christie's fiction) for more adventurous escapades abroad at the periphery of the British Empire. In her capers through Melbourne, Phryne becomes a tool with which Greenwood reprises the unsavory aspects of Australia's colonial past to depict colonial Melbourne as a freer and more equitable space. These and other aspects of her work, Ryan-Fazilleau maintains, suggest Greenwood's "intention to undertake a postcolonial 'rewriting' of the Queen of Crime."[4]

Ryan-Fazilleau's interpretation of Greenwood's postcolonial re-writing of Christie's work is a salient one, but one that I argue does not take into consideration the full complexity of the Australian postcolonial relationship with England in general, and that therefore misses, in particular, Greenwood's more subtle relationship with the work of the Queen of Crime. One of Ryan-Fazilleau's contentions, for example, is that Greenwood revises and reverses the terms of Christie's "elitist ideology" to present a more egalitarian Australian system, appealing to contemporary readers.⁵ She contrasts the two detective protagonists of Greenwood and Christie—Phryne and Poirot—to highlight her point. Revealing that while Poirot makes "disdainful remarks about [his offsider's] lack of intelligence and frequently humiliates him," Ryan-Fazilleau shows that in contrast, Phryne "treats her offsider [her maid and companion, Dot] with far more respect."⁶ While this observation is accurate, Ryan-Fazilleau's analysis of these characters cuts across the premise of postcolonial texts, which, as Elleke Boehmer suggests, resist hierarchical structures from a marginalized position.⁷ Ryan-Fazilleau's analysis of Phryne as Dot's superior is a top-down approach, and her critical discussion centers on a person in authority (Phryne) treating her subordinate (Dot) well. This formula is problematic in that it can redeploy the hierarchical relations of superior and subordinate typically critiqued within postcolonial theory.

I suggest that it is more productive to observe how Greenwood elevates the marginalized and disenfranchised (including Phryne herself) from positions of weakness to positions where they have agency and autonomy. Phryne's upward social movement from a street urchin in the slums of pre–World War I Melbourne to a titled, wealthy lady, for example, is mirrored in Dot's elevation from a low socio-economic status to social and financial security. Indeed, Phryne rejects and challenges suggestions that Dot is lower than her in social status, despite her own newly-attained aristocratic position. In *Death by Water* (2005), for example, Dot assumes she will be dining with the maids in the second-class dining room, yet Phryne insists, "No.... You're dining with me. Second Class indeed. I did not bring you here to be patronised, Dot."⁸ Furthermore, the way Greenwood writes back to Christie lacks the antagonism that some postcolonial texts possess, such as Jean Rhys's *Wide Sargasso Sea* (1966), in which Jane Eyre's Mr. Rochester is presented as an imperious British villain who causes the insanity and subsequent death of Bertha Mason, his subaltern wife. Instead, I argue, that the Phryne Fisher mystery novels can be labeled a postcolonial *tribute* series, a term which I have employed to signal the way they pay homage to the *grand dame* of detective fiction, as well as undercut or critique aspects of the framework of classical British detection in which Christie wrote. Drawing on settler postcolonial theory, I show that this form of tribute is marked by ambivalence, rather than the outright rejection or "writing back" which Ryan-Fazilleau's interpretation presupposes.

One form of tribute Greenwood pays to Christie is the way she models her heroine upon Christie's characters, for many similarities can be drawn between Phryne and three of Christie's main detectives. Christie's sleuth, Tuppence Beresford (née Cowley) from *The Secret Adversary* (1922), can be seen as a model for Phryne as an "adventuress." Phryne, like Tuppence, is a 1920s flapper-type, with bobbed hair and a stylish wardrobe; she also loves the good life and smokes, and both characters exhibit a desire to break away from their father's Victorian patriarchal control. While the Detection Club's rules of fair play rule out feminine intuition, both Tuppence and Phryne subvert this interdiction and rely on their sixth sense to solve crimes. In *The Secret Adversary*, Tuppence uses her female intuition to detect that the antagonist is somewhere at hand. She then cries out to the infamous Sir James Peel Edgerton and to Julius P. Hersheimer, "I can't help it. I know Mr. Brown's somewhere in the flat! I can *feel* him"[9] and, as the reader finds out later, she was right. Likewise, in Greenwood's novel *Raisins and Almonds* (2007), Phryne tells her wharfie friend Bert that she *feels* there is something underhanded going on in the Eastern Markets, and as the novel progresses, she is also proved right. Bert asks her if she knows this by "female intuition" and Phryne retorts, "absolutely."[10] Further, both adventuresses make reference to Doyle's Sherlock Holmes series by employing irregulars. Tuppence employs a young assistant, Albert, after she notices a "threepenny detective novel protruding from Albert's pockets."[11] Phryne likewise employs an irregular with a similar sounding name to Tuppence's coadjutor—Herbert—and notices that he, too, reads detective stories. However, unlike Tuppence's reliance and subsequent marriage to Tommy, her fellow sleuth, Phryne prefers—and operates from—an independent status, much like Miss Jane Marple.

Christie's Miss Marple could be considered another strong female character to whom Greenwood pays tribute via a number of inter-textual references. Miss Marple's methods of detection stem from her perceptive understanding of human nature, combined with her ability to listen carefully and ask loaded questions from an apparently naïve point of view. Similarly, Phryne is considered "very perceptive about people"; she asks questions constantly and deciphers people's motives with consistent accuracy.[12] Crucially, the two sleuths operate under the radar in some sense, as both are women and often dismissed as innocuous. Miss Marple is an unassuming old lady; Phryne is a young and glamorous flapper who "looked perfectly harmless" because, presumably, her interests are in men, society and fashion. However, in both cases the detectives' eyes reveal their intelligence and astuteness, and Phryne's guise of harmlessness is only an apparent one: "unless you caught her eye, in which case you felt that you were stripped down to component molecules, weighed in the balance, and found wanting."[13] Greenwood pays particular tribute to Miss Marple in *Urn Burial* (2003). Here, Phryne and an older lady sleuth called Miss Mary Mead (itself a reference to St. Mary Mead, the village where Miss Marple lives), together solve some mysteries at a mansion in country Victoria and light-heartedly discuss their experiences as female detectives. The collegiality between the two characters parallels the relationship between Greenwood and her precursors, as she fondly draws on Christie's characters. However, while Miss Marple is portrayed as celibate,

Phryne is sexually active and regularly beds handsome and intelligent men. One reviewer has labeled Phryne as "Miss Marple's naughty niece."[14] This might be seen as a tactic by which Greenwood updates Christie's iconic female sleuth.

There is an even more significant relationship between Christie's iconic male detective and Phryne. Hercule Poirot and Phryne share a penchant for the finer things in life, and are similar in the breadth of their social acquaintance and engagement with the police. Poirot has a preference for exotic food, is markedly cosmopolitan, and has an unusual degree of access to the middle and upper classes. Phryne, too, is a food connoisseur, travels the world, and speaks numerous languages—including Poirot's French. Because of her prefix, the Honorable Phryne Fisher moves in high society, but her egalitarian nature also positions her favorably and in sympathy with the middle to lower classes. Both detectives also develop good relations with the police. While Poirot has a long-standing friendship with Chief Inspector Japp, Phryne has a mutually beneficial partnership with Detective Inspector Robinson. It must be noted, however, that Phryne's methods of detection differ from Poirot's: while Poirot famously relies on his "little grey cells," Phryne (as noted earlier) relies more on instinct and her subconscious. In *The Green Mill Murder* (1993), Phryne witnesses a murder, yet who the murderer is and how the victim has met his end initially escape her notice. Phryne often muses throughout the novel that "her subconscious [is] trying to tell her something,"[15] and rather than isolating herself like Poirot to think and use rational methods of deduction, Phryne eschews reflection and just goes to bed. Because she disengages her conscious mind, and allows her dreams and subconscious to reveal answers, Phryne awakes with the solution to the mystery. Greenwood also affectionately parodies Poirot, as Phryne admits that she wishes

> the real world [would conform] to Hercule Poirot's rules.... She would love to gather all the suspects together and state, on the authority of the little grey cells, exactly how each one could have been the murdered but wasn't, until she reached the last person, who was, and who always confessed instantly.[16]

The textual examples already cited show that Greenwood's work can be seen as a tribute to, rather than an undermining of, Christie and her British detective fiction. Further titles in Greenwood's series cement this relationship of tribute: *Murder on the Ballarat Train, Dead Man's Chest, Death on Victoria Dock* and *Murder in Montparnasse* play on Christie's *Murder on the Orient Express, Dead Man's Folly, Death on the Nile* and *Murder in Mesopotamia*. Greenwood also makes explicit reference to one of Christie's novels in her short story collection, *A Question of Death* (2007), in which one of the stories is titled "The Body in the Library." However, a postcolonial response to Christie's work can indeed be traced in Greenwood, although it is one that is subtle rather than aggressive, and focused more on detective fiction in general rather than on Christie herself.

Greenwood responds in an ambivalent manner to dominant interwar detective fiction's conventions in that she subverts many of the Detection Club's rules of fair play, as indicated above. The club members insisted, for example, that authors should not rely on "mumbo jumbo" in solving mysteries, and that they should only use ghosts and Chinese characters in moderation.[17] By contrast, in *Death Before Wicket* (1999), "mumbo jumbo" is a thematic thread throughout the novel as two characters practice black magic and manipulate the behavior of other characters. Even Phryne participates in some of their rituals in order to solve the mystery. In many of the Miss Fisher Mystery novels, supernatural themes underpin the plot. In *Ruddy Gore* (1995), for example, a ghost haunts the set of a theatre and appears to make frequent spectral appearances, even leaving a mysterious smell. Moreover, Phryne's recurring love interest is a handsome Chinese man, Lin Chung. In these ways, Greenwood's series demonstrates resistance to British canonical detective fiction prescriptions. Consequently, I maintain that ambivalence is key to understanding the relationship between Greenwood and her precursors, in Australia and England, and to understanding the literary register in which she works.

Settler Narratives and Greenwood

Because of its emphasis on the roles of ambivalence and the status of a settler colony as "occup[ying] a site of struggle between contending 'regimes of value,'"[18] settler postcolonial theory, rather than postcolonialism *per se*, is more useful for analyzing Greenwood's series and its relationship to Christie's work because it is more relevant to writing in and about Australia than straightforward models of postcolonial "writing back." Settler postcolonial theory opens a space to consider what Alan Lawson has identified as settlers' ambivalent engagement with colonialism and the manifestation of this in literature. Lawson defines the settler subject as simultaneously colonizing and colonized, and explains that settlers have an ambivalent relationship to two points of reference: the old place of "authority" and new the place of "authenticity." The settler subject constantly oscillates, Lawson suggests, between these two poles and occupies a place of "double subjectivity," which makes settler narratives unstable and ambiguous.[19]

A similar dynamic can be seen in Greenwood's novels. On the one hand, the series manifestly draws from a place of *authority*—in this case from Christie—and it clearly refracts canonical detective fiction conventions onto an Australian milieu, even while subverting them. On the other hand, Greenwood does establish Australia as her place of *authenticity*, the place in which she engages with late colonial history. In her discussion of historical fiction in settler postcolonial domains, Victoria Kuttainen has shown that these narratives have particularly "shifty qualities."[20] Historical fiction in settler domains, she has argued, often displays an ambivalent relationship to time and history: a desire to be free of both the authority of empire and the guilt of a colonial past. Kuttainen draws on Tom Griffiths' proposal that Australian settler literature is fraught with a psychological guilt relating to colonial violence and dispossession. This guilt, she argues, manifests itself in texts exhibiting a compulsion to eradicate colonial wrongs and re-write history in order to reconstruct a more positive national image. In this vein, Greenwood attempts to revise an era of history burdened by the aftermath of colonial racial prejudice and to break from Christie's British milieu, stratified by class and race. Not only does Greenwood attempt to revise and reverse elitist imperial ideology, also she responds to these historical tensions by positively presenting an imagined community of characters who are not racist, as demonstrated in Phryne's and her household's close relationship with Lin Chung and his Chinese culture. In fact, Phryne's household represents a slice of society where racism during the interwar period is either non-existent or rapidly diminishing.

Still, whereas Greenwood's positive depictions of the Chinese in Australia show her attempt to confront past racism toward this group, they also present the fantasy of an inclusive multicultural interwar society. In reality, this was the era of the White Australia policy, fraught with prejudice and racial tensions, exemplified in the discourse that proliferated concerning the "yellow peril." Contemporary readers could be lulled into imagining that justice towards this marginalized group had already been served in Phryne's 1920s, but this is only a confection of Greenwood's, not a reflection of social or cultural reality. The Fisher series, then, appears structured by what Lawson classifies as settler postcolonial "ambivalence"[21]; oscillating between sympathy for the plight of the marginalized suffering at the hands of settlers and colonists, and complicity with colonization in continuing the erasure of history and seeking to assert a conciliatory narrative that places the white settler in a sympathetic and anachronous position. This does not mean that historical narratives within a postcolonial domain should be dismissed, but it does open a space for serious consideration of the cultural work undertaken by historical fiction, such as Greenwood's series, that engages with Australia's past.

Even with the fantasy element in the Fisher series, its attempts to correct the wrongs of a settler colonial past could be viewed as not merely escapist. More saliently, other readings point to ways the series provides not only entertaining fiction, but a potentially instructive agenda beneath its sleek surface, especially in terms of feminist and middlebrow interpretations. In fact, this is what is most exciting about the connections between the Australian contemporary author and a precursor like Agatha Christie. Greenwood's novels are not just a postcolonial tribute series: she draws out the "middlebrow" aspects of Christie's authorship and readership, and plays upon these, too.

The Phryne Fisher Series and Its Middling Position

In *The Feminine Middlebrow Novel 1920s to 1950s*, Nicola Humble offers this definition:

> The middlebrow novel is one that straddles the divide between the trashy romance or thriller on the one hand, and the philosophically or formally challenging novel on the other: offering narrative excitement without guilt, and intellectual stimulation without undue effort.[22]

In contrast to the recent recuperative criticism of scholars like Humble who affirm this middling position, Virginia Woolf derided the category of the middlebrow as inauthentic literature. She argues that there is a battle between "highbrows and lowbrows joined together in blood brotherhood against the bloodless and pernicious pest who comes between."[23] Until the rise of middlebrow studies, there has remained a persistent aversion in academia to scholarly study of books from this middling category, including Christie's fiction, even though they comprise a large portion of the books the public actually read. This is also because middlebrow fiction is supposedly driven not by artistic integrity but by commercial success.

If "brows" still matter and continue to inform assessments of literary value, then perspectives of the middlebrow could be useful in reading Greenwood's Phryne Fisher series and in exploring, again, another form of ambivalence in how the series dazzles readers with glamor and lures them with confection on the one hand, but also offers intellectual puzzle work and cultural critique on the other. In this way, I argue, Greenwood's fiction links two forms of "middling position"—as settler postcolonial writing positioned midway between colonial and colonizing writing, and as middlebrow literature between serious fiction and entertainment. In addition, the middlebrow has been linked by critics such as Humble to women's experience, and reading with an eye to this aspect of Greenwood's fiction alerts us to similar aspects of her precursor, Agatha Christie.

Humble has argued that between the 1920s and the 1950s, the feminine middlebrow novel in Britain was concerned with shifting gender roles, and elements of this can be seen in Christie's fiction. This is demonstrated by a break from old Victorian and Edwardian feminine molds with her inclusion of modern 1920s flapper-like figures. Tuppence Beresford and Lady Eileen "Bundle" Brent are two examples. Both exhibit a lack of Victorian sentimentality, are fearless and are accorded traditionally masculine attributes. For example, Tuppence plunges boldly into solving the mystery in *The Secret Adversary*, and the reader is told that she is "accustomed to take the lead" in her partnership with Tommy Beresford. At one point she is even labeled with the infamous name of Sherlock.[24] Further, she knows that she would not fit into the old mold of dutiful daughter because her father "has that delightful early Victorian view that short skirts and smoking are immoral. You can imagine what a thorn in the flesh I am to him," indicating her movement from Victorian standards of feminine behavior to more modern ones.[25] Bundle also proves to be more fearless and daring than her male counterparts in *The Seven Dials Mystery* (1929), willing to risk her safety by confining herself in a cramped cupboard in the perceived deadly Seven Dials enemy clubrooms in order to spy on their meeting. However, even with these headstrong, seemingly independent characters, marriage is never far from the plot and, with it, the suggestion that a woman's true identity lies in the domestic realm. Yet this is both complicated and affirmed by Christie. In *Partners in Crime* (1929), Tuppence, married and at home in her modern flat in suburbia, complains that that her domestic life is "satisfactory, but dull."[26] She longs for some excitement away from the monotony of her domestic duties, her exercise routine and her numerous shopping trips.[27] Her desire for something exciting is met when the chief of British Intelligence, Mr. Carter, suggests that Tuppence should again "try her hand at a little detective work" alongside her husband.[28] In this, Christie seems to suggest that marriage can be a partnership or a "joint venture" (as she repeatedly reminds us with Tuppence and Tommy in *The Secret Adversary*), rather than a hierarchy of gender roles. The multiple and sometimes ambivalent images of women in Christie's fiction— such as independent and strong women, and those who are married and enmeshed in domesticity—serve as a commentary on interwar modernity, where new roles for women were being carved out in unprecedented ways concurrent with the tensions that this created. This complex social undercurrent in Christie's work is a middlebrow theme, and one which Greenwood's series picks up.

Phryne's reverse migration and settlement back into Australia's interwar society, the tensions this brings, the resistance she encounters, and the new ground she occupies also reflects women's experience during this period, and this theme forms the backbone of the Fisher series. Angela Woollacott has noted that women of the 1920s were acquiring new skills for the workplace, which enabled them to be independent both financially and socially.[29]

Phryne's own flourishing career aligns with the increasingly independent status of women during this time, as does her refusal to be married and dependent on a man and his income, which is the case for Tuppence. Instead, Phryne's private detective services provide her income in part, supplemented by her investments in real estate and government stocks.[30] In the novel *Away with the Fairies* (2001), Phryne agrees with a female editor of a women's magazine, in whose opinion

> every woman can be educated, can have a career, can be the breadwinner for her family, can run a household and go into parliament or medicine or law, and when there are enough of us as doctors and lawyers and parliamentarians, when there are many women in public life, the Man cannot ignore us. We will take our rightful place.[31]

Throughout the Fisher series Phryne encourages other women to become independent and pursue careers, giving special attention to the development of her own adopted daughters, Jane and Ruth. She provides both girls with an education, formally and informally, encourages them to pursue future careers and gives them opportunities to foster their intellectual talents. Linked to this 1920s shift in women's work and independence is the increase in women's social freedom, and Phryne also exemplifies this change. Phryne's freedom to be mobile both spatially and socially helps further establish her status as a 1920s modern woman. Woollacott notes that "modernity, for white women, was linked to physical freedoms and mobility."[32] Phryne and Christie's Bundle exemplify Woollcott's claim, for both characters drive Hispano-Suiza sports cars, and Phryne, like Bundle, drives fast enough to terrify both her passengers and nearby pedestrians. The social and cultural issues that Greenwood and Christie engage with are historical concerns that framed the 1920s, and through the Fisher series, readers are provided with a window onto this pivotal period of Australia's colonial modernity, as Christie provides another such window onto British modernity. Even though Phryne is a fantasy figure in terms of her classlessness, her sexual liberty and her anachronistic attitude to race, she nonetheless may be seen to represent the 1920s woman and her gains in independence and autonomy.

Though Phryne reflects the shifting status of women during this period and indicates Greenwood's engagement with serious social themes, literary critics attached to notions of highbrow or serious literature may not find this enough to regard it an artefact worthy of scholarly attention. In particular, Greenwood's use of the detective fiction genre may itself be enough for critical, although not popular dismissal. This is another point at which Greenwood and Christie's work meets, as Christie's fiction has often been rejected in the academic domain. For Q. D. Leavis middlebrow fiction is a *"faux-bon,"* a consumable that leaves readers "with the agreeable sensation of having improved themselves without incurring fatigue."[33] Leavis also draws links between class, taste and gender:

> In the bestseller as we have known it since the author has poured his own daydreams, hot and hot, into dramatic form, without bringing them to any such touchstone as the "good sense, but not common-sense" of a cultivated society: the author is himself—or more usually herself—identified with the leading character, and the reader is invited to share the debauch.[34]

Leavis's dismissive attitude toward bestsellers here in particular, which she extends also to the middlebrow, provides evidence for Erica Brown and Mary Grover's contention that the middlebrow "is a nexus for prejudice towards the lower middle classes, the feminine and domestic, and towards narrative modes regarded as outdated."[35] Leavis is not the only esteemed critic to have scorned middlebrow literature and its place in the literary landscape. Max Horkheimer and Theodor Adorno labeled the "idiotic women's serial" as an object that "embraces the whole of mass culture" and exemplifies the way the culture industry can lull society into a mediocre existence that "corrupts" the individual.[36] Such comments are provocative for feminist scholarship. This is because these pejorative undertones perpetuate gender hierarchies, linking books, authors and judgments of taste with gender. In addition, as Faye Hammill points out, "much middlebrow writing has been ignored by the academy because of a misperception that it is so straightforward as to require no analysis, while in fact, its witty, polished surfaces frequently conceal unexpected depths and subtleties."[37] The historical, cultural and social depths of Greenwood's fiction are at least partially concealed by the novels' glossy covers and their protagonist's glamorous persona. Greenwood is honest enough, though, to acknowledge the fantasy aspect of her protagonist. She states:

> Because I wanted her to be a female wish-fulfilment figure, I wanted her to be like James Bond, with better clothes and fewer gadgets.... All I really did was take a male hero of the time and allow her to be female. No one thinks it odd that James Bond has blondes and no regrets.... The modern women detectives are afflicted with self-doubt, neglect their diets, worry about exercise, think they may be growing fat (as if fat was a disfigurement), and are generally burdened with low self-esteem and guilt.[38]

However, a fantastic surface does not signify a complete absence of depth, as Light and Kaplan have shown separately with Christie's fiction. Alison Light argues: "For Christie it was by denying the feminine (in its late Victorian and Edwardian dress) and by ventriloquizing what had been the male part, cheerily domesticated, that she could find ways of speaking as a modern woman. Reticence could be a form of conservative self-protection but also if a new-found power."[39] Light affirms the depths that can be plumbed in Christie's fiction, beyond its entertaining surface. So too are there depths to be explored in Greenwood's fiction, even though it is something with which few critics have engaged. Yet Bookscan data shows that Greenwood is in the top twenty Australian authors for the early twenty-first century and, outside the scholarly domain, her novels are widely discussed in terms of Australia's literary landscape.[40] The popularity of her novels is compounded by the success of the television series, *Miss Fisher's Murder Mysteries* (2012–present), which has been met with acclaim in Australia and overseas. Of course, much like Christie's fiction, Greenwood's market success may itself suggest the series' commercial ambitions and its place in commodity culture rather than literature, and this success may be one reason the series could be dismissed as an escapist fantasy that is too facile for scholarly critique.

Recent critical work on production and reception in the Australian literary field offers insight into the reception and classification of Greenwood's series, along with other fiction written by women. Bode analyzes the increasing number of female fiction writers in Australia's literary landscape. Her statistical analysis demonstrates that "women now dominate the Australian novel field." However, Bode suggests, "far from being a sign of women's liberation ... this gender trend in authorship has produced a de-valuing of this literary form, and a re-establishment of male novelists at the centre of critical discussion and acclaim."[41] At this center she places Peter Carey, David Malouf, David Williamson, Les Murray and Patrick White, who are the top five Australian authors discussed in the academic domain.[42] Her argument echoes scholars of the middlebrow, who claim that cultural devaluation and gender are linked: "constructions of modernism are gendered, associating literary value with masculinity and exile, and thus implicitly associating the feminine and domestic with the devalued middlebrow."[43] Bode does not discuss women writers in terms of middlebrow authors, but she does mention in her notes that "when I refer to literary fiction I am [also referring to] the broader category of middlebrow fiction ... the books we find in the 'good book stores.'"[44] Greenwood is included in her discussions on authors of literary fiction, and Bode points out that despite much general dialogue around Greenwood's work, it is "not prominent in academic journals."[45] The link between the devaluation of women's fiction, the preference for male novelists in critical scholarship, and the middling category of Greenwood's fiction may explain why the Fisher series has been overlooked by most literary scholars. The series' market success, its tentative alignment with a middlebrow perspective, and its potential to enable critical readings, can nevertheless be easily dismissed in a scholarly domain that, as Bode has shown, prefers male fiction over female fiction. Yet as discussed in this chapter, middlebrow scholars have sought to recover fiction dismissed as too facile for scholarly analysis, especially during the golden age of this mid-range fiction that appealed to massifying and professionalizing urban readerships: Christie's milieu of the 1920s. These scholars have argued for the value of middlebrow fiction in that it can provide a means to comment on social change and shifting values, and they affirm that this fiction can also provide a window onto women's experience. Humble, Kaplan and Light's work on Christie serves as an exemplar for this type of project. Likewise, as Greenwood gestures to Christie and signals to the middlebrow in general, even so far as enabling her fiction to be positioned within this category, the Fisher series can also provide insights into society and culture. It can urge readers, as Christie's fiction does, to consider women's experience critically. Even with the obvious fantasy element in the series, to dismiss it on literary value only affirms the downward trend for profiling and assessing women's writing that Bode's work highlights.

I have attempted to show that Kerry Greenwood's fiction offers much to consider, not least in its tentative tribute to, and ambivalent critique of, canonical British detective fiction. In such a way, Greenwood's Phryne Fisher series can be read in terms of its settler postcolonial relationship to its British precursor, namely Agatha Christie. This characteristic ambivalence is also a theme in Greenwood's work, as well as a structuring principle. I have argued that Greenwood's engagement with both history and social themes can be read in terms of another position of ambivalence: the middlebrow. Partly a confected fantasy, yet partly also a serious social critique that reaches a wide readership, the Fisher series connects with and highlights women's experience in Australia. As the Fisher series connects two "middling" aspects of Greenwood's writing—the settler postcolonial and the middlebrow—these draw out fresh ways of reading the work of her precursor: Christie. Greenwood arguably plays with the canonical conventions of the golden age of British detective fiction, but reading her fiction from an affirmative middlebrow position also draws attention to the ways in which Christie's strong heroines subvert some dominant aspects of the British literary tradition. Greenwood comments on Australia's late colonial modernity, and draws the reader's attention away from male pioneer and bush narratives that have dominated Australian literature, towards a period of modernity where women were carving out new roles in a distinctly urban environment. Christie's fiction possesses similar qualities of social critique and comment. These middlebrow feminist and settler postcolonial frames of interpretation force clever forms of analysis, not merely on solving fictional crimes. They suggest that further work might be productively undertaken on Christie's own engagement with imperial and colonial themes.

NOTES

1. Mitzi M. Brunsdale, *Icons of Mystery and Crime Detection: From Sleuths to Superheroes* (Westport: Greenwood Press, 2010), p. 615; Hallie Ephron, "'The Deadly Dozen' Mistakes in Mystery Writing," *The Writer* 121 (2008), pp. 26–29 (p. 26).

2. Sue Ryan-Fazilleau, "Kerry Greenwood's 'Rewriting' of Agatha Christie," *Journal of the Association for the Study of Australian Literature* 7 (2007), pp. 59–70 (p. 59).

3. See Bill Ashcroft, Gareth Griffiths and Helen Tiffin's *The Empire Writes Back* (London: Routledge 1989).
4. *Ibid.*
5. *Ibid.*, p. 60.
6. *Ibid.*, p. 61.
7. Elleke Boehmer, "Postcolonialism" in Patricia Waugh (ed.), *Literary Theory and Criticism: An Oxford Guide* (Oxford: Oxford University Press, 2006), pp. 340–61 (p. 342).
8. Kerry Greenwood, *Death by Water* (Scottsdale: Poisoned Pen Press, 2005), p. 15.
9. Agatha Christie, *Agatha Christie 1920s Omnibus: The Secret Adversary* (London: HarperCollins, 2006), p. 101. Emphasis added.
10. Kerry Greenwood, *Raisins and Almonds* (Scottsdale: Poisoned Pen Press, 2002), p. 130.
11. Christie, *The Secret Adversary*, p. 59.
12. Kerry Greenwood, *Dead Man's Chest* (Scottsdale: Poisoned Pen Press, 2002), p. 55.
13. Kerry Greenwood, *Murder and Mendelssohn* (Crow's Nest: Allen & Unwin, 2013), p. 16.
14. Greenwood, *Raisins and Almonds*, back cover.
15. Kerry Greenwood, *The Green Mill Murder* (Scottsdale: Poisoned Pen Press, 1993), p. 83.
16. Greenwood, *Murder and Mendelssohn*, p. 166.
17. Brunsdale, *Icons of Mystery and Crime Detection*, p. 615.
18. Graham Huggan, *The Postcolonial Exotic: Marketing the Margins* (New York: Routledge, 2001), p. 5.
19. Alan Lawson, "Difficult Relations: Narrative Instability Is Settler Cultures" in Matria-Alzira Seixo, John Noyes, Garça Abreu, and Isabel Moutinho (eds.), *Proceedings of The Paths of Multiculturalism: Travel Writings and Postcolonialism* (Lisboa: Edicoes Cosmos, 2000), pp. 49–60 (p. 50).
20. Victoria Kuttainen, *Unsettling Stories: Settler Postcolonialism and the Short Story Composite* (Newcastle-upon-Tyne: Cambridge Scholars, 2010), p. 7.
21. Lawson, "Difficult Relations," p. 53.
22. Nicola Humble, *The Feminine Middlebrow Novel, 1920s-1950s* (Oxford: Oxford University Press, 2001), p. 11.
23. Woolf, "Middlebrow," p. 156.
24. Christie, *The Secret Adversary*, pp. 80, 40.
25. *Ibid.*, p. 8.
26. Agatha Christie, *Partners in Crime* (London: HarperCollins, 2001), p. 14.
27. *Ibid.*, pp. 9–11.
28. *Ibid.*, p. 16.
29. Angela Woollacott, "White Colonialism and Sexual Modernity: Australian Women in the Early Twentieth Century Metropolis" in Antoinette Burton (ed.), *Gender, Sexuality and Colonial Modernities* (London: Routledge 1999), pp. 49–62.
30. Kerry Greenwood, *Murder on the Ballarat Train* (Scottsdale: Poisoned Pen Press, 1991), p. 419.
31. Kerry Greenwood, *Away with the Fairies* (Scottsdale: Poisoned Pen Press, 2001), p. 38.
32. Woollacott, "White Colonialism and Sexual Modernity," p. 58.
33. Q. D. Leavis, *Fiction and the Reading Public* (London: Chatto & Windus, 1939), pp. 39, 37.

34. *Ibid.*, p. 236.
35. Erica Brown and Mary Grover (eds.), *Middlebrow Literary Cultures: The Battle of the Brows, 1920–1960* (Houndmills: Palgrave Macmillan, 2012), p. 1.
36. Max Horkheimer and Theodore W. Adorno, "Dialectic of Enlightenment" in Vincent B. Leitch (ed.), *The Norton Anthology of Theory and Criticism*, 2d ed. (New York: Norton, 2010), pp. 1107–1126 (p. 1122).
37. Faye Hammill, *Women, Celebrity, and Literary Culture Between the Wars* (Austin: University of Texas Press, 2007), p. 6.
38. Kerry Greenwood, *A Question of Death: An Illustrated Phryne Fisher Treasury* (Scottsdale: Poisoned Pen Press, 2007), p. xi.
39. Alison Light, *Forever England: Femininity, Literature and Conservatism Between the Wars* (London: Routledge, 1991), p. 108.
40. Katherine Bode, *Reading by Numbers: Recalibrating the Literary Field* (London: Anthem Press, 2012), p. 161.
41. *Ibid.*, p. 6.
42. *Ibid.*, p. 161.
43. Brown and Grover, *Middlebrow Literary Cultures*, p. 10.
44. Bode, *Reading by Numbers*, p. 205.
45. *Ibid.*, p. 161.

Bibliography

Boehmer, Elleke. "Postcolonialism" in Patricia Waugh (ed.), *Literary Theory and Criticism: An Oxford Guide*. Oxford: Oxford University Press, 2003, pp. 340–61.
Bode, Katherine. *Reading by Numbers: Recalibrating the Literary Field*. London: Anthem Press, 2012.
Brown, Erica, and Mary Grover (eds.). *Middlebrow Literary Cultures: The Battle of the Brows, 1920–1960*. Houndmills: Palgrave Macmillan, 2012.
Brunsdale, Mitzi M. *Icons of Mystery and Crime Detection: From Sleuths to Superheroes*. Westport: Greenwood Press, 2010.
Carter, David. "The Mystery of the Missing Middlebrow or the C(o)urse of Good Taste" in Judith Ryan and Chris Wallace-Crabbe (eds.), *Imagining Australia: Literature and Culture in the New World*. Cambridge: Harvard University Press, 2004, pp. 173–201.
Christie, Agatha. *Partners in Crime* (1929), London: HarperCollins, 2001.
_____. *The Secret Adversary* (1922). *Agatha Christie 1920s Omnibus*. London: HarperCollins, 2006, pp. 1–218.
_____. *The Seven Dials Mystery* (1929). *Agatha Christie 1920s Omnibus*. London: HarperCollins, 2006, pp. 645–841.
Ephron, Hallie. "'The Deadly Dozen' Mistakes in Mystery Writing." *The Writer* 121 (2008), pp. 26–29.
Greenwood, Kerry. *Away with the Fairies*, Scottsdale: Poisoned Pen Press, 2001.
_____. *Cocaine Blues*. Scottsdale: Poisoned Pen Press, 1989.
_____. *Dead Man's Chest*. Scottsdale: Poisoned Pen Press, 2010.
_____. *Death Before Wicket*. Scottsdale: Poisoned Pen Press, 2003.
_____. *Death by Water*. Scottsdale: Poisoned Pen Press, 2005.
_____. *The Green Mill Murder*. Scottsdale: Poisoned Pen Press, 1993.
_____. *Murder and Mendelssohn*. Crows Nest: Allen & Unwin, 2013.

_____. *Murder on the Ballarat Train.* Scottsdale: Poisoned Pen Press, 1991.
_____. *A Question of Death: An Illustrated Phryne Fisher Treasury.* Scottsdale: Poisoned Pen Press, 2007.
_____. *Raisins and Almonds.* Scottsdale: Poisoned Pen Press, 2002.
_____. *Ruddy Gore.* Scottsdale: Poisoned Pen Press, 1995.
_____. *Urn Burial.* Scottsdale: Poisoned Pen Press, 2003.
Griffiths, Tom. "A Haunted Country" in Jennifer McDonnell and Michael Deves (eds.), *Land and Identity.* Sydney: Association for the Study of Australian Literature, 1998.
Hammill, Faye. *Women, Celebrity, and Literary Culture Between the Wars.* Austin: University of Texas Press, 2007.
Horkheimer, Max, and Theodore W. Adorno. "Dialectic of Enlightenment" in Vincent B. Leitch (ed.), *The Norton Anthology of Theory and Criticism*, 2d ed. New York: Norton, 2010, pp. 1107–1126.
Humble, Nicola. *The Feminine Middlebrow Novel 1920s to 1950s: Class, Domesticity, and Bohemianism.* Oxford: Oxford University Press, 2001.
Kuttainen, Victoria. *Unsettling Stories: Settler Postcolonialism and the Short Story Composite.* Newcastle-upon-Tyne: Cambridge Scholars, 2010.
Lawson, Alan. "Difficult Relations: Narrative Instability is Settler Cultures" in Matria-Alzira Seixo et al. (eds.), *Proceedings of The Paths of Multiculturalism: Travel Writings and Postcolonialism.* Lisboa: Edicoes Cosmos, 2000, pp. 49–60.
Leavis, Q. D. *Fiction and the Reading Public.* London: Chatto & Windus, 1939.
Light, Alison. *Forever England: Femininity, Literature and Conservatism Between the Wars.* London: Routledge, 1991.
Radway, Janice A. *A Feeling for Books: The Book-of-the-Month Club, Literary Taste, and Middle-Class Desire.* Chapel Hill: University of North Carolina Press, 1997.
Ryan-Fazilleau, Sue. "Kerry Greenwood's 'Rewriting' of Agatha Christie." *Journal of the Association for the Study of Australian Literature* 7 (2007), pp. 59–70.
Woolf, Virginia. "Middlebrow." *The Death of the Moth and Other Essays* (1932). Harmondsworth: Penguin, 1942, pp. 152–60.
Woollacott, Angela. "White Colonialism and Sexual Modernity: Australian Women in the Early Twentieth Century Metropolis" in Antoinette Burton (ed.), *Gender, Sexuality and Colonial Modernities.* London: Routledge, 1999, pp. 49–62.

Autobiography in *Agatha* (1979)
"*An imaginary solution to an authentic mystery*"

SARAH STREET

On December 4, 1926, Agatha Christie, aged 36, disappeared inexplicably. Her car was found on the Surrey Downs with few clues as to her whereabouts. The case became a *cause célèbre* as detectives and the public searched for the author. After eleven days she turned up in a hotel in Harrogate where she had registered under a false name. While speculation ensued that she had been suffering from memory loss, or mental instability following her mother's death, the full story behind the episode was never revealed, not least in her autobiography published posthumously in 1977.[1] Kathleen Tynan published a novel in 1978 about the incident which formed the basis for her screenplay for *Agatha* (directed by Michael Apted, 1979), a film starring Vanessa Redgrave and Dustin Hoffman.[2] Released at a time when interest in Christie was particularly intense—her death, the autobiography, a spate of film adaptations of her novels—the film represents a desire to know, to "write" those missing sections of the autobiography in a way that Tynan and others involved in the film's production felt to be true to her character. This essay discusses how a controversial biographical incident became translated into a film that was similarly controversial, but not just because of its subject matter. Through the twists and turns of a tortuous film production, I examine broader issues relating to celebrity, authenticity, memory and fiction related to those eleven "lost" days of Agatha Christie's life.

The title of this essay is a quotation from Kathleen Tynan. "An imaginary solution to an authentic mystery" is an epigraph at the beginning of her book *Agatha*; the phrase also opens the film. It is appropriate because the book and film explore the tension between notions of authenticity and imagination arising from an incident in Christie's life (authenticity) about which she thereafter kept silent (giving rise to imagination). This situation has led to many interpretations of what might have happened—Christie's fame as a mystery writer compounds curiosity about her real life and public desire for the author of thrillers to have a suitably mysterious life. Yet as a popular figure she commanded great respect, which influenced responses to Tynan's book and the film.

In her autobiography Christie writes that she hates recalling a part of her life that was unhappy. Her mother had died and her husband Archie was of little support during her period of grieving. He stayed in London and started a relationship with Nancy Neele, the former secretary of one of his business associates, while Agatha cleared away her beloved mother's possessions. She felt lonely and recalls becoming tearful and absent-minded, forgetting her name on one occasion when signing a check. When Archie returned, she felt him to be a stranger; he told her he was in love with someone else and wanted a divorce: "He would hardly speak to me or answer when he was spoken to … he was fighting for his happiness."[3] Ill, depressed and unable to write fiction since her mother's death, Christie was haunted by self-reproach during this dark period: "If I'd been cleverer, if I had known more about my husband—had troubled to know more about him instead of being content to idealize him and consider him more or less perfect—then perhaps I might have avoided all of this."[4] Despite these elements of self-reflection and introspection, the autobiography makes no reference to the eleven days when she was missing, implying that it was a chapter Christie preferred to be kept private: forgetfulness should be forgotten.

At the time, the disappearance attracted great speculation. The first sign of anything wrong was when Christie's car was found abandoned down a slope at Newlands Corner near Guildford.[5] In the car were her fur coat, a suitcase and an expired driver's license; Christie was nowhere to be found. The newspapers had a field day reporting the case while the Silent Pool, a natural spring near the scene of the car accident, was searched in case the novelist had drowned. Theories abounded—some suspected her husband of foul play—and even the crime writer Dorothy L. Sayers visited the scene of the disappearance in search of clues. Some sources claim that Christie had written letters before she disappeared, one to Archie which he burned, one instructing her secretary to cancel reservations for a trip to Yorkshire and, confusingly, a letter to her brother-in-law Campbell saying she was going to Yorkshire for a recuperating break. Inclined towards spiritualism, Sir Arthur Conan Doyle took one of Agatha's gloves to a medium. Christie was eventually found in the Hydropathic Hotel, Harrogate where she had registered as "Mrs. Teresa Neele of Cape Town," Neele being the surname of Archie's lover. Several people there had suspected her real identity, including journalist Peter Ritchie-Calder who was probably the basis of the character Wally Stanton in Tynan's novel. Without any clear information forthcoming from Agatha Christie about what had happened, her disappearance was put down to a loss of memory. Yet her silence on the matter did not result in drawing a line under the incident. Public curiosity was insatiable regarding this moment of non-conformity, which appeared both shocking and fascinating at the same time.

Many years later, these known facts—sparse but intriguing—interested novelist Kathleen Tynan, who turned to them for her screenplay and book, her "imaginative" response to an "authentic mystery." The memory loss was referred to in Tynan's book by the doctor who examines Agatha in Harrogate as *la belle indifférence*, apparently a medical description of amnesia. In the novel Agatha translates this as "a fine indifference ... or perhaps "blithe" would be a better translation?"[6] This implies a sagacious knowingness about the disappearance, a desire to be someone else for a brief time in order to cope with personal trauma. This sympathetic premise is key to Tynan's vision for *Agatha*, one that became embroiled in the machinations of filmmaking practice as the production proceeded. Apart from exploiting intense public interest in Christie, the film involved conflict between other celebrities and professionals who in their different ways struggled to make sense of this puzzling event in Christie's life.

Adapting Agatha *for the Screen*

Agatha was a tortuous film production that went ahead in spite of many difficulties. Registered as a British film but financed mostly by American capital, many British and American personnel were involved in the complex development and production process. British director Michael Apted was particularly distinguished for his work in television and all of the location shooting took place in the UK including at Harrogate, Bath, York and at Bray Studios. The production team consisted of Gavrik Losey, David Puttnam and Jarvis Astaire, British producers who contributed particular expertise at key stages, but Losey had the greatest creative input. The American production companies that financed the film were Sweetwall Productions, Warner Bros. and First Artists. Sweetwall Productions was owned by actor Dustin Hoffman, the main co-star in *Agatha*, who also had an interest in the film via First Artists. First Artists was a somewhat unusual operation since as a subsidiary of Warner Bros. it had been founded in 1969 by very high-profile actors: Barbra Streisand, Sidney Poitier and Paul Newman, who were subsequently joined by Steve McQueen and Dustin Hoffman. The company's aim was to give these actors greater artistic control over productions than was usual, and Hoffman's two films for the company were *Agatha* and *Straight Time* (1978). This meant that Hoffman's expectations for having considerable executive control over *Agatha* were high and his First Artists contract stipulated that he could only star or co-star in a film rather than be a supporting actor. However, correspondence on the film held at the Bill Douglas Cinema Museum in the University of Exeter shows that Hoffman's personal ambitions for a high degree of creative control were frustrated by a number of factors that make the film fascinating for reasons that extend beyond the controversial nature of its subject matter.[7] During production many people became concerned for different reasons—financial, creative and personal.

Public interest in Agatha Christie, combined with renewed curiosity about her brief disappearance following the publication of her autobiography and Tynan's book, made for an excellent prospect for screen adaptation. Any speculations about the disappearance so soon after Christie's death were, however, bound to require great care in showing how a novelist with Christie's popular profile might have responded to common experiences of family bereavement and marital betrayal. Before the various revisions of the screenplay are considered, along with the difficulties that made the production so tortuous, a brief account of the film's narrative is necessary in order to evaluate its final speculations about the disappearance in comparison with the book and first screenplay. The film is not a straightforward adaptation of Tynan's book, but many key details are similar, contributing to a well-acted and in many ways powerful and evocative screen account of those lost days in Harrogate.

Agatha starts with the lead-up to the disappearance of Agatha Christie (Vanessa Redgrave) and concentrates on her retiring manner at a literary luncheon, her husband Archie's (Timothy Dalton) coldness towards her and his announcement over breakfast that he wants a divorce. Key plot points are revealed early on, such as Agatha finding out that Archie's lover Nancy Neele plans to visit to a spa to undertake weight-loss treatment. The important character Wally Stanton (Dustin Hoffman), an American journalist visiting the UK who attends the literary luncheon, is introduced. He befriends local journalist John Foster (Paul Brooke) who is also interested in following Christie's increasing fame as a popular novelist after the publication of *The Murder of Roger Ackroyd* (1926), the book being celebrated at the luncheon. Stanton tries to see Agatha at her house but is sent away by Archie who is angered by the intrusion. Agatha leaves and we see her car crash as she swerves to avoid a dog, a detail not in Tynan's book, which simply states that "she drove off wildly and at speed in the direction of Newlands Corner."[8] The car is found empty and a major search begins at the Silent Pool and surrounding area. Archie does not seem too perturbed, dismissing the idea of suicide as "ridiculous."

The film then shows Agatha on the train to Harrogate where she registers as Teresa Neele from Cape Town. The shots of her journey are particularly effective in suggesting a temporal and emotional break with her past life. A close-up of her sitting on the train at first has her face obscured but the flicker of the light then illuminates her face intermittently as she stares ahead, responding to the staccato strobe effect by shutting her eyes. The screen fades to black and we next see her face more fully lit, presumably after sleeping, and she looks more engaged as the train enters the station in Harrogate. In a few seconds of screen-time a rupture has been suggested that is similar to the dreaming effect in *Brief Encounter* (David Lean, 1945), another film dealing with a female protagonist in the midst of a personal crisis and with train travel as suggestive of both contemplation and transgression.

At the hotel Agatha befriends Evelyn Crawley (Helen Morse), a resident who is receiving treatment at the baths. Agatha avidly follows the arrival of Nancy Neele (Celia Gregory) without confronting her and pretending to Evelyn that she is curious about Nancy as a possible relative. At the baths Agatha becomes fascinated with the workings of the equipment, taking notes and conducting research as if she is a detective. Meanwhile, Wally has been following Agatha Christie's disappearance. He learns of Archie's affair indirectly from John Foster and then from Agatha's secretary and confidant Charlotte Fisher (Carolyn Pickles) via an advertisement Agatha has put in the *Times* under the name of Teresa Neele, which Charlotte takes as a signal that she is safe. Wally goes to Harrogate suspecting that Agatha has gone in search of Nancy. Soon after arriving he befriends Teresa Neele and gradually falls in love with her, knowing she is Agatha Christie but not letting her know he has seen through her pretense. While Teresa/Agatha is wary at first, she appears to some extent attracted by Wally, enjoying dancing, swimming and talking with him at the hotel. It seems that Agatha's research at the baths covers how to cause a fatal accident with the electrical equipment, planting the suspicion that she is going to use this knowledge to kill Nancy. But we eventually learn that her plan, which involves Agatha pretending to work at the baths and switching around crucial electricity current dials on the apparatus, is for Nancy to unintentionally kill Agatha; suicide by proxy. Wally becomes suspicious of Agatha's behavior and guesses her plan. After a suspenseful sequence involving Wally running to the baths, desperately searching for Agatha in the treatment rooms, he interrupts the "accident" in time to revive Agatha after her brief exposure to electric shock. Nancy had turned up for treatment and was asked by someone (Agatha) she mistook for Mrs. Braithwaite, the usual person who administered treatment, to turn on the electric current. Not realizing that the "on" and "off" dials had deliberately been tampered with, Nancy ignites a terrifying blast of electricity. Wally rushes in and, to Nancy's horror, they find that that the person shaking in the chair is Agatha. Wally revives her after switching off the current.

Agatha is saved by Wally's timely intervention. Producer Gavrik Losey wanted it to be clear in the film that Agatha's attempt would not have worked, that she was an amateur blundering in the world of electricity and that "all she would succeed in doing is blowing the rheostat and giving herself some sharper, nastier shocks than the machine normally gives."[9] Nevertheless, these finer details were not included in the film; instead, Wally tells her when she recovers that her plan was "very clever." In addition, the need for great care over Christie's image in the film explains why in Tynan's book Agatha tries, but fails due to an interruption, an experimental "dry run" of murder on Nancy, an incident that does not feature in the film. Tynan did not approve of this omission—she thought the "dry run" was "essential to the plot ... she must appear to be carrying out one of her own stories."[10] To imply that Agatha was in the end not planning a perfect murder, the book refers to a letter written to Evelyn explaining about the suicide intention. In the film, neither the "dry run" nor the letter were included, nevertheless leaving the impression that she did indeed intend to kill herself. Both book and film were caught between needing to maintain suspense for much of the plot, while taking care to suggest that even though Christie wrote murder mysteries she would never entertain committing murder herself.

After the news of the missing author being found spreads, Archie reveals little about the incident at a press conference, puts down Agatha's disappearance to illness and denies that he has been having an affair. Agatha visits Wally for a final time before leaving Harrogate; he tells her he loves her and that he will not publish the story. By this time their relationship is mutually respectful even if Agatha cannot return Wally's affections. Agatha says she will go back to Archie because they must get a divorce, a remark that Wally comments on as a "surprise ending." He watches as Agatha and Archie leave Harrogate on the train. Echoing the final words of the book at the end of the film, a title informs us that two years later the Christies divorced.[11]

A Contested Production and the Hoffman Factor

The above version of events that reached the screen only reflects part of Kathleen Tynan's original vision, which related more closely to her book. Many compromises were reached along the way, making the production a highly contested one for creative as well as financial reasons. The credited screenwriters were Kathleen Tynan with revisions by Arthur Hopcraft. Murray Schisgal and Christopher Hampton also contributed but they were not credited. By examining the screenplay's evolution during the production process, it becomes clear that key details and nuances of character were omitted, some more striking than others. When films are adapted from books, the editing of details and even the cutting of major elements is often necessary, but with *Agatha* the process caused an unusual amount of contention that started in autumn 1977 and continued during 1978 before the film was completed and finally released in February 1979.

Tynan was made aware of the need for changes to the original script but was not entirely comfortable with them all, writing to director Michael Apted that she felt "let down" and that "some of the tone of the film and the meat are being irretrievably lost."[12] One major change was the reduction of the significance of the character Evelyn, Agatha's new friend in Harrogate. In the book she is a close confidante who accompanies her on shopping and bathing trips, and who Agatha generally uses to gauge the impact of her new persona as Teresa Neele. Losey later commented: "The principle of the script, which would have made a better film, was that it was the tale of two women" (Agatha and Evelyn).[13] Changes in casting might have influenced the decision to reduce the role of Evelyn after Julie Christie, forced by ill health to pull out of the production, was replaced by Helen Morse, a less high-profile actor. Tynan was not entirely happy with the reduction of Evelyn's role, but accepted it. She wrote to Michael Apted on 20 November 1977: "The film must ... work as a psychological thriller; a study of a woman in crisis who because of the experience she undergoes, and with the help of two catalysts—Wally and Evelyn—changes and grows. Of course Evelyn's part had to be curtailed, both from the plot point of view, as well as her relations with Agatha. Wally can do the same but better."[14] Advertising for the book and film reflects the augmentation of Wally as a character and also Hoffman's co-star billing. The book features Vanessa Redgrave as Agatha in the foreground with Hoffman as Wally in the background whereas in the film poster this positioning is reversed.[15]

Tynan's comments do show some agreement with changes to Wally's role but in view of her criticism of some of the script changes it seems she was not happy with the extent of this, even claiming that Hoffman did not want this:

> In principle I think it's daft to write in scenes for Dustin that don't carry the film forward plotwise or emotionally. It's quite evident how magical Dustin and Vanessa are together. I think it would only be damaging to Dustin's part to overexpose it just for the sake of putting him on camera whenever we can. He's always opposed that idea from the very first meetings we had.[16]

There is great stress on Agatha's vulnerability in the book and her state of mind is signaled very early on, but as an inevitable result of adaptation from page to screen there is less opportunity for quite this depth of despair to surface in the film, Redgrave's performance notwithstanding. In both the book and the film, however, Agatha's assumed identity as Teresa Neele allows her to step outside of herself, a process observed most keenly by Wally who understands that this helps her psychologically. His collusion with her pretense is clearly motivated by a desire to be close to the famous writer, while at the same time allowing him to collect the information he needs as a journalist.

Despite the fact that much was made of the augmentation of Wally's role as a result of Hoffman's First Artists contract that stated he could only star or co-star in a film, Wally was always a central character in the book. The main difference in the film is that there is more physical intimacy and suggestion of romance, for example in a scene when Wally asks Teresa/Agatha if she would "care for a kiss" which she refuses at first, although she later returns the question with the opposite result. There is also a scene in which Wally and Teresa/Agatha are swimming, with him supporting her body tenderly as she appears to struggle against the water. These scenes risk cheapening their relationship, which in the book is more subtle, a point Tynan was keen to stress must be handled carefully in the absence of a more prominent role for Evelyn. Giving Evelyn more emotional weight in the book was arguably safer than exaggerating the romance angle with Wally to the extent that it is in the film, since the latter is in danger of making Agatha more akin to Archie who is cast as unloving and unfaithful.

As the production progressed Tynan was less involved and additional writers were brought in to work on the script; Hoffman also made many suggestions for re-shooting scenes. *Agatha* went well over budget which prevented Hoffman from having the executive control over final cut he desired. The film started out with a relatively modest budget of £1,728,004 but this rocketed as re-shoots commenced, largely demanded by Hoffman who was eager to extend his role as Wally Stanton. Hoffman was keen to explain that in asking for re-shoots he was trying to perfect his performance rather than wanting to be on screen simply for the sake of his personal aggrandizement. This can be ascertained from a long report published in *Variety* early in 1979 where Hoffman defends his position, claiming that First Artists and not he pushed for the augmentation of his role.

> I feel somewhat passionate about this ... because First Artists has tried to use the old reliable ego formula with stars in the press. The star wanted it rewritten for him, they seem to be saying. Number one, I would have just as well preferred to have a part that was supporting, but they wouldn't allow it. Number two, when it was to be made co-starring and I asked for the extra three weeks of rehearsal, that was *all* I asked for.[17]

Despite these protestations and even though Wally's romantic attachment to Agatha was accentuated in the finished film, Hoffman was frustrated at not being able to exert more of an influence in the editing stage. We get a fairly detailed sense of his wishes for the film in a letter from editor Jim Clark to Phil Feldman, First Artists' president and chief executive, in which some of Hoffman's suggestions are discussed.[18] Cross-cutting different scenes was one preferred strategy; for example, in the film's opening scene Hoffman wanted the film to convey a greater sense of the complex emotions going through Agatha's head as she watches an engraver completing work on a gift for Archie, a tankard engraved: "Archie, my love, my friend, Agatha." Clark records that they tried cross-cutting this scene with footage of publishers Collins & Fisher waiting for Agatha to go to the literary reception, but "this became scrappy and confusing." Similarly in the literary lunch scene, Hoffman wanted more cross-cutting between Agatha and Wally but Clark interpreted this request as Hoffman wanting to make up for an inadequate performance: "I feel we can't go any further than we have.... If Dustin wanted more out of this he should have played the scene in a less passive manner at the time. I get a little tired of actors who expect the editor to "create" something they didn't deliver when they had the opportunity."

On the other hand some of Hoffman's recommendations were carried out: for example, he requested that a scene of Teresa/Agatha and Wally joyfully dancing in the hotel should be intercut with the desperate searches for Christie. This underlines the stark contrast between the personal abandon in a luxury hotel experienced by Agatha and the great number of people and level of resources and seriousness behind the nationwide search for the missing author. For the scene in the swimming pool that represented "the peak of trust" between them, Hoffman wanted even more explicit suggestion of romance, an idea that Clark was not sympathetic toward: "I searched through all that footage for the most 'romantic' elements, and cannot believe we had anything more touching." Clark writes: "If Dustin believes there was footage with 'so much love in it' which I haven't used, let him come find it. Maybe our definition of the word 'love' is different. I've been through that footage a 1000 times and it hasn't yielded more riches." Hoffman's suggestions were clearly interpreted as unhelpful interference by professionals such as Clark who were unused to actors trying to assume a major role beyond their performance.

It would seem, then, that Hoffman did exert a degree of influence in spite of his overall impression of being reined-in as the budget spiraled out of control. He was allowed to shoot a key scene towards the end of the film in which Wally once again declares his love for Agatha in a hotel as she recovers from her ordeal. It represents the conclusion of their relationship as Wally says he will not publish the story, which would surely have been a great professional scoop, and Agatha appears to care a little for Wally even though she makes it clear that she will return to Archie. Wally hands her his story, which she places in his suitcase as she gently folds his shirts, kneeling down and handling his clothes with loving care. Such gestures of tenderness are to convince the viewer that they have formed a deep friendship for which she is grateful. As Jim Clark's comments reveal, this was about as far as the rest of the production team was prepared to go with the romance angle, a view that chimed with Losey's awareness that it needed to remain as one-sided as possible. Despite the controversy Hoffman was pleased with aspects of the final film, including Vanessa Redgrave's performance and the cinematography, as well as claiming that he always maintained respect for Kathleen Tynan's original screenplay.[19] These may have been diplomatic remarks to the press just before the film's release but as an example of a well-crafted film with top stars, beautifully shot by award-winning Italian cinematographer Vittorio Storano with astute direction and a fascinating story-base, *Agatha* subsequently enjoyed wide release and eventually made a modest profit.[20]

Beyond the perspective of Hoffman's personal situation, the wrangling over script re-writes and requests for reshoots created instability within the film's financial infrastructure. Despite being largely American this was dependent on a completion bond provided by the British company Film Finances.[21] Film Finances worked as a form of insurance for film productions. In return for a percentage of the budget, Film Finances guaranteed to the lenders that the contracted film would be delivered to the distributor and undertook to meet any overspend. But it would only issue a bond once it was satisfied that the independent producer was able to meet a set of stringent conditions relating to the production of the film. In the very few cases where a guaranteed production got into serious difficulties, Film Finances had the right to take over and finish the film. With *Agatha* it seems that in the end, and in spite of their attempts to halt the accumulating overspend, they gave up, withdrawing the bond and returning £60,000 in settlement. The production companies ended up financing the project's overspend. The collapse of one of the film's major sources of external regulation created difficulties for the producers who largely blamed Hoffman for pushing for re-shoots at a time when money was running out. Disgruntled at being unable to complete the film quite as he desired, Hoffman sued First Artists. Hoffman was in dispute primarily with Phil Feldman of First Artists, claiming that his contract was the root of all of the difficulties; he was only taking it to its logical conclusion and to do so he needed the full support of First Artists. What the case demonstrated was the impracticality of actors taking executive control over a production that involved several professional producers already as well as a financial infrastructure that required accountability at all stages.

The production's troubled development led to another key figure's disgruntlement. Co-producer David Puttnam pulled out once principal photography had commenced, and as the demands for re-shoots started to be made. At the time he was becoming immersed in finishing *Midnight Express* (1978), but he felt that that *Agatha* was becoming too complicated. His feelings of frustration escalated in October when he wrote to producer Jarvis Astaire that the production was out of control:

> My own prognosis of the current situation is that the creative elements have (wrongly) lost confidence in the script. This, as any hardened filmmaker can tell you always happens immediately prior to shooting, and the temptation to "improve the piece to death" becomes irresistible unless someone stops it. The script is always the target for attack because it can't argue its own case and relies on an element of "faith" to keep it intact; this "faith" being a commodity in short supply in an atmosphere in which a multiplicity of egos and ambitions are under considerable pressure.[22]

Puttnam felt his cautions against alterations to the script and additional shooting at the end of the schedule were not being heeded and that his professionalism was being undermined. He was also concerned about the vulnerable financial position regarding the guarantee bond from Film Finances, a warning that turned out to be true. Puttnam's reference to "a multiplicity of egos and ambitions" is certainly pertinent to clashes between the production's personnel, including himself, but it seems that most of the resentment was directed at Hoffman. While some of this may have been exaggerated, and inspired by the fact that Hoffman was an assertive American film star with unusual interests in production, as we have seen, he certainly made a decisive mark on the finished film.

The Christie Estate

Problems with *Agatha* were not only located within the film production team. Rosalind Hicks, Agatha Christie's daughter, tried to stop the film being made. Grounds for this were based on a U. S. court ruling on "right to publicity" regarding the heirs and successors of famous deceased persons. The view was conveyed by her lawyer: "Mrs. Hicks and the other living relatives of Agatha Christie are most distressed and are in fact shocked that responsible producers and production companies would so blatantly trade upon the name of a recently deceased individual of the stature of Agatha Christie."[23] They did not succeed in stopping the film but correspondence shows that concern over Rosalind Hicks's reaction meant that in the film Christie's daughter does not appear whereas she is mentioned in the book. At one point David Puttnam wanted to include a nursery scene but was advised against this by lawyers. The producers received legal opinion on treading very carefully in this respect. Kathleen Tynan also feared for her book and the possibility that she too was in danger of being sued by the Christie Estate. But the grounds concerning the "right to publicity" were less easily targeted at the film when the *Daily Mail* serialized Christie's autobiography in October 1977 and at the same time published a "reconstruction" of what might have happened when she disappeared. This was quite close to the version suggested by the book and film, so it was hardly the case that only the filmmakers were interested in the incident. In the event all was well for the production but the Christie Estate's reaction did not help the increasingly complex issues regarding the script and Hoffman's case for greater involvement.

Losey was sensitive to the need to respect Christie's reputation throughout the production; his attitude was extremely reverential towards the novelist. He argued, for example, that great care should to be taken that the audience should not think Agatha was trying to pin a murder on Nancy Neele. As his notes cautioned:

> We may be and are playing a fictional Agatha Christie but we cannot break the rules. The selling power of the film is the fact that it is about "the mystery of Agatha Christie herself," to use the words of the *Daily News* at the time. The script drew on what is known, I have drawn on what is known and although we all of us would truthfully say along with everyone else, this is fiction, the power of the fiction will be, amongst other things, that it is drawn out of her world and her rules as she, the "real" Agatha Christie, saw and expressed them.[24]

This awareness of the impact of fictional representations of public figures was astute since the film's success to a great extent depended on the portrayal of Christie as being both believable and sensitive. Vanessa Redgrave did not look like Agatha Christie but her performance was appropriate for depicting the uncharacteristic nature of the disappearance. Her ethereality, otherworldliness and physical grace communicated an essence of the troubled novelist very well. The lack of physical resemblance arguably helped the film because it went well with its general fictional latitude and reliance on an audience's continuing curiosity about the mysterious affair at Harrogate.

Aftermath

Many people wanted to forget the disappearance, film and book. Agatha Christie herself preferred the eleven days to be unrecorded, as part of life that was unhappy before she met archaeologist Max Mallowan to whom she was happily married for the rest of her life. Yet as this case shows, the past cannot be erased and the meaning of earlier events is never fixed. The eleven days were clearly significant for Agatha Christie, marking a moment when she took action that influenced the subsequent divorce. Maybe it was necessary for her to come to terms with the present, to "disappear" for a short time, even if it was marked by amnesia or even a breakdown. In a Freudian sense such life markers are important, even if their significance is not fully understood at the time, as a palimpsest of the unconscious when meaning can be repressed and subject to endless "re-writing" of the same event. In many respects this is what happened concerning this contested incident as Christie's biographers came up with many theories about what might have happened in Harrogate.[25] Christie's silence about her disappearance gave others the incentive to "write" their own versions. Andrew Norman's 2006 biography, for example, claimed to have solved the mystery by using medical case studies to show that Christie was suffering from a "fugue state," or period of "out-of-body amnesia" induced by stress and which put her into a trance.[26]

Tynan's script similarly became the subject of contested meaning as other voices sought to change its inflections as the production became increasingly complicated. Losey's vision was for the disappearance to be all about Archie— "a distress signal.... She hopes her husband will be distressed and that he will be shocked into realizing that he does love her.... She also wants to hurt him, not with the aim of revenge—but to get him back."[27] While the drive to extend Wally's role and heighten the film's romantic elements is in part explained by the reduction of the character Evelyn's significance, Hoffman's First Artists' contract and status as a major film star, the impact on the production's budget was profound. It also complicated the focus on Agatha, the depths of her personal despair and experience of grief and rejection. The contestations over the film's creative direction also reflect broader anxieties over celebrity and the need to take care with Christie's national and international image. The enduring fascination with the case itself is testament to Christie's fame extending beyond her reputation as a writer of popular fiction. The significance placed on the incident and the various creative and journalistic responses to it sheds light on Agatha Christie as an author whose celebrity exceeded her writing even if she was reluctant to accept this status.

As *Agatha* demonstrates, the Christie Estate could not control "the right to publicity" since it proved impossible to regulate comments about a figure with such a popular profile. By trying to base the film on "her world and her rules" that Losey felt Tynan had come close to conveying in her book, *Agatha* was nevertheless pulled towards deviation, bordering on the unacceptable as Hoffman's role was in danger of distorting this core premise. It was the production's financial base and the views of key professionals such as editor Jim Clark that ensured the production did not go even more out of control. Compromises were reached all-round, from the perspectives of Hoffman, Losey, the Christie Estate and Tynan. As released in 1979, *Agatha* was marked by the series of interconnected machinations which this chapter has sought to unravel.

Trying to write those "lost" days has been compelling for other producers; one of the most fanciful interpretations was in an episode of *Doctor Who* in 2008 entitled "The Unicorn and the Wasp," in which Christie's amnesia is explained by her role in helping the Doctor defeat a deadly alien in the form of a giant wasp at the Silent Pool. But perhaps Christie herself should have the last word. In 1934 she published a novel, *Unfinished Portrait*, under the pseudonym Mary Westmacott.[28] The character Celia is undergoing a divorce, she has also lost her mother and is suicidal. She comes to terms with her past when she confides in an artist while travelling. While one must take care not to read too much autobiography into this, it was perhaps another way for Christie to address the unhappiness that had beset her in 1926, to turn to writing something of her experience via a fictional character. As the character Celia experiences healing, Christie too went on to achieve personal happiness and even greater fame as a writer. The celebrated moment of *la belle indifférence* in Harrogate clearly served a purpose of transition, of stepping outside of herself as a celebrity and wife, in order to move forward. The eleven days indeed remain an enigma, continuing to fascinate with their apparently endless possibilities for re-writing ever more fantastic "imaginary solutions" to an "authentic mystery."

NOTES

1. Agatha Christie, *An Autobiography* (London: Collins, 1977).
2. Kathleen Tynan, *Agatha: The Agatha Christie Mystery* (London: Star, W. H. Allen, 1978).
3. Christie, *An Autobiography*, p. 353.
4. *Ibid.*, p. 352.
5. For an overview of the disappearance and the various theories about what happened see James Hobbs's website *Hercule Poirot Central*, accessed October 16, 2014, www.poirot.us.
6. Tynan, *Agatha*, p. 179.
7. The files were donated by Gavrik Losey to the Bill Douglas Cinema Museum.
8. Tynan, *Agatha*, p. 33.
9. Gavrik Losey, "Notes on How Plot Is Developed," n.d., Bill Douglas Center, Exeter (thereafter BDC), BDC 6/1/1/8.
10. Kathleen Tynan to Michael Apted, 20 November 1977, BDC 6/1/1/3.
11. The book however adds that four years later in 1930 Agatha Christie married Max Mallowan and lived happily ever after.
12. Kathleen Tynan to Michael Apted, 20 November 1977, BDC 6/1/1/3.
13. Gavrik Losey interviewed by Paul Newland, 18 May 2007, BDC.
14. Tynan to Apted, 20 November 1977, BDC 6/1/1/3.
15. The paperback edition with this cover image was published by Ballantine, New York, 1978. This is the only book cover I have located that used the film actors. Other editions featured a silhouette of Agatha Christie or a drawing of her abandoned car.
16. Tynan to Apted, 20 November 1977, BDC 6/1/1/3.
17. *Variety*, 26 January 1979 in BDC 6/1/1/20.
18. Jim Clark to Phil Feldman, 9 September 1977, BDC 6/1/1/18. All subsequent quotations in this paragraph refer to the same document.
19. *Variety*, 26 January 1979 in BDC 6/1/1/20.
20. Figures for U.S. box office to date are $7.5 million, www.the-numbers.com.
21. The information on Film Finances was obtained from their files, Conduit Street, London, July 2013.

22. David Puttnam to Jarvis Astaire, 29 October 1977, BDC 6/1/1/14.
23. Greenbaum, Wolff and Ernst, solicitors to Puttnam and production companies of *Agatha*, 21 October 1977. BDC 6/1/1/21.
24. Losey, "Notes on How Plot Is Developed."
25. See Jared Cade, *Agatha Christie and the Eleven Missing Days*, rev. ed. (London: Peter Owen, 2011).
26. Andrew Norman, *The Finished Portrait* (Stroud: The History Press, 2006).
27. Losey, "Notes on How Plot Is Developed."
28. Mary Westmacott, *Unfinished Portrait* (London: Collins, 1934).

Bibliography

Archival materials housed in the Bill Douglas Centre, University of Exeter.
Apted, Michael (dir.). *Agatha*. Warner Bros., 1979.
Christie, Agatha. *An Autobiography*. London: Collins, 1977.
Cade, Jared. *Agatha Christie and the Eleven Missing Days*, rev. ed. London: Peter Owen, 2011.
Hobbs, James. *Hercule Poirot Central*. Website (2004). www.poirot.us
Norman, Andrew. *The Finished Portrait*. Stroud: The History Press, 2006.
Tynan, Kathleen. *Agatha: The Agatha Christie Mystery*. London: Star, W. H. Allen, 1978.
Westmacott, Mary. *Unfinished Portrait*. London: Collins, 1934.

Editorial
Fans Have the Final Word

J. C. BERNTHAL

In August 2015, the international press got hold of some research I had produced with Queens University Belfast's Dominique Jeannerod and data analyst Brett Jacob. We had produced a "formula" for readers to solve Agatha Christie puzzles. The whole thing, commissioned by a cable television network, was, we assured people, "a bit of fun," and an indication that more is going on in Christie than meets the eye. Some journalists were unforgiving: Britain's *Daily Mail* called the formula "daunting," a BBC World Service interviewer asked if we were "sapping the fun" from reading, and *Quill and Quire*'s Steven Beattie accused us of murdering the books' appeal.[1]

None of this was unexpected but what surprised me was the overwhelmingly positive responses from fan communities the world over. Christie's admirers—there are millions, and I am one—enjoyed our research for what it was: a tribute. There are a lot of stereotypes surrounding Agatha Christie enthusiasts, who have been maligned by journalists and ignored by scholars. Just as the final word in this book's introduction went to Christie herself, the final word in this seminal volume should go to her diverse and loyal fans.

The Agatha Christie fan community is a multigenerational and international affair. Most fans started reading Christie at a very young age and they always remember their first encounter. Robert, from Lancashire, England, started at the age of eight, "as a result of travel sickness." To take his mind off things, his mother recommended *Five Little Pigs* (*Murder in Retrospect*). "I soon forgot the sickness and was enthralled," he says. "I spent all my pocket money" investing in Christie, and she still hasn't lost her readability. "Christie is the perfect companion for a lazy summer afternoon relaxing in the garden." Robert has been welcomed into the online Christie fan community, through Facebook, which came at just the right time:

It has started a new chapter in my life that is the most enjoyable time, I have met some of [my online friends] and they are as nice in person as they are on the faceless Facebook. They are wonderful friends and I have Agatha Christie to thank for it.

Another member of the online fan community, Linda, 60, lives on the island of Anguilla, part of the British West Indies. After outgrowing Nancy Drew at the age of twelve, she wandered to the local library looking for a challenge, and the librarian recommended *The Murder of Roger Ackroyd*. "I was delighted by the surprise ending," says Linda, "and I was hooked. I thank that librarian as this one book started my life-long love of Agatha Christie and her books and she is still my favorite author to this day." For Linda, Agatha Christie has struck that rare balance between reflecting the atrocity of murder and lightening the blow with a "subtle sense of humor woven throughout." "Murders are serious matters. Her sense of humor lightens the seriousness of the murder but doesn't disrespect it."

Linda is not alone in thinking we should take Christie more seriously. Graham, 21, from Oxford, England, has come to learn that the pleasure Christie gives him is not the mark of a bad writer, but its opposite. Graham's mother collected every Christie title and one day he picked up her copy of *Cards on the Table*. "Even though to this day I do not understand Bridge, which features so prominently, I found it an enjoyable read." When Graham took his A-level exams at school, he wanted to write about Poirot and Hastings but was informed that "there wasn't enough substance in an Agatha Christie to analyze." Graham only stopped believing this at university when he wrote his dissertation, "a study of the way in which authors bid farewell with their 'final' works," which ended up drawing on *Curtain: Poirot's Last Case*. "The excitement of everyone in the department finally laid those A-level demons to rest." He fell in love with the book and the author. "*Curtain* … is a novel of contradictions.… It is a fitting ending for Poirot and Hastings … but it breaks all the rules." Now, with Christie as an intellectual core, he is ready to face the world.

Anne, 51, lives in The Lizard, a village in Cornwall. She has been reading Agatha Christie for almost forty years. Her first book was *The Hollow* (*Murder After Hours*): "I was staying at an Aunt's and bored stiff when I saw the book in her bookcase. I was attracted by the cover [which featured a] hedgehog and box of matches. I started to read and that was it–I was off to the library the following week and haven't stopped reading and re-reading since then." Anne collects the various paperback editions, and has an impressive collection of around two thousand. They belong in a purpose-built wall-to-wall and ceiling-to-floor bookcase.

> I also collect as much memorabilia as I possibly can. I have attended the [International Agatha Christie Festival, in Torquay] for the last couple of years and really enjoy meeting up with other fans and talking all things Agatha.… Even

though I disagree with the more recent TV adaptations it doesn't stop me going location spotting whenever I can.

For Scott, in Melbourne, Australia, it is a question of "obsession" which "began as a youngster." "Agatha Christie," he explains, "quite literally changed my life." And as a valued fan, he has met Christie's family, attended the International Agatha Christie Festival in Torquay, England, four times, and even "been given the rare honor of a backstage tour of 'The Mousetrap'—a thrilling experience, considering the monumental history!" Scott explains: "My home is decorated from cellar to attic with things I have collected, and I have let out my artistic side by creating tributes to my favorite books, little groupings of found objects featuring in the stories." The Christie Estate voted him "Australia's Biggest Agatha Christie Fan" in 2013, an honor he takes pride in. "What would my life be without Agatha Christie? I can't help but think it would be extremely dull!"

Scott and Anne are not alone in collecting. Ralf, who lives in Nuenen, a village in the Netherlands, has devoted a huge amount of time to building up a library of Agatha Christie editions. The "Queen of Crime" library, which has a strong online presence, "contains over 5,700 books in fifty-five languages/dialects by and about Agatha Christie." Fans, publishers and Agatha Christie Limited send him new books to add to the shelves, often in advance of publication. The aim is "to build up a library for future purposes, so authors, journalists, and theatre people can borrow [the] works." The whole project is professional, but it is a labor of love. Ralf read his first Christie, *A Murder Is Announced*, at age eleven, while camping.

Jaclyn, from New York, started reading Christie for work, not pleasure: she was assigned *And Then There Were None* in eighth grade. "I was hooked." Jaclyn travels to England every year to make the International Agatha Christie Festival, and to meet fellow admirers "who enjoy a challenging puzzle, a little romance and lots of (vicarious) drama, but without the gratuitous sex and violence that permeates some murder mysteries and thrillers." Is there something specifically "English" about this alternative world; this world where tension, confusion and difficulties exist but in a sanitary, not sordid, way?

Jeff, "50 years young," from California, San Diego, thinks so. He also started young, after reading Poirot's obituary on the front page of the *New York Times* in 1975. "I stumbled across one of her books at a local secondhand bookshop—it was *The Murder at the Vicarage*, and even though my copy is falling apart, I still have it.... I took it home and read it voraciously—all in one sitting." Soon he was "hitting used bookstores every few weeks," but he quickly learned to slow down, "to savor the flavor" and even sometimes to work out "whodunit." The one book he saved, for over two decades after buying it, was *Curtain: Poirot's Last Case*. When he made the pilgrimage to the United Kingdom for the International Agatha Christie Festival, Jeff "decided to reread all the Agathas again," this time "in the order they were published" and culminating in *Curtain*. "Yes, I knew whodunit ... but on this read-through I could slow down.... It turned into an appreciation of the author and her very real art."

For Tito, 49, from São Paulo, Brazil, it all started with his aunt's verbatim account of the spy thriller *Destination Unknown*. "The destination was really unknown," he notes, because no one would have guessed that once he had read everything in translation he would fly to England to "research her documents," "build a fantastic network of friends around the world" and eventually write two books: "one about Agatha Christie's England and the other about her life and work." This very English lady has given Tito a colorful, varied life.

Many of what Agatha Christie Limited has branded "superfans" have spoken about the joys of meeting and getting to know Tom Adams. It was Adams' iconic cover art from the 1960s to 1980s that got many readers interested in Christie in the first place. Each eerie painting stands as a work of art in its own right, while also providing hawk-eyed readers with valuable clues to the books' puzzle solutions. Scott, who has a website devoted to these images, states: "I own four of his original paintings and several limited-edition prints, something I never could have dreamt of! And better still, I now count Tom and his wife, Georgie as friends."

Can fans solve the mystery of Agatha Christie's appeal? Everyone has a different opinion. Graham gets animated on this topic:

> I think the secret to Agatha Christie's enduring success is her almost mercurial tendency for subversion. There is almost always some sort of trick to be played. ... Christie sometimes gets pigeon-holed as a conservative, formulaic writer. But I think she is still widely read because you open her novels often expecting that, and then are confronted with something different altogether...

Tito has a completely different solution. "I think that in the trees of Ashfield [the young Agatha's family home], there was a magical gate that she crossed." She became "blessed with the power to tell stories like no others could do and she became a magical personality, attracting adoration for her work and herself forever."

Scott notes that "her combination of the macabre and delightful characters is second-to-none. I'm probably more in love now than ever before." Linda puts it down to Christie's humanity: "she ... provides a calm and comfortable world" peppered with people from "all walks of life": "From Inch the taxi driver to Mr. Pye ... from old spinsters to Lords of the Manors ... from fastidious Belgian detectives to vicars, no one is excluded and everyone is welcome." Jeff echoes Christie herself, as quoted in the introduction: from plots to settings to dialogue to character, "Christie's books really had something for everyone.... That sausage machine worked gloriously until the end.... The stories seem fresh and even relevant." But ultimately, he suggests, "that is for academics to argue."

Note

1. Katherine Rushton, "Sorry, Poirot: Now There's a Formula to Tell Us Whodunnit," *Daily Mail* (August 3, 2015), p. 29; Steven Beattie, "Who Killed the Fun in Agatha Christie? (Spoiler: Academics), *Quill and Quire* (August 4, 2015), accessed August 4, 2015, www.quillandquire.com/authors/2015/08/04/who-killed-the-fun-in-agatha-christies-novels-spoiler-academics.

Bibliography

Beattie, Steven. "Who Killed the Fun in Agatha Christie? (Spoiler: Academics)." *Quill and Quire* (August 4, 2015). www.quillandquire.com

Rushton, Katherine. "Sorry, Poirot: Now There's A Formula to Tell Us Whodunnit." *Daily Mail* (August 3, 2015), p. 29.

About the Contributors

Sarah Bernstein is a PhD candidate in the Department of English, University of Edinburgh, Scotland. Her research focuses on post-war writing by women and its engagement with social sciences and the British Welfare state. Other research interests include representations of girlhood, detective fiction, the Frankfurt School, nature writing and ecocriticism.

J. C. Bernthal received a PhD from the University of Exeter, England. He works for the crime writer Sophie Hannah. His monograph, *Queering Agatha Christie*, is forthcoming with Palgrave. He has carried out research for the BBC and UKTV, with publications on Christie in *Clues: A Journal of Detection* (2014); *Women: A Cultural Review* (2015); and *The Detective* (ed. Barry Forshaw, Intellect, 2016).

Charlotte Beyer is a senior lecturer in English studies at the University of Gloucestershire, England. She has published widely on contemporary literature and genre, especially fiction. She is the co-editor of *Mothers Without Their Children* (Demeter Press, 2016) and editor of a special issue on contemporary crime fiction for the *Journal of American, British and Canadian Studies* (2017).

Meg Boulton is affiliated with the History of Art Department at the University of York, England, from which she received her AHRC-funded PhD. Her research focuses on the conceptualization of (sacred) space, and the importance of space and place in creating institutional identities. She is also a freelance lecturer at the University of York and the Oxford University Department for Continuing Education.

Brigitta Hudácskó is a PhD candidate and instructor at the University of Debrecen, Hungary, where she has taught on Sherlock Holmes adaptations. Her thesis is "Sherlock Holmes in the War on Terror: Crime Dramas Featuring the Character of the Great Detective." Research interests include detective fiction, television studies and translation studies.

Michelle M. Kazmer is a professor in the School of Information, Florida State University. She conducts research in the area of distributed knowledge and applies theories from information science to detective fiction. Her research has been published in *Library & Information Science Research* (2013) and the *Journal of the Association for Information Science & Technology* (2014).

About the Contributors

Jilly Lippmann is a tutor in English literature and a doctoral candidate in the College of Arts, Society and Education at James Cook University, Australia. Her research focuses on the "New Woman" in late colonial modernity in mainstream print culture and Australian literature. She has also been a research assistant and a learning advisor and course facilitator for first-year bridging courses.

Merja Makinen is an associate professor in English literature at Middlesex University, England. She is the author of *Agatha Christie: Life and Letters* (forthcoming, Palgrave Macmillan); *Agatha Christie: Investigating Femininity* (Palgrave Macmillan, 2001); the entry for Agatha Christie in the *Blackwell Companion to Crime Fiction* (eds. Lee Horsley and Charles Rzepka, Blackwell, 2010); and an article in *The Human* (June 2015).

Rebecca Mills is an associate lecturer at Plymouth University, England. She completed her PhD thesis, "Post-World War II Elegy and the Geographic Imagination," supported by the European Fund, at the University of Exeter. Research interests include elegy, detective fiction, modernism, literary geographies, the uncanny, the Gothic, rites of passage and death.

Sarah Street is a professor of film and the foundation chair of drama at the University of Bristol, England. She has published widely on British cinema, costume and cinema, European film set design and color film. Her book *Colour Films in Britain: The Negotiation of Innovation, 1900–55* (BFI/Palgrave Macmillan, 2012) was awarded Best Monograph prize by the British Association of Film, Television and Screen Studies.

Index

Adams, Tom 179
adaptation 1, 6–7, 91–93, 98–112
Adorno, Theodor 155
"The Adventure of Johnny Waverley" 105–106, 110
After the Funeral 5, 29, 33–36, 40–42
Agatha 8, 161–174
The Agatha Christie Hour 90
Agatha Christie's Poirot 6, 8, 82, 90–93, 98–112
And Then There Were None 8, 41, 53n36, 178
anti-Semitism 25
Apted, Michael 161, 163, 167
Astaire, Jarvis 163, 171
At Bertram's Hotel 41n53
Auriti, Marino 106–107
Austen, Jane 30
An Autobiography (memoir by AC) 12, 162

Bachelard, Gaston 100–101
Baráth, Katalin 131n3
Bargainnier, Earl F. 86
Barnard, Robert 3
Bart, István 131
Barzun, Jacques 29–30
Bax, Arnold 16
Bellos, David 131, 136, 139
Beresford, Prudence "Tuppence" (fictional character) 7, 147–148, 153
Berger, John 65
the Bible 38, 54–55
The Big Four 85, 131n4
Birns, Margaret Boe 34, 37
Birns, Nicholas 34, 37
Bloom, Harold 11–12, 19, 25–26
Bode, Katherine 156
The Body in the Library 116–117, 123
Boehmer, Elleke 147
Bowen, Elizabeth 89
Brady, Orla 92
Brief Encounter 91, 165
Brown, Erica 155
Brownson, Charles 84

Buck, Michele 99
Burnett, Gary 115

"The Capture of Cerberus" 81, 88–89
Cards on the Table 177
Carey, Peter 155
A Caribbean Mystery 116n8, 121
Chan, Jackie 134n17
Chatman, Elfreda 115
childhood 5–6, 45–57
Christie, Archie 162, 164–165, 168, 169
Christie, Campbell 162
Christie, Julie 167
Clark, Jim 168–170, 173
Cleopatra (Queen of Egypt) 65
Cole, Cathy 66
Conan Doyle, Arthur 6, 83, 86, 88, 89, 91, 134, 148, 162; *see also* Holmes, Sherlock; Watson, John H.
Cook, Michael 61–62, 63, 65
Cox, Pamela 47, 49, 56
Crooked House 45, 47–49, 50, 52–53, 54–56
Csanády, Katalin 137–138, 140, 141
Curran, John 102, 102n12
Curtain: Poirot's Last Case 53n36, 85, 177, 178–179

d'Alambert, Jean 139
Dalton, Timothy 164
Dead Man's Folly 47, 53, 54–55, 149
Death on the Nile 8, 41, 149
Derrida, Jacques 48
Destination Unknown 179
Detection Club 145, 148–150
Doctor Who 174
Dömötör, Edit 140
"The Double Clue" 85–88, 91

Eagleton, Terry 11
Eastman, Brian 99, 100, 203
Eco, Umberto 137
Edelman, Lee 45–46, 48, 55, 57
Einstein, Albert 16

183

Eliot, T.S. 11
empire 5, 7, 18, 18n23, 37, 131–132, 134, 146, 151–157
enlightenment era 102, 103–105, 107
Evans, Mary 63–64, 67
Evil Under the Sun 31
Exton, Clive 99, 103

fandom 1, 8, 83, 93, 176–180
Farnham, Brian 108
Feldman, Phil 168, 170
feminism 1, 4, 5, 62, 83, 145, 151–152, 155–157
Fisher, Charlotte 165
Fisher, Phryne (fictional character) 145–157; see also Greenwood, Kerry
Five Little Pigs 176
foreignness 7, 82, 84, 86–91, 130, 135, 136–141
forensic science 110, 114, 116–117
Foucault, Michel 26
"Four and Twenty Blackbirds" 110
4.50 from Paddington 120, 121
Freud, Sigmund 12, 53, 55, 172–173
Fry, Roger 16
Funerals Are Fatal see *After the Funeral*

Gálvölgyi, Judit 137, 139, 140, 141
Garbo, Greta 87
Giant's Bread 13–15, 16, 18, 20–21, 24–25
Gildersleeve, Jessica 70, 76
Giles, Judy 47
Gill, Gillian 11
Gioni, Massimiliano 107
golden age of detective fiction 29, 68, 86, 131, 134–135, 145–150, 157
Greenwood, Kerry 7, 145–157
Gregory, Celia 165
Griffiths, Tom 151
Grover, Mary 155

Habermas, Jurgen 115
Hall, Stuart 48
Hallowe'en Party 47, 49, 51–52, 53, 54–55
Hammill, Faye 155
Hastings, Arthur (fictional character) 6, 81, 83–85, 87, 99, 103, 108, 177
Hawkes, Gail 87
Helen of Troy 65–67, 65n25
Hercule Poirot's Christmas 137–141
heredity 18, 41, 56
heteronormativity 6, 15–19, 54–55, 62–64, 69, 71, 75–77, 81–93, 84n15
Hickory Dickory Death see *Hickory Dickory Dock*
Hickory Dickory Dock 88, 89, 101, 110–111
Hicks, Rosalind 171
Hoffmann, Dustin 161, 163–164, 167–169, 173
The Hollow 11–19, 21–23, 24–26, 177
"The Hollow" (play) 13
Holmes, Sherlock (fictional character) 6, 30, 81–82, 83–85, 84n15, 88, 89, 107, 134, 148; see also Conan Doyle, Arthur

Holst, Gustav 16
homosexuality 51, 51n25, 53, 81, 84, 85, 90–91
Horkheimer, Max 155
Horowitz, Anthony 108
"How Does Your Garden Grow?" 101, 108
Humble, Nicola 4, 152

information behavior 1, 104–111, 114–125

Jackson, Philip 92, 99
Jaeger, Paul 115
Joyce, James 3

Keating, H.R.F. 3
Knepper, Marty S. 4
Knepper, Paul 49
Knight, Stephen 30, 84
Kondor, Vilmos 131n3
Kuttainen, Victoria 151

"The Labors of Hercules" (TV episode) 82, 92
Lawrence, D.H. 12, 17
Lawson, Alan 150
Leavis, Q.D. 154–155
Lee, Bruce 134n17
Lemon, Felicity (fictional character) 6–7, 82, 89–90, 92–93, 98–112
Light, Alison 3, 9, 11, 30, 31n9, 32, 47, 48, 68, 72, 83, 155, 157
Linda 134n17
Lord Edgware Dies 108–109, 110, 111
Losey, Gavrik 163, 166–167, 172–173

Makinen, Merja 5, 6, 11–28, 46, 47, 53, 61, 70, 74, 76
Malleus Maleficarum 38
Mallowan, Max 172
Malouf, David 155
The Man in the Brown Suit 90
Mansfield, Katherine 63, 67n36
Markham, Kika 91
Maróti, Andor 133–134
Marple Jane (fictional character) 3, 7, 31, 33, 50, 114–125, 134, 148–149
Marshall, Andrew 108
Mary I (Queen of Scotland) 65
Mauriès, Patrick 105
McQueen, Steve 163
mental illness 30, 46, 47–49, 51–53, 52n31, 140–141, 161, 165, 167–168
Meyerhold, Vsevolod 16
middlebrowism 4, 5, 7, 26, 71, 135–136, 141, 145–157
The Mirror Crack'd from Side to Side 120
modernism 1, 4–5, 11–12, 16–17, 24–26, 63, 66–67, 73–74, 76, 89–90
modernity 4, 29–44, 45–49 51–52, 55–57, 71–75, 100, 106–107
Moers, Ellen 71
Moore, Sarah H. E, 64
Moran, Pauline 92–93

Morse, Helen 165, 167
"The Mousetrap" 1, 9, 70, 178
The Moving Finger 5, 29–33, 34, 35, 36, 38, 39, 40–42, 119, 124–125, 179
Muncie, John 52
Murder After Hours see *The Hollow*
The Murder at the Vicarage 114, 119–120, 121, 122, 178
Murder in Mesopotamia 149
Murder in Retrospect see *Five Little Pigs*
A Murder Is Announced 120, 121, 122–123, 178
The Murder of Roger Ackroyd 8, 30, 131n4, 164, 177
The Murder on the Links 131n4
Murder on the Orient Express 8, 149
Murder on the Orient Express (TV movie) 90
Murder in the Calais Coach see *Murder on the Orient Express*
Murray, Les 155
The Mysterious Affair at Styles 3, 83, 84
The Mysterious Mr. Quin 6, 61–77
"The Mystery of the Spanish Chest" 89

N or M? 31
Neele, Nancy 162–166, 168, 172
Nemesis 41, 45, 59
Newman, Paul 163
Norman, Andrew 173

objects 29–42, 100–102, 104, 106–107, 111–112
Oliver, Ariadne (fictional character) 4n9, 51, 55, 82

The Pale Horse 5, 29, 37–40, 42
Partners in Crime 153
Peril at End House 30, 41
Pickles, Carolyn 165
Plain, Gill 31, 33
A Pocket Full of Rye 117–118, 120
postcolonialism 7, 145–147, 149–152, 157
Poirot, Hercule (fictional character) 3, 6, 13–15, 17, 23, 36, 49, 51, 53, 64, 81–93, 98–112, 134, 137–138, 147, 149, 177
Poitier, Sydney 163
Prokofiev, Sergei 16
Puttnam, David 163, 170–171
Pyne, J. Parker (fictional character) 89, 100

queer theory 1, 4, 45–46, 50–51, 55, 81, 82, 84, 93

Redgrave, Vanessa 161, 164, 167, 170, 172
Rejtő, Jenő 136
Réz, Lola Kosáryné 137, 140–141
Rhys, Jean 89, 147
A Room of One's Own 12; *see also* Woolf, Virginia
The Rose and the Yew Tree 21
Rowland, Susan 18n23
Ryan-Fazillea, Sue 146–147

Sad Cypress 30
Savoy, Bert 88
Sayers, Dorothy L. 162
Schaub, Melissa 62, 74
Schoenberg, Arnold 16
Scotland Yard 110, 116–118, 134
The Secret Adversary 131n4, 147–148
Sedgwick, Eve Kosofsky 81, 84, 85
The Seven Dials Mystery 153
Shakespeare, William 37
Sherlock 107
Sinclair, May 12, 76
Sleeping Murder 120–121, 123
Sparkling Cyanide 41n54
Stockton, Kathryn Bond 46, 50–51, 53–57
Stravinsky, Igor 16
Streisand, Barbara 163
Suchet, David 90–92
Super Sleuths (TV documentary) 99
Symonds, Julian 83

Tatlin, Vladimir 16
Ten Little Indians see *And Then There Were None*
theatricality 13–14, 16, 29, 35, 37–41, 41n53, 54–55, 64–65, 70, 87, 110, 124
They Do It with Mirrors 123–124
Timmer, Damien 99
RMS *Titanic* 24
To the Lighthouse 11–16, 17–20, 23–25, 73–74; *see also* Woolf, Virginia
Tyler, Robert 87
Tynan, Kathleen 161–162, 163–164, 166–168, 170, 171, 173

Unfinished Portrait 174

Valaki csenget see *Hercule Poirot's Christmas*
Varga, Bálint 134
Vermeer, Johannes 35–36
Victoria (Queen of Great Britain) 5
Victorian era 4, 34–36, 76, 83, 147–148, 153, 155

Watson, John H. (fictional character) 6, 83–85, 84n15; *see also* Conan Doyle, Arthur
West, Rebecca 13
Westmacott, Mary (pseudonym of AC) 5, 12, 21, 26, 174
What Mrs McGillicudy Saw! see *4.50 from Paddington*
White, Patrick 155
Williams, Ralph Vaughan 16
Williamson, David 155
Woolf, Virginia 3, 4, 5, 11–14, 16, 20, 22, 67, 73–74, 152
Woollacott, Angela 153–154
World War I 5, 13, 36, 36n30, 83, 84, 147
World War II 5, 22, 29–31, 33–34, 35–36, 38, 45–48, 51, 130, 131–132

York, R.A. 35, 38, 41, 47

www.ingramcontent.com/pod-product-compliance
Ingram Content Group UK Ltd.
Pitfield, Milton Keynes, MK11 3LW, UK
UKHW042014140426
5217IPUK00015B/1166